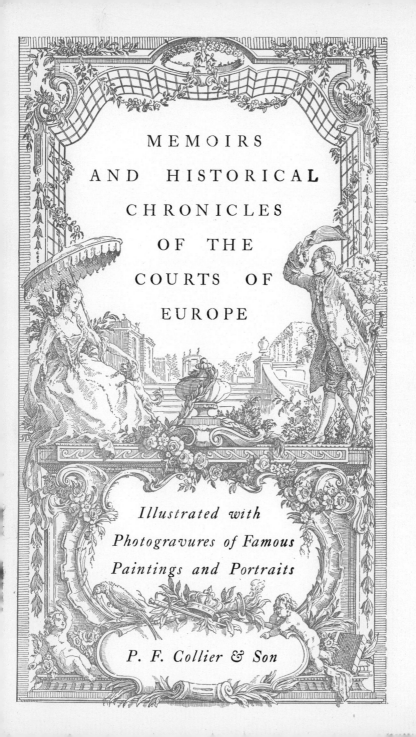

MEMOIRS AND HISTORICAL CHRONICLES OF THE COURTS OF EUROPE

Illustrated with Photogravures of Famous Paintings and Portraits

P. F. Collier & Son

MEMOIRS OF
THE EMPRESS JOSEPHINE

BY MADAME DE RÉMUSAT
Lady-in-Waiting to the Empress

VOLUME II

*With a Special Introduction
and Illustrations*

VIGILANS ET AUDAX

NEW YORK
P F COLLIER & SON
PUBLISHERS

MEMOIRS OF THE
EMPRESS JOSEPHINE

CHAPTER XVI
(1805-1806.)

I HAVE already described the dullness and depression of Paris during this campaign, and the sufferings of every class of society from the renewal of war. Money had become still more scarce; in fact, it attained such a price that, being obliged to send some in haste to my husband, I had to pay ninety francs merely for obtaining gold for a thousand-franc bank-note. Such an opportunity of spreading and increasing the general anxiety was, of course, turned to advantage by the malcontents. Warned by former experience, and alarmed by the imprudence of certain utterances, I held aloof from every one, seeing only my own friends and persons who could not involve me in any difficulty.

When the Princes or Princesses of the Imperial family held their receptions, I went, as did others, to pay my respects to them, and also to the Arch-Chancellor Cambacérès, who would have been highly displeased at any neglect. He gave grand dinners, and held receptions twice a week. He resided in a large house on the Carrousel, which has since been converted into the Hôtel des Cent Suisses.* At seven

* This hotel was pulled down in the reign of Louis Philippe. —P. R.

in the evening a line of carriages would generally
stretch across the Carrousel, and Cambacérès would
note its length from his window with delight. Some
time was occupied in getting into the courtyard and
reaching the foot of the staircase. At the door of the
first reception-room an attendant announced the
guest's name in a loud voice; this was repeated until
the presence-chamber was reached. There an immense crowd would be collected; there were two or
three rows of women; the men stood close together,
forming a sort of passage from one angle of the room
to the opposite corner. Up and down this walked
Cambacérès with great gravity, covered with decorations, and usually wearing all his orders and diamonds; on his head an enormous powdered wig. He
kept on making civil little speeches right and left.
When we felt quite sure he had seen us, especially if
he had spoken, it was the custom to retire, and thus
make room for others. We frequently had to wait
a long time for our carriages, and the surest way to
be agreeable to Cambacérès was to tell him, the next
time, of the inconvenience caused by the numberless
vehicles in the Place all crowding toward his house.

Fewer persons went to the receptions of the Arch-
Treasurer Le Brun, who seemed to attach less importance to these outward observances, and lived
quietly. But, although he had not the foibles of his
colleague, he was also deficient in some of his qualities. Cambacérès was a kind-hearted man; he received petitions graciously, and, if he promised to support them, his word could be relied on. Le Brun's
only care was to amass a fortune, which became considerable. He was a selfish, cunning old man, who
never did any good to anybody.

The member of the Imperial family whom I saw
most frequently was Mme. Louis Bonaparte. People

came to her house of an evening to hear the news.

In December, 1805, a report having been spread that the English were likely to descend on the Dutch coast, Louis Bonaparte received commands to travel through Holland, and to inspect the Army of the North. His absence, which gave a little more freedom to his wife, and was a relief to his household, who held him in awe and aversion, enabled Mme. Louis to pass her evenings pleasantly. Music and drawing at a large table in the center of the *salon* were the chief amusements. Mme. Louis had a great taste for the arts: she composed charming ballads; she painted well; she liked the society of artists. Her only fault, perhaps, was in not maintaining the ceremonious demeanor in her house demanded by the rank to which she had been elevated. She always remained on intimate terms with her school-fellows, and with the young married women who habitually visited her, and her manners retained something of the freedom of those school-days. This gave rise to remark and censure.

After a long silence respecting the movements of the army, which produced general uneasiness, Le Brun, aide-de-camp to the Emperor, and a son of the Arch-Treasurer, was dispatched from the battle-field of Austerlitz, and arrived one evening with news of the victory, of the succeeding armistice, and of the well-founded hope of peace. The news was announced at all the theatres, and posted up everywhere on the following day. It produced a great effect, and dispelled the gloom and apathy of Paris.

It was impossible not to be elated by so great a success, and not to take the side of glory and of fortune. The French were carried away by the description of the victory, to which nothing was wanting, since it terminated the war; and this time again there was no need to prescribe public rejoicing: the nation identified itself with the success of its army.

I look upon this period as the zenith of Bonaparte's good fortune, for his mighty deeds were made their own by the bulk of his people. Afterward, doubtless, he increased in power and in authority, but he had to bespeak enthusiasm, and, though he sometimes succeeded in enforcing it, the efforts he was obliged to make must have lessened the value of the applause.

In the midst of the pride and delight displayed by the city of Paris, it may well be believed that the great bodies of the State and the public officers did not neglect the opportunity of expressing the general admiration in high-flown language. When we now read the speeches delivered on the occasion in the Senate and the Tribunate, the orations of prefects and mayors, the pastoral letters of bishops, one wonders if it be possible that a human head should not be turned by such excess of praise. Every glory of the past was to fade before that of Bonaparte; the greatest names were to drop into obscurity; fame would thenceforth blush at what she had formerly proclaimed, etc., etc.

On the 31st of December the Tribunate was assembled, and Fabre de l'Aude, the President, announced the return of a deputation which had been sent to the Emperor. Its members had brought back a glowing account of the marvels they had witnessed. A great number of flags had also arrived. The Emperor bestowed eight on the city of Paris, eight on the Tribunate, and fifty-four on the Senate; the entire Tribunate was to present the latter.

On the conclusion of the President's speech, a crowd of tribunes rushed forward to propose what was called *des motions de vœux*. One of them moved that a gold medal should be struck; another, that a public monument should be erected; that the Emperor should receive the honors of a triumph, after the old fashion of imperial Rome; that the whole city of Paris should go forth to meet him. " Language," said one member, " can not attain such height of grandeur, nor express the emotions it calls forth."

Carrion-Nisas proposed that, on the proclamation of the general peace, the sword worn by the Emperor at the battle of Austerlitz should be solemnly consecrated. Each speaker endeavored to surpass the others, and certainly, during this sitting, which lasted several hours, all that flattery could suggest to the imagination was exhausted. And yet this very Tribunate was a source of anxiety to the Emperor, because it contained in itself a semblance of liberty; and he subsequently abolished it in order to consolidate his despotic power, even in the smallest outward signs. When Bonaparte " eliminated " the Tribunate (this was the technical expression for that measure), he did not shrink from using these words: " This is my final break with the Republic."

The Tribunate, having arranged to carry the flags to the Senate on the 1st of January, 1806, decided that on the same occasion it should be proposed to erect a column. The Senate hastened to pass a decree to this effect, and also decreed that the Emperor's letter, which had accompanied the flags, should be engraved on marble and placed in the Hall of Assembly. The senators on this occasion rose to the height attained by the tribunes.

Preparations were now made for the rejoicings which were to take place on the return of the Emperor. M. de Rémusat sent orders, through me, for the performance of various pieces containing appropriate passages at the theatres. The Théâtre Français having selected " Gaston et Bayard," some slight

changes were made by the police in certain lines that
were deemed inadmissible.   The Opera House prepared a new piece.

Meanwhile the Emperor, after receiving the signature of the peace, was preparing to quit Vienna,
and addressed its inhabitants in a proclamation full of
compliments, both to themselves and to their sovereign.   It ended thus:

" I have shown myself little among you, not from
disdain or a vain pride, but I did not wish to interfere
with the feelings due to your sovereign, with whom
it was my intention to make a prompt peace."

We have already seen what were the Emperor's
real motives for remaining in retirement at Schônbrunn.

Although, in point of fact, the French army had
been kept under tolerable discipline while in Vienna,
there can be no doubt that the inhabitants were over-
joyed at the departure of the guests they had been
obliged to receive, to lodge, and to feed liberally.   To
give an idea of the consideration with which our vanquished enemies were forced to treat us, it will be
sufficient to state that Generals Junot and Bessières,
who were quartered on Prince Esterhazy, were daily
supplied from Hungary with every delicacy of the
table, including Tokay.   This was due to the generosity of the Prince, who defrayed the whole cost.

I recollect hearing M. de Rémusat relate that, on
the arrival of the Emperor at Vienna, the Imperial
cellars were explored in search of this same Tokay,
and much surprise was expressed that not a single
bottle was forthcoming; all had been carefully removed by the orders of Francis.

The Emperor reached Munich on the 31st of December, and on the next day proclaimed the Elector
of Bavaria King.   He announced this in a letter to

the Senate, in which he also made known his adoption of Prince Eugène, and the marriage of the latter, which was to take place before the Emperor's return to Paris.

Prince Eugène hastened to Munich, having first taken possession of the States of Venice, and reassured his new subjects, as far as possible, by dignified and moderate proclamations.

The Emperor felt himself bound also to bestow some praise on the army of Italy. A bulletin says: " The Italians have displayed great spirit. The Emperor has frequently said: ' Why should not my Italian people appear gloriously on the world's stage? They are full of intelligence and passion; it will be easy henceforth to give them soldierly qualities.' " He made a few more proclamations to his army, in his usual turgid style, but they are said to have produced a great effect on the army.

He issued one decree which would have been good if it had been put into execution. " We adopt," he said, " the children of those generals, officers, and privates who lost their lives at the battle of Austerlitz. They shall be brought up at Rambouillet and at St. Germain, and placed out in the world, or suitably married by our care. To their own names they shall add that of Napoleon."

The Elector, or rather the King, of Bavaria, is a younger son of the house of Deux-Ponts, who came to the Electorate through the extinction of that branch of his family which was governing Bavaria. In the reign of Louis XVI. he was sent to France and placed in the King's service. He soon obtained a regiment, and resided for a considerable time either in Paris or in garrison at one of our towns. He became attached to France, and left behind him the recollection of much kindness of disposition and cordiality of manner. He was known as Prince Max. He declined, however, to marry in France. The Prince de Condé offered him his daughter; but his father and his uncle, the Elector, objected to the match on the grounds that Prince Max, not being rich, would probably have to make canonesses of some of his daughters, and that the admixture in their veins of the blood of Louis XIV. with that of Mme. de Montespan would be an obstacle to their admittance into certain chapters.

When, at a later period, this Prince succeeded to the Electorate, he always retained an affectionate remembrance of France, and a sincere attachment to her people. Having become King by the will of the Emperor, he took pains to prove his gratitude by a splendid welcome, and he received all the French with extreme kindness. It may well be imagined that not for one moment did he dream of declining the proposed marriage for his daughter. The young Princess was then seventeen or eighteen years of age, and possessed attractive qualities, as well as personal charms. The marriage, which was due to political reasons, became the source of uninterrupted happiness to Eugène. Princess Augusta of Bavaria attached herself warmly to the husband chosen for her; she aided him in no small measure to win the hearts of the Italians. With beauty, sense, piety, and amiability, she could not fail to be tenderly beloved by Prince Eugène, and at the present day they are settled in Bavaria, and enjoy the happiness of a perfect union.

During the Emperor's stay at Munich, he took it into his head, by way of recreation after his labors of the past months, to indulge a fancy, partly political, partly amorous, for the Queen of Bavaria. That Princess, who was the King's second wife, without being very beautiful, was of an elegant figure and pleasing though dignified manners. I think the Emperor pretended to be in love with her. The lookers-on said it was amusing to watch the struggle between his imperious temper and rude manners and the desire to please a Princess accustomed to that kind of etiquette which is never relaxed in Germany on any occasion whatever. The Queen of Bavaria contrived to exact respect from her strange admirer, and yet seemed to be amused with his devotion. The Empress considered her to be more coquettish than was desirable, and the whole business made her anxious to get away quickly from the Bavarian Court, and spoilt the pleasure she would otherwise have felt in her son's marriage.

At the same time, Mme. Murat took offense because the new Vice-Queen, who had become the adopted daughter of Napoleon, took precedence of her on ceremonial occasions. She feigned illness in order to avoid what seemed to her an affront, and her brother was obliged to get into a rage with her, to prevent her from too plainly exhibiting her discontent. Had we not actually witnessed the rapid rise of certain pretensions in those who are the favorites of fortune, we should have been astonished at these sudden bursts of temper in princes of so recent a date that they could scarcely yet have become accustomed to the advantages and rights appertaining to their rank. This spectacle we have, however, beheld so frequently that we are not surprised, but merely admit that no human passion is so easily aroused, or grows so rapidly, as vanity.

Bonaparte had always been well aware of this, and he used the knowledge as his surest method of governing. While at Munich, he made many promotions in the army. He gave a regiment of Carbineers to his brother-in-law, Prince Borghese. He rewarded several officers by promotion, or by the Legion of Honor. Among others, he created M. de Nansouty, my brother-in-law, grand officer of the order. He was a brave man, esteemed in the army, straightforward, and endowed with a keen sense of duty, not very common, unfortunately, among our military chiefs. He left behind him in a foreign country a reputation which is very honorable to his family.

The Emperor's military Court, encouraged by their master's example, and, like him, flushed with victory, took great pleasure in the society of the ladies who had accompanied the Empress. It seemed as if Love was now to have his share of power in a world which had hitherto somewhat neglected him; but it must be admitted that not much time was allowed to him for the establishment of his reign, and his attacks were of necessity rather brisk.

We may date from this period the passion which the beautiful Mme. de C—— inspired in M. de Caulaincourt. She had been appointed Lady-in-Waiting in the summer of 1805. When quite young she had married her cousin, who was at that time equerry to the Emperor, and she drew all eyes on herself by her striking beauty. M. de Caulaincourt fell desperately in love with her, and this feeling, which was for several years more or less reciprocal, deterred him from thinking of marriage. Mme. de C—— became more and more estranged from her husband, and at last took advantage of the law of divorce. When the return of the King condemned M. de Caulaincourt, otherwise the Duke of Vicenza, to a life of obscurity, she resolved to share his ill fortune, and married him.

I have already said that the Emperor announced during this campaign his consent to the evacuation of the kingdom of Naples by our troops; but before long he again quarreled with the sovereign of that kingdom, either because the King did not exactly carry out the treaty that had been concluded with him, and was too much under the influence of the English, who were continually threatening his ports, or because the Emperor wished to accomplish his project of subjecting the whole of Italy to his own authority. He also thought, no doubt, that it would be his best policy to eject the house of Bourbon by degrees from the thrones of the Continent. Be this as it may, according to custom, and without any previous communication, France learned by an order of the day, dated from the Imperial camp at Schônbrunn, 6th Nivôse, year 14, that the French army was marching to the conquest of the kingdom of Naples, and would be under the command of Joseph Bonaparte, who accordingly repaired thither.

" We will pardon no longer," so runs the proclamation. " The dynasty of Naples has ceased to reign. Its existence is incompatible with the repose of Europe and the honor of my crown. Soldiers, forward! . . . and delay not to tell me that all Italy is subject to my laws or those of my allies."

It is in this summary tone that Bonaparte, fresh from signing treaties of peace, began another war, gave new offense to the sovereigns of Europe, and incited the English Government to stir up fresh enemies against himself.

On the 25th of January the Court of Naples, under the pressure of a skillful and victorious enemy, embarked for Palermo, abandoning the capital to its new sovereign, who would soon take possession of it. Meanwhile the Emperor, having been present at the marriage of Prince Eugène on the 14th of January, left Munich, and, having received on his way through Germany the honors that were invariably offered him in every place, reached Paris on the night of the 26th to the 27th of January.

I have thought it well to conclude here the history of what was to me Bonaparte's second epoch, because, as I said before, I look upon the close of this first campaign as the highest pitch of his glory; and for this reason, that now the French people again consented to bear their share in it.

Nothing, perhaps, in the history of circumstances and of men, can be compared to the height of power to which he attained after the peace of Tilsit; but, if at that time all Europe bent before him, the spell of victory had been strangely weakened in France, and our armies, although consisting of our own citizens, were beginning to be aliens to us.

The Emperor, who often appreciated things with mathematical accuracy, was well aware of this; for, on his return from concluding the above treaty, I heard him say, " Military glory, which lasts so long in history, is that which fades the quickest among its contemporaries. All our recent battles have not produced in France half the effect of the one victory of Marengo."

Had he carried his reflections further, he would have seen that the people who are governed need eventually a glory that will be of solid use, and that admiration for that which bears but a barren brilliancy is soon exhausted.

In 1806 England was again accused, rightly or wrongly, of inciting enmity against us. Supposing her to be with justice jealous of our returning prosperity, we did not think it impossible that she might endeavor to molest us, even if we had in perfect good faith shown every sign of intended moderation. We did not think the Emperor had been the cause of the last rupture which had destroyed the treaty of

Amiens; and, as it seemed impossible for a long time to come to compete with the naval power of the English, it did not appear to us to be politically wrong to endeavor to balance the weight which commerce gave to our enemies by the constitution given to Italy—that is, by a powerful influence on the Continent.

With such feelings as these, the marvels of this three months' campaign could not fail to impress us deeply. Austria had been conquered; the united armies of the two greatest sovereigns of Europe had fled before ours; the Czar had retreated; the Emperor Francis had personally sued for peace—a peace as yet bearing signs of moderation; kings had been created by our victories; the daughter of a crowned sovereign had been given in marriage to a mere French gentleman; finally, the prompt return of the conqueror, which gave hopes of permanent peace, and perhaps also a desire to retain our illusions respecting our master—a desire inspired by human vanity, for men do not like to blush for him by whom they are ruled—all these things again roused national admiration, and were only too favorable to the ambition of the victor. The Emperor perceived the progress he had made in popularity, and he concluded, with some appearance of probability, that glory would make up to us for all the losses we were about to sustain at the hands of despotism. He believed that Frenchmen would not murmur were but their slavery brilliant, and that we would willingly barter all the liberty that the Revolution had so hardly won for us, for his dazzling military success.

Finally, and this was the worst, he saw in war a means of stifling the reflections which his mode of government was sure sooner or later to evoke, and he reserved it to dazzle us, or at least to reduce us to silence.　As he felt himself perfectly master of the science of war, he had no fear of its results; and, when he could engage in it with such immense armies and such formidable artillery, he felt there was scarcely any danger to himself.　Although in this I may be mistaken, I do believe that, after the campaign of Austerlitz, war was rather the result of his system than the gratification of his taste.　The first, the real ambition of Napoleon was for power, and he would have preferred peace if it could have increased his authority.　There is a tendency in the human mind to bring to perfection anything with which it is exclusively occupied.　The Emperor, who was continually bent on increasing his power by every possible means, and who was becoming accustomed to the exercise of his own will on every occasion, became more and more impatient of the slightest opposition. The European phalanxes were gradually giving way before him, and he began to believe that he was destined to regulate the affairs of every continental kingdom.　He looked with disdain on the progress of the age, regarding the French Revolution, which was so solemn a warning to sovereigns, only as an event whose results he might use to his own advantage; and he came to despise the cry for liberty which for twenty years had been uttered at intervals by the people.　He was persuaded that he could, at any rate, trick them by accomplishing the destruction of what had existed, and replacing it by sudden creations, which would appear to satisfy that longing for equality which he believed with reason to be the ruling passion of the time.

He tried to turn the French Revolution into a mere freak of fortune, a useless disturbance which had merely upset individuals.　How often has he not made use of these specious words, in order to allay apprehension: " The French Revolution need fear nothing, since the throne of the Bourbons is occupied by a soldier! " And at the same time he would assume toward kings the attitude of a protector of thrones —" for," he would say, " I have abolished republics." Meanwhile he was dreaming of I know not what half-feudal project, the execution of which must inevitably be full of danger, since it drove him to war, and had besides the deplorable effect of diminishing the interest he ought to have taken in France itself. Our country soon ceased to be anything more to him than one large province of that empire which he desired to bring under his rule. Less interested in our prosperity than in our grandeur, which, in point of fact, was only his own, he conceived the idea of making every foreign sovereign a feudatory of his own power. He believed he should attain to this by placing members of his family on the various thrones which at the time actually sprang from himself; and we may assure ourselves that this was really his project, by attentively reading the form of oath which he exacted from the kings or princes created by him. He sometimes said: " It is my intention to reach such a point that the kings of Europe shall be forced, each one of them, to have a palace in Paris; and, at the time of the coronation of an Emperor of the French, they shall take up their residence in it, be present at the ceremony, and render it more imposing by their homage." This, it seems to me, was a sufficiently plain declaration of his intention of renewing in 1806 the empire of Charlemagne.

But times were changed, and, as the light of knowledge spread, the people became capable of forming a judgment as to the mode in which they ought to be governed. Besides this, the Emperor perceived that the nobles could never again exercise influence over the people, which had often been an obstacle to the authority of our kings; and he conceived the idea that it was from popular encroachment he must defend himself, and that the spirit of the age required him to take a contrary course to that which for centuries past had been the custom of kings.

It was the fact that, whereas formerly the nobles had almost always hampered the royal authority, at the present time some intermediary creation was needed by that very authority, which, in this age of liberal opinions, would naturally lean to the side of the sovereign, and retard the march of pretensions which, from being merely popular, had now become national. From this came the reëstablishment of a nobility, and the renewal of certain privileges which were always prudently distributed among distinguished members of the ancient nobility, and plebeians who had been ennobled by an act of the Imperial will.

All these things are a proof that the Emperor entertained this project of a new kind of feudality fashioned in accordance with his own ideas. But, besides the obstacles which England continually placed in his way, there was another, absolutely inherent in his own character. There would seem to have been in him two different men. The one, rather gigantic than great, but nevertheless prompt to conceive and also prompt to execute, laid from time to time some of the foundations of the plan he had formed. This man, actuated by one single idea, untouched by any secondary impression likely to interfere with his projects, had he but taken for his aim the good of mankind, would, with such abilities as he displayed, have become the one greatest man of the earth; even now he remains, through his perspicacity and his strength of will, the most extraordinary.

The other Bonaparte, forming a kind of uneasy conscience to the first, was devoured by anxiety, agitated by continual suspicion, a slave to passions which gave him no rest, distrustful, fearing every rival greatness, even that which he had himself created. If the necessity of political institutions was made plain to him, he was struck at the same moment by the rights which they must confer on individuals, and then, gradually becoming afraid of his own handiwork, he could not resist the temptation to destroy it piecemeal. He has been heard to say, after he had restored titles of nobility and given inalienable possessions* to his marshals: " I have made these people independent; but I shall know how to reach them and prevent them from being ungrateful." When seized upon by this spirit of distrust of other men, he gave himself up to it entirely, and thought only of how to create divisions among them. He weakened family ties, and applied himself to promote individual rather than general interests. Sole center of an immense circle, he would have liked it to contain as many radii as he had subjects, that they might meet nowhere save in him. This suspicious jealousy, which incessantly pursued him, fastened like a canker on all his undertakings, and prevented him from establishing on a solid foundation any of the schemes which his prolific imagination was continually inventing.

After the campaign of Austerlitz he was so inflated with success, and with the worship which the people, half dazzled and half subjugated, paid to him, that his despotism became more than ever intensified. Every citizen felt the yoke that was laid on him heavier; heads were bowed almost perforce before his glory, but it was discovered afterward that he had taken means to prevent their being lifted again. He

* Majorats.

surrounded himself with new splendor in order to put a greater distance between himself and other men. He copied, from German customs which he had carefully observed, the whole etiquette of courts, which he made a daily slavery, and no one was exempt from minute observances which he brought to the utmost perfection.

It must be owned, however, that immediately after a campaign he was almost obliged to take measures which would silence the clamorous pretensions of his followers; and, when he had put these down, it did not occur to him that he ought to treat with greater consideration the other classes of citizens, of far less importance in his eyes. Military men, still flushed with victory, would assume a haughty position from which it was difficult to bring them down. I have kept a letter from M. de Rémusat, written from Schônbrunn, which describes very exactly the inflation of the generals, and the prudence that was required in order to live peaceably with them. " The military profession," he writes, " gives to a man's character a certain blunt sincerity, so that he does not try to hide the meanest passions. Our heroes, who are accustomed to open war with their enemies, acquire a habit of disguising nothing, and see a battle-field in any opposition they may meet with, of whatever kind. It is curious to hear them speak of civilians, and indeed, afterward, to hear them discuss each other—each depreciating the deeds of the others, attributing a large share of their success to luck; blackening reputations which we outsiders had thought firmly established; and, in their behavior to us, so puffed up with their newly acquired glory that one needs much tact and many sacrifices of pride, even of proper pride, to procure toleration from them."

The Emperor noticed this somewhat belligerent attitude of the officers of his army. He cared little that it was annoying to civilians, but he would not have it reach a point which might be inconvenient to himself. Therefore, while still at Munich, he thought proper to rebuke the arrogance of his marshals, and on this occasion self-interest induced him to use the language of reason. " Recollect," he said, " that you are to be soldiers only when with the army. The title of marshal is merely a civil distinction, which gives you the honorable rank at my Court that is your due, but it carries with it no authority. On the battle-field you are generals; at Court be merely great nobles, belonging to the State by the civil position I created for you when I bestowed on you the title which you bear."

This warning would have produced a greater effect had the Emperor ended it with such words as these: " In camp or in Court, recollect that your first duty everywhere is to be good citizens." He should have held similar language to all classes, to whom he was bound to be a protector as well as a master; he should have spoken the same words to all Frenchmen, and so have united them in a new equality, not adverse to distinctions won by valor. But Bonaparte, as we have seen, was always in dread of natural and generous ties, and the iron chain of despotism is the only bond he employed, because it binds each man, as it were, separately, leaving him no commerce with his fellows.

CHAPTER XVII

(1806.)

WHEN the Emperor arrived in Paris, at the end of January, 1806, the death of Pitt, at the age of forty-seven, had just occurred in England. His loss was deeply felt by the English, and a truly national regret did honor to his memory. Parliament, which had just opened, voted a large sum to defray his debts, for he died leaving no fortune, and he was splendidly buried in Westminster Abbey. When the new Ministry was formed, Mr. Fox, his opponent, was made Foreign Secretary. The Emperor looked upon the death of Pitt as a fortunate event for him, but he soon perceived that English policy had not changed, and that the British Government would not relax its endeavors to excite enmity against him among the continental Powers.

During the month of January, 1806, the debates in the English Parliament had been very warm. The Opposition, led by Mr. Fox, asked the Government for explanations as to the carrying out of the late war; it asserted that the Emperor of Austria had not been faithfully assisted, and that he had been left to the mercy of the conqueror. The Ministers then laid on the table the text of the conditions of the treaty between the various Powers at the beginning of the campaign. This treaty proved that subsidies had been granted to the coalition which had undertaken to drive the Emperor from Hanover, Germany, and Italy, to replace the King of Sardinia on the throne of Piedmont, and to secure the independence of Holland and Sweden. The rapid victories of our troops had upset these plans. The Emperor of Austria was blamed for having begun the campaign too precipitately, without waiting for the arrival of the Russians; and the King of Prussia, whose neutrality had been the principal cause of the failure of the coalition, was especially blamed. The Czar's anger was roused, and he might have been tempted to punish this fatal inaction, had not the lovely and fascinating Queen of Prussia interceded between the two sovereigns. A rumor then arose in Europe that her beauty had disarmed the Emperor of Russia, and that to it he had sacrificed his just displeasure. Napoleon, who had subdued the King of Prussia by the fear of his arms, thought it well to reward him for his neutrality by handing over Hanover to him until the very uncertain epoch of general peace. On his side, the King ceded Anspach to Bavaria, and abandoned in favor of France his claims to the duchies of Berg and of Cleves, which were bestowed shortly afterward on Prince Joachim, otherwise Murat.

The report laid before the English Parliament on the treaty of which I speak was published in our newspapers, and accompanied, as may be imagined, by remarks hostile to the continental Powers. The weakness of those kings who place themselves at the mercy of the *shopkeepers* of Europe was deplored.

" If England," so ran the comment, " should succeed in forming a fourth coalition, Austria, who lost Belgium by the first, Italy and the left bank of the Rhine by the second, Tyrol, Swabia, and the Venetian States by the third, would by the fourth lose her own crown.

" The influence of the French Empire on the Continent will secure the well-being of Europe, for with it will have begun the age of civilization, of science, of light, and of law. The Emperor of Russia has imprudently embarked, like a young man, in a dangerous policy. As to Austria, we must forget her faults, since she has suffered for them. However, it is right to say that if the treaty now made public in England had been known, perhaps Austria might not have obtained the terms which have been granted to her; and we may remark, in passing, that Count de Stadion, who concluded this treaty of subsidies, is still at the head of affairs under the Emperor Francis."

These remarks, which were the expression of an ill-concealed irritation, began to cause some little uneasiness in the early part of February, and to make attentive observers fear that peace would not be of long duration.

No treaty had been concluded with the Czar. Under pretext that he had only acted as auxiliary to the Austrians, he refused to be included in the negotiations; and I have heard it said that the Emperor, impressed by this conduct, looked upon him, from that time forth, as the veritable antagonist who would dispute with him the empire of the world. He always endeavored to depreciate him as much as possible.

There is an order in Russia which can only be worn by a general whose services have on some great occasion been useful to the empire. When Alexander returned to his capital, the knights of this order came to offer him the decoration. The Emperor declined it, replying that he had not held the chief command during the campaign, and therefore had not merited the honor, as he had only imitated the intrepidity of his brave soldiers to the best of his ability.

While our journals praised his modesty, they added: " The Czar deserved this decoration if, in order to wear it, it is sufficient to be in command without being victorious. It is well known that it was not the Emperor Francis who decided on joining battle at Austerlitz, still less did he direct operations. Certainly, by accepting the decoration, Alexander would have taken on himself the oversights of his generals; but that would have been better than to attribute the defeat of the Russians to a small number of Austrians, who fought with courage. They did all that could have been expected of them by their allies."

It was on the 2d of February that this article appeared in our public prints; on the preceding day they had published the proclamation to the Army of Italy, which announced the invasion of the kingdom of Naples. Joseph Bonaparte, seconded by Marshal Masséna, was very shortly to occupy the capital; Prince Eugène was taking possession of Venice. Thus the whole of Italy was becoming dependent on the French Empire. On another side, northern Germany was subject to us, the kings whom we had set up bound themselves to our interests, and we were shortly to witness another marriage, which would be likely to further the projects in which the Emperor was secretly indulging.

On the occasion of his journey from Munich, he had made a few hours' stay at Augsburg. While there, the former Elector of Trèves, uncle to the King of Saxony, had presented to him the young Hereditary Prince of Baden, who, confused and almost trembling in the presence of Napoleon, had humbly implored the honor of alliance with him by a marriage with some member of his family. The Emperor accepted this respectful request, and promised to bear it in mind on his return to his own states.

Finally, he had just dispatched his brother Louis on an expedition to Holland, in order to establish some acquaintanceship between the Prince and a coun-

try which was soon to receive the Imperial command
to erect a throne for Louis on the wreck of the
republic.

Such was the political situation of the Emperor.
Such a position would surely have satisfied any views
less ambitious than his own, nor can it be denied that
he had made full use of the eighteenth month of his
reign, now just expired.

In France, party spirit seemed absolutely to have
died out. All bent under the yoke; no class could be
indifferent to so much glory; and the Emperor endeavored to increase the prestige which surrounded
him still further by numerous public works, simulta-
neously undertaken. As soon as it became possible
for him to divert his attention for a moment from
foreign affairs, he devoted it to the improvement of
the finances of the country, which had suffered during his absence. M. Barbé-Marbois, Minister of the
Treasury, having incurred his displeasure, was
replaced by M. Mollien, who was a skillful financier.
The Emperor was ably seconded by his Minister of
Finance, Gaudin, whose prefect integrity and sound
knowledge sustained credit and improved the system
of taxation. Indirect taxes were ventured on to a
greater extent than before; luxury, which would
render these taxes more productive, was encouraged;
and the heavy contributions which the Emperor had
everywhere levied upon his conquered enemies
afforded him the means, without burdening his people,
of keeping up the strength of his army, and undertaking all the improvements which were begun throughout France, as if by magic, at his command.

Roads over Mont Cenis and the Simplon were
actively pushed on; bridges were built, roadways
repaired; a town was founded in Vendée; canals were
dug at Ourcq and at Saint Quentin; telegraphs (i. e.,

signals) were established to accelerate correspondence; Saint Denis was about to be repaired; the Vendôme column and the triumphal arch at the Carrousel were commenced. A plan for embanking the Seine with new quays, and for embellishing the whole neighborhood lying between the Tuileries and the Boulevards, was adopted, and the work of demolition had already made some progress. The Rue de Rivoli was planned, the colonnade of the Louvre nearly completed; Lemot, the sculptor, was intrusted with the decoration of the pediment. We could observe the gradual rise of the Pont des Arts, and the commencement of the bridge near the Jardin des Plantes, which was to bear the name of Austerlitz. The conservatories in these gardens had been enriched with spoils from those of Schônbrunn; scientific men were encouraged in the pursuit of fresh discoveries; painters received orders for pictures to commemorate our victories; the Academy of Music was encouraged; the first musical artists in Italy came to France to direct our vocal music; literary men received pensions, and large grants were made to actors; military schools were founded at Fontainebleau and at Saint Cyr; and the Emperor himself inspected the public schools of Paris. Finally, in order that the industry of the nation might be encouraged in every branch at once, he conceived the idea of an exhibition, to be held in the spring, and in commemoration of the campaign, in which every product of industry, of whatever kind, should be represented.

M. de Champagny, the Minister of the Interior, wrote a circular letter to all the prefects, directing them to inform the departments over which they presided that, on the 1st of May, there would be exhibited on the Place des Invalides, under tents erected for the occasion, everything deserving of notice in articles of use and of luxury. Trade was in this manner awakened from the torpor in which it had been plunged by the war. The Emperor ordered the splendor and the cost of his Court to be increased. He gave his approval to the growing elegance of the women's dress, to the sumptuous decoration of his own palaces, and to that of the houses of his sisters and his great nobles. The French nation, which is naturally prone to vanity and extravagance, gave itself up to the comforts and luxuries of life; and as for us, whose fortunes were but annuities depending not only on the life but on the caprice of our master, with an utter disregard of prudence, influenced by the example of others and by the fear of displeasing him, we were ruled by the will of Bonaparte alone in the use to which we put the greater or less sums he distributed to us, and which he gave with the intention of subduing rather than of enriching us.

I say *we,* and yet at this time neither M. de Rémusat nor I had any share in his gifts. The cross of Saint Hubert had been given to my husband as a recompense for his recent journey, but he never stood in the full light of Imperial favor. As for myself, I led an unobtrusive life in the midst of the Court, whose numbers were greatly augmented. To speak frankly, although I had taken pleasure in the prominence assigned to me by my masters when I first entered their service, the little experience I had acquired warned me not to endeavor to regain any position of importance, now that the interior of the palace was no longer the same. I shall devote the following chapter to the details of Court life, as it was now regulated, but I will return for the present to my narrative of events.

Immediately on the Emperor's return to his capital, he was congratulated by the respective bodies of the State.

During his stay at Munich he had witnessed a German ceremonial, in which the King and Queen of Bavaria, having taken their places on the throne, received all the persons belonging to their Court, who passed before them in succession, each making a low salutation. He desired to establish a similar custom in France, and we received orders to prepare for this new " etiquette."

The fact is that, at that time, everything had to be constructed afresh. Revolutionary liberty had suppressed all the rules of politeness. People no longer knew how to salute each other when they met, and all we court ladies suddenly discovered that the art of making a courtesy had been omitted in our education. Despréaux, who had been dancing-master to the last Queen, was thereupon summoned to give us lessons. He taught us how to walk and how to bow; and thus a little boundary-line, trifling enough in itself, but which acquired some importance from its motive, was drawn between the ladies of the Imperial Court and those belonging to other circles. We took with us into society ceremonious manners, which distinguished us everywhere; for a spirit of opposition caused those women who kept aloof from the new Court to retain the free and rather abrupt manners which the absence of the habits of society had given them. In France, opinions make themselves felt everywhere; they now showed themselves in the different way in which a lady-in-waiting and a lady from the Faubourg Saint Germain would enter a drawing-room. But, putting motives aside, it must be owned that the advantage was ours. This was evident after the return of the King: those ladies who had a real right to be about him, either from the habit of freedom of manner which they had acquired, or from the relief they affected to feel at finding themselves on what great people call *their own ground,* introduced at the Tuileries a bold manner and loud tones of voice, which contrasted sharply with the quiet and graceful behavior that Bonaparte's punctilious etiquette had made habitual to us.

On an appointed day, therefore, the Emperor placed himself on his throne, having the Empress on his left, the Princesses and the Lady of Honor seated on court tabourets, and the grand officers standing on either side. The ladies-in-waiting, the wives of the marshals, of the great officials, and of the ministers, all in full court dress, then came in slow procession to the foot of the throne, where they courtesied in silence. They were followed by the gentlemen.

The ceremony was very long. At first the Emperor was delighted. He took pleasure in etiquette, especially when invented by himself; but he ended by being mortally wearied. Toward the end, every one was hurried past; there was some difficulty in inducing him to remain on the throne until the close, and he was almost angry with us for our share in a ceremonial which he himself had imposed on us, in the exercise of his own will.

A few nights afterward he went to the Opéra, and was received with applause by an immense crowd. A piece by Esménard, author of the " Poème de la Navigation," was given.

The scenery at the Opéra represented the Pont Neuf. Persons of all nationalities were rejoicing together, and singing verses in honor of the conqueror. The pit joined in the choruses; branches of laurel were distributed throughout the house, and waved aloft with cries of " Vive l'Empereur ! " He was touched, as well he might be. It was, perhaps, the very last time that public enthusiasm for him was spontaneous.

Shortly afterward the Emperor received a similar

ovation at the Comédie Française, but an unforeseen circumstance threw a slight shadow over the evening. Talma was acting the part of Abner in the tragedy of " Athalie." During the performance Bonaparte received a messenger bringing the news of the entry of the French troops into Naples. He immediately dispatched an aide-de-camp to Talma, with orders to interrupt the play, and to announce the news from the foot-lights. Talma obeyed, and read the bulletin aloud. The audience applauded, but I remember thinking that the applause was not so spontaneous as that we had heard at the Opéra.

On the following day our newspapers announced the fall of her whom they designated as the modern Athalie; and the vanquished Queen was grossly insulted, with total disregard of the social propriety that generally enforces respect toward misfortune.

It was remarked shortly afterward that, on the opening of the Legislative Assemblies, M. de Fontanes displayed great tact, when he praised Bonaparte, in avoiding any insult to the fallen sovereigns whom he had dethroned. He dwelt chiefly, in his eulogium, on the moderation which had promoted peace, and on the restoration of the tombs in St. Denis. M. de Fontanes's speeches during this reign are, on the whole, distinguished by propriety and good taste.

After having thus shown himself to the public and exhausted every form of adulation, the Emperor resumed his life of hard work at the Tuileries, and we our life of etiquette, which was regulated with extreme precision. He began from this period to surround himself with so much ceremonial that none of us thenceforth could be said to have any familiarity with him. In proportion as the Court became more numerous, it assumed a greater appearance of monotony, each one doing his own task by clockwork; but no one

thought of emancipating himself from the one groove
of thought belonging to a narrow circle of small duties.
A daily growing despotism, the fear we all felt of it—
a fear which consisted simply in our dread of receiving a rebuke for the smallest fault—and the silence
we observed on every subject, placed the various inhabitants of the Tuileries on the same level. It was useless to have either opinions or talents, for there was
never any possibility of experiencing a feeling of any
kind, nor of exchanging an idea.

The Emperor, feeling secure of France, gave himself up to his grand projects, and kept his eyes fixed
on Europe. His policy was no longer directed to
securing his power over the opinions of his fellow
citizens. In like manner, he disdained the little successes of private life, which we have seen him at an
earlier period anxious to obtain; and I may say that
he looked upon his Court with the indifference which
a complete conquest inspires, when compared with
one as yet unattained. He was always anxious to
impose a yoke on every one, and to succeed in this he
neglected no means to his end; but, from the moment
he perceived his power to be established, he took no
pains to make himself agreeable.

The dependence and constraint in which he held the
Court had at least this one advantage: anything
resembling intrigue was almost unknown. As each
individual was firmly convinced that everything depended on the sole will of the master, no one attempted
to follow a different path from that traced out by him;
and in our dealings with each other there was a feeling
of security.

His wife was almost in the same position of dependence as others. In proportion as Bonaparte's affairs
increased in magnitude, she became a stranger to
them. European politics, the destiny of the world,

mattered little to her; her thoughts did not reach to heights which could have no influence on her own fate. At this period she was tranquil as to her own lot, and happy in that of her son; and she lived a life of peaceful indifference, behaving to all with equal graciousness, showing little or no special favor to any one, but a general good will. She neither sought for amusement nor feared *ennui;* she was always gentle and serene, and, in fact, was indifferent to nearly all things. Her love for her husband had greatly declined, and she no longer suffered from the jealousy which had in former years so much disturbed her. Every day she judged him with greater clearness, and, being convinced that her greatest source of influence over him consisted in the sense of restfulness imparted to him by the evenness of her temper, she took pains to avoid disturbing him. I have said long ago that such a man as he had neither time nor inclination for much display of affection, and the Empress at this period forgave him all the fancies which sometimes take the place of love in a man's life; nay, more, she became his confidante in these little affairs.

On his return from Austerlitz, he again met Mme. de X——, but seemed to take no notice of her. The Empress treated her precisely as she treated others. It has been said that Bonaparte occasionally returned to his former fancy for this lady; but, if so, it was so temporarily that the Court barely perceived the fact, and, as it gave rise to no new incident, it awakened no interest. The Emperor, who was convinced that the influence of women had harmed the kings of France, was irrevocably resolved that they should never be more than an ornament to his Court, and he kept his resolution. He had persuaded himself, I know not how, that in France women are cleverer than men, or at any rate he often said so, and that the education they receive develops a certain kind of ability, against which one must be on one's guard. He felt, therefore, a slight fear of them, and kept them at a distance on this account. He exhibited a dislike of certain women's temper which amounted to weakness.

He banished Mme. de Staël, of whom he was genuinely afraid, and shortly afterward Mme. de Balbi, who had ventured on some jesting remarks concerning himself. She had indiscreetly made these observations in the hearing of a person whom I will not name, and who repeated all he had heard. This individual was a gentleman and a Chamberlain. I mention the fact in order to prove that the Emperor found persons in every class who were willing to serve him in his own way.

We began to perceive, during the winter of this year, how unhappy Mme. Louis was in her home life. Her husband's tyranny was exercised in every particular; his character, quite as despotic as his brother's, made itself felt throughout his household. Until now his wife had courageously hidden the excess to which he carried his tyranny; but a circumstance occurred which obliged her to confide some of her troubles to her mother.

The health of Louis Bonaparte was very bad. Since his return from Egypt he had suffered from frequent attacks of a malady which had so weakened his legs and his hands that he walked with difficulty, and was stiff in every joint. Every remedy known to medicine was tried in vain. Corvisart, who was medical attendant to the whole family, advised him to try, as a last resource, a disgusting remedy. He imagined that a violent eruption on the skin would perhaps draw out the poison which had defied other treatment. It was therefore decided that on the state bed of Louis, under its embroidered canopy, should be spread the hospital

sheets of some patient suffering from the itch; and his
Imperial Highness placed himself between them, and
even put on the sick man's night-shirt. Louis, who
wished to hide this experiment from everybody, insisted that nothing should be changed in the habits of
his wife. They usually slept in the same room, though
not in the same bed; he had always obliged her to
pass the night near him on a small bed placed under
the same canopy. He imperatively commanded that
she should continue to occupy this bed, adding, in a
spirit of strange jealousy, that no husband should
ever omit to take precautions against the natural in-
constancy of women. Mme. Louis, notwithstanding
her disgust, submitted in silence to this gross abuse of
conjugal authority.

Meanwhile, Corvisart, who was in attendance on
her, and who remarked a change in her appearance,
questioned her respecting the details of her life, and
obtained from her an admission of her husband's
strange fancy. He thought it his duty to inform the
Empress, and did not conceal from her that, in his
opinion, the atmosphere of Louis's bedroom was very
unwholesome for his wife.

Mme. Bonaparte warned her daughter, who replied
that she had thought as much; but, nevertheless, she
earnestly entreated her mother not to interfere between
her husband and herself. Then, no longer able to
restrain herself, she entered into particulars which
showed how grinding was the tyranny from which she
suffered, and how admirable the silence she had
hitherto kept. Mme. Bonaparte appealed to the
Emperor, who was attached to his stepdaughter, and
he expressed his displeasure to his brother. Louis
coldly replied that, if his private affairs were interfered with, he should leave France; and the Emperor,
who could not tolerate any open scandal in the family,

and who was perhaps, like the others, daunted by Louis's strange and obstinate temper, advised Mme. Louis to have patience. Happily for her, her husband soon gave up the disgusting remedy in question, but he owed her a deep grudge for not having kept his secret.

Had her daughter been happy, there was nothing at this time to disturb the tranquillity of the Empress. The Bonaparte family, full of their own affairs, no longer interfered with her; Joseph was absent and about to ascend the throne of Naples; Lucien was exiled for ever from France; the youthful Jérôme was cruising along our coasts; Mme. Bacciochi was reigning at Piombino; and the Princess Borghese, alternating between physic and dissipation, meddled with nobody. Mme. Murat only might have caused annoyance to her sister-in-law, but she was engaged in promoting her husband's interests, to which the Empress made no opposition; for she would have rejoiced greatly at Murat's obtaining a principality which would have removed him from Paris.

Mme. Murat used her utmost efforts, and was even importunate with the Emperor, in order to attain her ends. She connived at his gallantries, lent him her house on occasions when it was convenient to him to use it, and tried to divert him by fêtes, and to please him by a display of luxury according to his taste. She interested herself in every detail of the etiquette that he wished to introduce, and assumed airs of dignity, somewhat stilted perhaps, which induced him to declare that his sister was in every respect fitted to be a queen. She neglected no means of success, paid attention to Maret, who had gradually gained the sort of influence that is acquired by assiduity, and flattered Fouché into a zealous attachment to her interests. The understanding between Mme. Murat and these two personages, who were both ill-disposed toward M. de Talleyrand, increased the dislike of the latter to Murat; and, as at this period he was in high favor, he often thwarted Mme. Murat's plans. Murat used to say, in the southern accent he never lost, " Would not Moussu dé Talleyrand like me to be broken on the wheel! "

Murat, relying on his wife to further his interests, contented himself with giving no cause of offense to the Emperor, behaved toward him with entire submission, and bore his alternations of temper without complaint. Brave to excess on the battle-field, he had not, it was said, any great military talent; and when with the army he asked for nothing but the post of danger. He was not wanting in quickness, his manners were obliging; his attitudes and his dress were always rather theatrical, but a fine figure and noble appearance saved him from looking ridiculous. The Emperor reposed no confidence in him, but he employed him, because he feared him in no wise, and because he could not help believing in every kind of flattery. A certain sort of credulity is not rarely combined in the same character with distrust; and those great men who are the most suspicious by nature are not the least amenable to flattery.

On his return from the campaign of Austerlitz the Emperor distributed further rewards to his generals. To some he gave considerable sums of money, to reimburse them for the expenses of the campaign. General Clarke was made Grand Officer of the Legion of Honor, in recognition of the manner in which he had fulfilled his duties as Governor of Vienna. Hitherto Clarke had been treated with some coldness; the Emperor showed him but little confidence, and accused him of retaining a secret affection for the house of Orleans; but he succeeded in convincing Bonaparte of

his obsequious devotion.   General Clarke, now Duc de
Feltre, has for the last three years played a somewhat
conspicuous part, and it may be well to give some
particulars of his career.

His uncle, M. Shee, who was made Senator by the
Emperor, and who is a peer of France, was previous
to the Revolution secretary-general to a division of
light cavalry, of which the Duke of Orleans was
colonel-general.   He was accompanied by his nephew,
Clarke, whom he had sent for from the country.   The
young man found himself specially attached to the
house of Orleans, and it is on this account, perhaps,
that Bonaparte suspected him of private leanings
toward that party.   He served the Revolution with
zeal, and was even employed, in 1794 and 1795, by the
Committee of Public Safety, in the war administration.

He accompanied Bonaparte into Italy, but haughty
manners were displeasing to the commander-in-chief.
Later on he was sent as ambassador to Tuscany, and
remained there for a considerable time, although he
frequently applied for his recall and for employment
in France.   On finally obtaining these, he applied himself to overcoming Bonaparte's prejudice against him:
he flattered him assiduously, solicited the favor of a
post in his personal service, displayed the absolute
submission demanded by such a master, and was
eventually made Councilor of State and private secretary.   He was very hard-working and punctual, and
never wanted recreation.   He was narrow-minded
and unimaginative, but clear-headed.   He accompanied
the Emperor in the first Vienna campaign, showed
capacity as Governor of the city, and received a first
reward on his return.   We shall hear of him later on
as Minister of War, and in every capacity as a man of
second-rate ability.   His integrity has always been

freely acknowledged; he amassed no fortune except that which resulted from the savings of his various salaries. Like M. Maret, he carried the language of flattery to its extreme limits.

His first marriage was unhappy, and he obtained a divorce. He had one daughter, a gentle and agreeable girl, whom he gave in marriage while he was in office to the Vicomte Emery de Montesquiou-Fezensac, whose military advancement, thanks to his father-in-law, was very rapid. This young man is at the present time aide-major-general in the Royal Guards. The Duc de Feltre's second wife was an excellent but insignificant woman. By her he had several sons.

Meanwhile, M. de Talleyrand's friendliness toward M. de Rémusat brought me into a closer acquaintance with him. He did not as yet visit at my house, but I frequently met him, and wherever this occurred he took more notice of me than formerly. He seldom missed an opportunity of praising my husband, and thus he gratified the feelings dearest to my heart; and, if I must speak the whole truth, he gratified my vanity also by seeking me out on all occasions. He won me over to him by degrees, and my former prejudice against him vanished. Yet he would sometimes alarm me by certain expressions for which I was unprepared. One day I was speaking to him of the recent conquest of Naples, and ventured to let him perceive that I disapproved of our policy of universal dethronement. He replied in the cold and deliberate tone that he knows so well how to assume when he means to permit no reply, " Madame, we shall not desist until there shall no longer be a Bourbon on a European throne." These words gave me pain. I thought little, I must admit, about our royal family; but still, at the sound of the name of Bourbon, certain recollections of my early days awakened former feelings that had faded rather than disappeared.

I could not, at the present time, attempt to explain this feeling without running the risk of being accused of insincerity, which is absolutely foreign to my character. It may be thought that, remembering the period at which I write, I want gradually to prepare the way for my own return to those opinions which everybody now hastens to parade. But this is not the case. In those days I admired the Emperor; I was still attached to him, although less fascinated by him; I believed him to be necessary to France; he appeared to me to have become her legitimate sovereign. But all these feelings were combined with a tender reverence for the heirs and all the kin of Louis XVI.; it pained me deeply when fresh misfortunes were prepared for them and I heard them evil spoken of. Bonaparte had often inflicted suffering of this kind on me. To a man who only appreciated success, Louis XVI. must have seemed deserving of little respect. He was entirely unjust toward him, and believed in all the popular stories against him, which were the offspring of the Revolution. When the conversation turned on that illustrious and unfortunate King, I endeavored as soon as possible to change the subject.

But to return. Such was M. de Talleyrand's opinion at that time; I will show by degrees, and when the time comes, how events subsequently modified it.

During the winter the heir of the King of Bavaria came on a visit to our Court. He was young, deaf, not very amiable; but he had very polished manners, and he showed great deference toward the Emperor. He had apartments at the Tuileries, two chamberlains and an equerry were placed at his service, and every attention was paid to him.

On the 10th of February the list of ladies-in-waiting

was increased by the names of Mme. Maret, on the request of Mme. Murat, and of Mmes. de Chevreuse, de Montmorency-Matignon, and de Mortemart.

M. de Talleyrand was an intimate friend of the Duchesse de Luynes, and he induced her to make her daughter-in-law accept a place at Court. The Duchess was greatly attached to Mme. de Chevreuse. The latter had very pronounced opinions of her own, and every one of them distinctly opposed to what was expected of her. Bonaparte threatened; M. de Talleyrand negotiated, and, according to custom, obtained his way. Madame de Chevreuse was pretty, although red-haired, and very witty, but excessively spoiled by her family, willful and fantastic. Her health even then was very delicate. The Emperor tried by coaxing to console her for having forced her into the Court. At times he would appear to have succeeded, and then at others she would take no pains to conceal her dislike to her position. Her natural disposition gave her an attraction for the Emperor, which others would have vainly endeavored to exert, the charm of combat and of victory. For she would sometimes seem to be amused with the fêtes and the splendor of the Court; and when she appeared there in full dress and apparently in good spirits, then the Emperor, who enjoyed even the smallest success, would laugh and say, " I have overcome the aversion of Mme. de Chevreuse." But, in reality, I do not think he ever did.

The Baronne de Montmorency (now Duchesse de Montmorency), who was extremely intimate with M. de Talleyrand, had been induced to join the Court, partly by his persuasions, and partly by her wish to regain some extensive forest-lands which were seized by Government during her emigration, but had not yet been sold. Mme. de Montmorency was extremely

pleasant at Court; she demeaned herself without either
pride or subservience, appeared to enjoy herself, and
made no pretense of being there against her will.   I
think she found court life very agreeable, and that
possibly she may have regretted it.   Her name gave
her an advantage, as it does in every place.   The
Emperor often said that he cared only for the nobility
of history, and he certainly paid it great honor.

This reminds me of an anecdote concerning Bonaparte.   When he resolved on reconstituting titles, he
decided by a stroke of his pen that all the ladies-in-
waiting should be countesses.   Mme. de Montmorency,
who stood in no need of a title, but found herself
obliged to take one, asked for the title of baroness,
which, she said laughingly, suited her name so well.
" That can not be," replied Bonaparte, laughing too;
" you, madame, are not a sufficiently good Christian."

Some years later the Emperor restored to MM. de
Montmorency and de Mortemart a large portion of
the fortune they had lost.   M. de Mortemart, declining to become an equerry on account of the too great
fatigue of the post, was made Governor of Rambouillet.   We have all known the Vicomte de Laval-
Montmorency, father of the Vicomte Mathieu de
Montmorency, a Gentleman of Honor to Madame,
Governor of Compiègne, and one of the most ardent
admirers of Bonaparte.

From this time forward there was increasing eagerness to belong to the Emperor's Court, and especially
to be presented to him.   His receptions became very
brilliant.   Ambition, fear, vanity, love of amusement
and novelty, and the desire of advancement, caused a
crowd of people to push themselves forward, and the
mixture of names and ranks became greater than ever.

M. Molé joined the Government in the month of
March of this year.   He was the heir and last descend-

ant of Mathieu Molé, and was then twenty-six years of age. He was born during the Revolution, and had suffered from the misfortunes it caused. His father perished under the tyrannical rule of Robespierre, and he became his own master at an early age. He made use of his freedom to devote himself to serious and varied study. His family and friends married him, at the age of nineteen, to Mlle. de la Briche, heiress to a considerable fortune, and niece to Mme. d'Houdetot, of whom I have already spoken. M. Molé, who was naturally of a grave disposition, soon became weary of a merely worldly life, and, having no profession, he sought to fill up his time by literary compositions, which he showed to his friends. Toward the end of 1805 he wrote a short treatise, extremely metaphysical and not very clear, on a theory of authority and the will of man. His friends, who were surprised at the research indicated by such a work, advised him to print the treatise. His youthful vanity readily consented to this. The public looked indulgently on the work on account of his youth; both depth and talent were recognized in it, but, at the same time, a tendency to praise despotic government, which gave rise to an impression that the author aimed at attracting the attention of him who at that time held the destinies of all in his hand. Whether this was really in the mind of the writer, or whether he was horrified at the abuse of liberty, and for the first time in his life believed his country to be at rest and in security under the guidance of a strong will, I do not know. At any rate, M. Molé gave his work to the public, and it made some sensation.

After the return from Vienna, M. de Fontanes, who had a great regard for M. Molé, read the book to Bonaparte, who was greatly struck by it. The opinions it advanced, the superior mind it attested,

and the distinguished name of Molé attracted his
attention. He sent for the author, and praised him
as he well knew how; for he had great skill in the use
of words seductive to the young. He succeeded in
persuading him to enter into public life, promising
him that his career should be rapid and brilliant; and,
a few days after this interview, M. Molé was appointed
one of the auditors attached to the Interior Section.
He was a familiar friend of M. d'Houdetot, his cousin,
a grandson of her whom the " Confessions " of J. J.
Rousseau have made famous, and M. Molé persuaded
him to enter together with himself on the same career.
M. d'Houdetot was made auditor to the Naval Section.
His father held a command in the colonies, and was
taken prisoner by the English on the capture of Martinique. He had passed a part of his life in the Isle
de France, and returned, bringing with him a beautiful
wife and nine children, five of them girls. His daughters were all handsome; they are now living in Paris.
Some of them are married; one of them is Mme. de
Barante, the most beautiful woman in Paris at the
present time.

The fusion that was spreading with so much rapidity
brought about social concord, by mingling the interests
of all. M. Molé, for instance, belonging on his own
side to a very distinguished family, and on his wife's
to people of rank—for Mme. Molé's cousins were
Mmes. de Vintimille and de Fezensac—became a link
between the Emperor and a large circle of society.
My intimacy with members of his family was of old
date, and I was glad to see them taking their share of
the new places which were within the reach of those
who chose to take them. Opinions abated in the face
of self-interest; party spirit began to die out; ambition, pleasure, and luxury drew people together; and
every day discontent was lessened.

If Bonaparte, who was so successful in conciliating individuals, had but gone a step further, and, instead of governing by force alone, had yielded to the reaction which longed for repose; if, now that he had conquered the present moment, he had made himself master of the future, by creating durable institutions independent of his own caprice—there is little doubt but that his victory over our recollections, our prejudices, and our regrets would have been as lasting as it was remarkable. But it must be confessed that liberty, true liberty, was wanting everywhere; and the fault of the nation consisted in not perceiving this in time. As I have said before, the Emperor improved the finances, and encouraged trade, science, and art; merit was rewarded in every class; but all this was spoiled by the stamp of slavery. Being resolved on ruling everything himself, and for his own advantage, he always put himself forward as the ultimate aim. It is said that on starting for the first campaign in Italy, he told a friend who was editor of a newspaper: "Recollect in your accounts of our victories to speak of *me*, always of *me*. Do you understand?" This "*me*" was the ceaseless cry of purely egotistical ambition. "Quote *me*," "Sing, praise, and paint *me*," he would say to orators, to musicians, to poets, and to painters. "I will buy you at your own price; but you must all be purchased." Thus, notwithstanding his desire to make his reign famous by gathering together every kind of prodigy, he neutralized his efforts and ours by denying to talent that noble independence which alone can develop invention or genius of any kind.

CHAPTER XVIII
(1806.)

I THINK it will not be amiss at this point to devote a few pages to the interior management of what was called "the Emperor's household." Although, at the present time, his own private concerns and those of his Court have even more completely passed away than his policy and his power, still there will be perhaps some interest in an account of his minute regulations of the actions and the expenditure of each person belonging to the Court. He was always and in all things the same, and this fidelity to the system he had irrevocably adopted is one of the most singular sides of his character. The details I am about to give relate to several periods of his reign; but from the year 1806 the rules of his household were pretty nearly invariable, and the slight modifications which they sometimes received scarcely altered the general plan of their arrangement. I shall therefore sketch this general plan, aided by the excellent memory of M. de Rémusat, who during ten years was both a spectator and an actor in the scenes I am about to describe.

The civil list of France, under Bonaparte, amounted to a sum of twenty-five millions; in addition to this, crown lands and forests brought in three millions, and the civil list of Italy eight millions, of which he granted four to Prince Eugène. From Piedmont, partly by the civil list and partly by crown property, he received three millions; after Prince Borghese had been appointed Governor, only half that sum. Finally, four millions came from Tuscany, which were also afterward shared with Mme. Bacciochi, when she became Grand Duchess of Tuscany. The fixed revenue of the Emperor amounted, therefore, to 35,500,000 francs.

He kept at his own disposal the greater part of the sum allotted to the secret service of foreign affairs, and also the eighteen hundred thousand francs allotted to the theatres, of which barely twelve hundred thousand were voted by the yearly budget for their support. He dispensed the remainder in presents to actors, artists, men of letters, or even to officers of his household.

The fund for the maintenance of the police, after subtracting the expenses of the department, was also at his disposal; and this yielded a considerable sum every year, being derived from the tax on gaming-houses, which amounted to more than four million francs. He could also dispose of the share that the Government had reserved to itself on all newspapers, which must have brought in nearly a million francs; and, finally, of the sum yielded by stamps on passports and on permits to carry arms.

The sums levied during war were placed to the extraordinary credit, of which Bonaparte disposed as he liked. He frequently retained a large portion, which he made use of to supply the cost of the Spanish war, and for the immense preparations for the Russian campaign. Finally, he converted a considerable portion into specie and diamonds; these were deposited in the cellars of the Tuileries, and defrayed the cost of the war of 1814, when the destruction of public credit had paralyzed other resources.

The utmost order prevailed in Bonaparte's house-

hold; liberal salaries were paid to every one, but all
was so regulated that no official could use for himself
the sums that were intrusted to him.

His great officers received a fixed salary of forty
thousand francs. The last two years of his reign he
endowed the posts of great officers with a considerable income, besides the sums granted to the individuals who filled them.

The posts of Grand Marshal, of Grand Chamberlain, and of Grand Equerry were each endowed with
one hundred thousand francs; those of High Almoner
and Grand Veneur with eighty thousand francs; that
of Grand Master of Ceremonies with sixty thousand.
The Intendant and the Treasurer each received forty
thousand francs. M. Daru was the first Intendant;
he was succeeded by M. de Champagny when the latter retired from the Ministry of Foreign Affairs.
The First Prefect of the Palace and the Gentleman of
Honor to the Empress each received thirty thousand
francs.

M. de Nansouty, my brother-in-law, was for some
time First Chamberlain to the Empress; but, this post
having been abolished, he was made First Equerry
to the Emperor. The Lady of Honor received forty
thousand francs; the Mistress of the Robes, thirty
thousand. There were eighteen Chamberlains.
Those of oldest date received either twelve, six, or
three thousand francs, varying according to a sum
fixed by the Emperor every year; the others were
honorary. Bonaparte, moreover, regulated every
salary in his household annually, augmenting thereby
the dependence of us all by the uncertainty in which
we were kept.

The Equerries received twelve thousand francs;
the Prefects of the Palace, or Maîtres d'Hôtel, fifteen
thousand, and the Master of Ceremonies a like sum.

Each aide-de-camp received twenty-four thousand, as an officer of the household.

The Grand Marshal, or Master of the Household, superintended all the expenses of the table, of the domestic service, lighting and heating, etc. These expenses amounted to nearly two millions.

Bonaparte's table was abundant and well served. The plate was of silver and very handsome; on great occasions the dinner service was of silver-gilt. Mme. Murat and the Princess Borghese used dinner-services of silver-gilt.

The Grand Marshal was the chief of the Prefects of the Palace; his uniform was amethyst-colored, embroidered in silver. The Prefects of the Palace wore the same colored uniform, less richly embroidered.

The expenditure of the Grand Equerry (Master of the Horse) amounted to three or four millions. There were about twelve hundred horses. The carriages, which were more ponderous than elegant, were all painted green. The Empress had some equipages, among them some pretty open carriages, but no separate stable establishment. The Grand Equerry and the other Equerries wore a uniform of dark blue, embroidered in silver.

The Grand Chamberlain had charge of all the attendance in the interior of all the palaces, of the wardrobe, the Court theatricals, the fêtes, the chapel choir, of the Emperor's Chamberlains, and of those of the Empress. The expenditure on all these scarcely exceeded three millions. His uniform was red, with silver embroidery. The Grand Master of Ceremonies received little more than three hundred thousand francs; his costume was of violet and silver. The Grand Veneur, or Master of the Hunt, received seven hundred thousand francs: he wore green and silver.

The expenditure on the chapel was three hundred thousand francs.

The decorations of the apartments, as well as the care of the buildings, was in charge of the Intendant. The expenses of these would amount to five or six millions.

It will be seen that, on an average, the expenditure of the Emperor's household would amount to fifteen or sixteen millions of francs annually.

In later years he built extensively, and the expenditure was increased.

Every year he ordered hangings and furniture for the various palaces from Lyons. This was with a view to encouraging the manufactures of that city. For the same reason he bought handsome pieces of furniture in mahogany, which were placed in storerooms, and also bronzes, etc. Porcelain manufacturers had orders to supply complete services of extreme beauty.

On the return of the King, the palaces were all found to be newly furnished, and the furniture stores quite full.

But, including all these things, the expenditure never exceeded twenty millions, even in the most costly years, such as those of the coronation and of the marriage.

Bonaparte's expenditure on dress was put down on the budget at forty thousand francs. Sometimes it slightly exceeded this sum. During campaigns it was necessary to send him both linen and clothes to several places at once. The slightest sense of inconvenience, or the smallest difference of quality in the linen or cloth, would make him throw aside a coat or any other garment.

He always said he wished to dress like a simple officer of his own Guards, and grumbled continually at what, as he said, " he was made to spend "; while, from his caprice or awkwardness, the entire renewal of his wardrobe was constantly necessary. Among other destructive habits, he had that of stirring the wood-fires with his foot, thereby scorching his shoes and boots. This generally happened when he was in a passion; at such times he would violently kick the blazing logs in the nearest fireplace.

M. de Rémusat was for several years Keeper of the Wardrobe, receiving no emoluments. When M. de Turenne succeeded to that post, a salary of twelve thousand francs was awarded to him.

Every year the Emperor himself drew up a scheme of household expenditure with scrupulous care and remarkable economy. During the last quarter of each year the head of each department regulated his expenses for the following twelvemonth. When this was accomplished, a council was held and everything was carefully discussed. This council consisted of the Grand Marshal, who presided, the great officers, the Intendant, and the Treasurer to the Crown. The expenses of the Empress's household were comprised in the accounts of the Grand Chamberlain, on whose budget they were entered. In these councils the Grand Marshal and the Treasurer undertook to defend the Emperor's interests. The consultation being over, the Grand Marshal took the accounts to the Emperor, who examined them himself, and returned them with marginal notes. After a short interval, the council met again, under the presidency of the Emperor himself, who went over each item of expenditure anew. These consultations were generally repeated several times; the accounts of each department were then returned to its chief, and fair copies of them were made, after which they passed through the hands of the Intendant, who finally inspected them, together with the Emperor, in presence of the Grand Marshal. By these means all expenditures was fixed, and seldom indeed did any of the great officers obtain the sums for which they had asked.

Bonaparte's hour for rising was irregular, but usually it was seven o'clock. If he woke during the night, he would resume his work, or take a bath or a meal. He generally awoke depressed, and apparently in pain. He suffered frequently from spasms in the stomach, which produced vomiting. At times this appeared to alarm him greatly, as if he feared he had taken poison, and then it was difficult to prevent him from increasing the sickness by taking emetics.

The only persons who had the right of entry into his dressing-room without being announced were the Grand Marshal and the principal physician. The Keeper of the Wardrobe was announced, but was almost always admitted. He would have wished M. de Rémusat to employ these morning visits in giving him an account of all that was said or done at Court or in the city; but my husband invariably declined the task, and persevered in his determination with praiseworthy obstinacy.

The other physicians or surgeons on duty might not come unless they were summoned. Bonaparte seemed to put no great faith in medicine—it was frequently a matter of jesting with him; but he had great confidence in Corvisart, and much esteem for him. He had good health and a strong constitution; but, when he suffered from any indisposition, he became uneasy and nervous. He was occasionally troubled with a slight affection of the skin, and sometimes complained of his liver. He ate moderately, drank little, and indulged in no excesses of any kind. He took a good deal of coffee.

While dressing, he was usually silent, unless a discussion arose between him and Corvisart on some medical subject. In everything he liked to go straight to the point, and, if any one was mentioned as being ill, his first question was always, " Will he die? " A doubtful answer displeased him, and would make him argue on the inefficiency of medical science.

He acquired with great difficulty the art of shaving himself. M. de Rémusat induced him to undertake this task on seeing that he was uneasy and nervous under the hands of a barber. After many trials, and when he had finally succeeded, he often said that the advice to shave himself with his own hand had been of signal service to him.

Bonaparte so thoroughly accustomed himself during his reign to make no account of those about him, that this habitual disregard pervaded all his habits. He had not any of the delicacy that is ordinarily imparted by training and education, and would make his toilet in the most thorough fashion in the presence of any person whomsoever. In the same way, if he got impatient while his valet was dressing him, he would fly into a passion, heedless of all respect for himself or others. He would throw any garment that did not please him on the floor or into the fire. He attended to his hands and nails with great care. Several pairs of nail-scissors had to be in readiness, as he would break or throw them away if they were not sufficiently sharp. He never made use of any perfume except eau de Cologne, but of that he would get through sixty bottles in a month. He considered it a very wholesome practice to sprinkle himself thoroughly with eau de Cologne. Personal cleanliness was with him a matter of calculation, for, as I said before, he was naturally careless.

When his toilet was concluded, he went to his cabinet, where his private secretary was in attendance.

Precisely at nine o'clock, the Chamberlain on duty, who had arrived at the palace at eight A. M., and had carefully inspected the whole suite of rooms, that all might be in perfect order, and seen that the servants were at their posts, knocked at the door and announced the *levée*. He never entered the cabinet unless told to come in by the Emperor. I have already given an account of these *levées*. When they were over, Bonaparte frequently gave private audiences to some of the principal persons present—princes, ministers, high officials or prefects on leave. Those who had not the right of entry to the *levée* could only obtain an audience by applying to the Chamberlain on duty, who presented their names to the Emperor. He generally refused to see the applicants.

The *levée* and audiences would last until the hour of breakfast. That meal was served at eleven o'clock, in what was called the *salon de service,* the same apartments in which he held private audiences and received his ministers. The Prefect of the Palace announced breakfast, and remained present, standing all the time. During breakfast the Emperor received artists or actors. He would eat quickly of two or three dishes, and finish with a large cup of coffee without milk. After breakfast he returned to his work. The *salon* of which I have just spoken was ordinarily occupied by the Colonel-General of the Guards on duty for the week, the Chamberlain, the Equerry, the Prefect of the Palace, and, on a hunting morning, one of the officers of the hunt.

The ministerial councils were held on fixed days. There were three State councils a week. For five or six years the Emperor frequently presided over them, his Colonel-General and the Chamberlain being in attendance on him. He is said to have generally displayed remarkable ability in carrying on or suggesting discussions. He frequently astonished his hearers by observations full of luminousness and depth on subjects which would have seemed to be quite beyond his reach. In more recent times he showed less tolerance for others in these discussions, and adopted a more imperious tone. The State council, or that of the Ministers, or his own private work, lasted to six P. M.

After 1806 he almost always dined alone with his wife, except when the Court was at Fontainebleau; he would then invite guests to his table. He had all courses of the dinner placed before him at once; and he ate without paying any attention to his food, helping himself to whatever was at hand, sometimes taking preserves or creams before touching the more solid dishes. The Prefect of the Palace was present during dinner; two pages waited, and were assisted by the footmen. The dinner-hour was very irregular. If there happened to be any important business requiring his immediate attention, Bonaparte worked on, detaining the Council until six, seven, or even eight o'clock at night, without showing the smallest fatigue, or appearing to feel the need of food. Mme. Bonaparte waited for him with admirable patience, and never uttered a complaint.

The evenings were very short. I have already said how they were spent. During the winter of 1806 there were many small dancing entertainments given, both at the Tuileries and by the Princes. The Emperor would make his appearance at them for a few minutes, and always looked excessively bored. The routine of the *coucher* (retiring for the night) was the same as it was in the morning, except that the attendants came in last to receive orders. The Emperor in undressing and going to bed had no one near him except the *valets de chambre*.

No one slept in his chamber. His Mameluke lay near the inner entrance. The aide-de-camp of the day slept in the anteroom with his head against the door. In the rooms on the other side of this *salon* or anteroom, a Marshal of the Home Guard and two footmen kept watch all night.

No sentinel was ever seen in the interior of the palace. At the Tuileries there was one upon the staircase, because the staircase is open to the public, and they were everywhere at the outer doors. Bonaparte was very well protcted by very few persons; this was the care of the Grand Marshal. The police of the palace was extremely well managed. The name of every person who entered its doors was always known. No one resided there except the Grand Marshal, who ate there, and whose servants wore the Emperor's livery; but of these there were only the *valets de chambre* and the *femmes de chambre*. The Lady of Honor had an apartment which Mme. de la Rochefoucauld never occupied. At the time of the second marriage Bonaparte wished Mme. de Montebello to live there altogether. In the time of the Empress Josephine the Comtesse d'Arberg and her daughter, who had come from Brussels to be Lady of the Palace, were always lodged in the palace. At Saint Cloud all the attendants resided there. The Grand Equerry lived at the stables, which were or are those of the King. The Intendant and the Treasurer were installed there.

The Empress Josephine had six hundred thousand francs for her personal expenses. This sum in no degree sufficed her, and she incurred many debts annually. A hundred and twenty thousand francs were allowed her for her charities. The Archduchess had but three hundred thousand francs, and sixty thousand for her private purse. The reason of this difference was, that Mme. Bonaparte was compelled to assist many poor relations, whose claims on her were great and frequent. She having certain connections in France and the Archduchess none, Mme. Bonaparte was naturally obliged to spend more money. She gave much away, but, as she never made her presents from her own resources, but bought incessantly, her generosity only augmented her debts to an appalling degree.

Notwithstanding the wishes of her husband, she could never submit to either order or etiquette in her private life. He was unwilling that any salesman of any kind should be received by her, but was obliged to relinquish this point. Her small private apartments were crowded by these people, as well as by artists of all kinds. She had a perfect mania for being painted, and gave her pictures to whomsoever wanted them—relations, friends, *femmes de chambre,* and even to her tradespeople, who brought her constantly diamonds and jewels, stuffs and gewgaws of all kinds. She bought everything, rarely asking the price, and the greater part of the time forgot what she had bought. From the beginning she had signified to her Lady of Honor and her Lady in Waiting that they were not to interfere with her wardrobe. All matters of that kind were arranged between herself and her *femmes de chambre,* of whom she had six or eight, I think.

She rose at nine o'clock. Her toilet consumed much time; a part of it was entirely private, when she lavished unwearied efforts on the preservation of her person and on its embellishment, with the aid of paint and powder. When all this was accomplished, she wrapped herself in a long and very elegant peignoir trimmed with lace, and placed herself under the hands of her hair-dresser. Her chemises and skirts were embroidered and trimmed. She changed all her linen three times each day, and never wore any stockings that were not new. While her hair was being dressed, if we presented ourselves at her door, we were admitted. When this process was finished, huge baskets were brought in containing many different dresses, shawls, and hats. There were in summer muslin or percale robes, much embroidered and trimmed; in winter there were redingotes of stuffs or of velvet. From these baskets she selected her costume for the day, and always wore in the morning a hat covered with feathers or flowers, and wraps that made considerable drapery about her. The number of her shawls was between three and four hundred. She had dresses made of them, coverings for her bed, cushions for her dog. She always wore one in the morning, which she draped about her shoulders with a grace that I never saw equaled. Bonaparte, who thought these shawls covered her too much, tore them off, and more than once threw them in the fire; after which she would then send for another. She purchased all that were brought to her, no matter at what price. I have seen her buy shawls for which their owner asked eight, ten, and twelve thousand francs. They were the great extravagance of this Court, where those which cost only fifty louis were looked at disdainfully, and where the women boasted of the price they had paid for those they wore.

I have already described the life which Mme. Bonaparte led. This life never varied in any respect. She never opened a book, she never took up a pen, and never touched a needle; and yet she never seemed to be in the least bored. She was not fond of the theatre; the Emperor did not wish her to go there without him, and receive applause which he did not share. She walked only when she was at Malmaison, a dwelling that she never ceased to improve, and on which she had spent enormous sums.

Bonaparte was extremely irritated by these expenditures. He would fly into a passion, and his wife would weep, promising to be wiser and more prudent; after which she would go on in the same way, and in the end he was obliged to pay the bills. The evening toilet was as careful as that of the morning. Everything was elegant in the extreme. We rarely saw the same dresses and the same flowers appear the second time. In the evening the Empress appeared without a hat, with flowers, pearls, or precious stones in her hair. Then her dresses showed her figure to perfection, and the most exquisite toilet was that which was most becoming to her. The smallest assembly, the most informal dance, was always an occasion for her to order a new costume, in spite of the hoards of dresses which accumulated in the various palaces; for she had a mania for keeping everything. It would be utterly impossible for me to give any idea of the sums she spent in this way. At every dressmaker's and milliner's in Paris, go in when we would, we were sure to find something being made for her or ordered by her. I have seen several lace robes, at forty, fifty, and even a hundred thousand francs each. It is almost incredible that this passion for dress, which was so entirely satisfied, should never have exhausted itself. After the divorce, at Malmaison, she had the same luxurious tastes, and dressed with as much care, even when she saw no one. The day of her death she insisted on being dressed in a very elegant *robe de chambre,* because she thought that the Emperor of Russia would come perhaps to see her. She died covered with ribbons and pale rose-colored satin. These tastes and these habits on her part naturally increased the expenses of those about her, and we found it difficult at times to appear in suitable toilets.

Her daughter was dressed with equal richness—it

was the tone of this Court; but she had order and
economy, and never seemed to take much pleasure in
dress. Mme. Murat and the Princess Borghese put
their whole souls into it. Their court dresses cost
them generally from ten to fifteen thousand francs;
and they supplemented them by rare pearls and jewels
without price.

With all this extreme luxury, the exquisite taste of
the Empress, and the rich costumes of the men, the
Court was, as may readily be imagined, most brilliant. It may even be said that on certain days the
coup d'œil was absolutely dazzling. Foreigners were
much struck by it. It was during this year (1806)
that the Emperor decided to give occasional concerts
in the Hall of the Marshals, as a certain large hall,
hung with portraits of the Marshals, was called.
These portraits are very likely there now. This hall
was lighted by an infinite number of candles, and to
it were invited all those persons who had any connection with the Government and those who had been
presented. Thus there were assembled usually between four and five hundred persons.

After having walked through the saloons where all
these people were assembled, Bonaparte entered the
hall and took his place at the end; the Empress on
his left, as well as the Princesses of his family, in the
most dazzling costumes; his mother on his right—
still a very handsome woman, with an air of great
distinction. His brothers were richly dressed, and
they with foreign princes and other dignitaries were
seated. Behind were the grand officers, the chamberlains, and all the staff, in their embroidered uniforms.
Upon the right and the left, in curved lines, sat two
rows of ladies—the Lady of Honor, the Lady in
Waiting, and the Ladies of the Palace, almost all of
them young, the greater number of them pretty and

beautifully dressed. Then came a large number of ladies—foreigners and Frenchwomen—whose toilets were exquisite beyond words. Behind these two rows of seated ladies were men standing—ambassadors, ministers, marshals, senators, generals, and so on— all in the most gorgeous costumes. Opposite the imperial chairs were the musicians, and as soon as the Emperor was seated they executed the best music, which, however, in spite of the strict silence that was enjoined and preserved, fell on inattentive ears. When the concert was over, in the center of the room, which had been kept vacant, appeared the best dancers, male and female, from the opera, and executed a charming ballet. This part of the entertainment of the evening amused every one, even the Emperor.

M. de Rémusat had all these arrangements under his charge, and it was no petty matter either, for the Emperor was extremely particular and exacting in regard to the most trivial details. M. de Talleyrand said sometimes to my husband, "I pity you, for you are called upon to amuse the unamusable."

The concert and the ballet did not last more than an hour and a half. Then the assembly went to supper, which was laid in the Gallery of Diana, and there the beauty of the gallery, the brilliancy of the lights, the luxury of the tables, the display of silver and glass, and the magnificence and elegance of the guests, imparted to the whole scene something of the air of a fairy-tale. There was, however, something lacking. I will not say that it was the ease which can never be found in a court, but it was that feeling of security which each person might have brought there if the powers that presided had added a little more kindliness to the majesty by which they surrounded themselves.

I have already spoken of Mme. Bonaparte's family. In the first years of her elevation she had brought four nephews and a niece to Paris from Martinique. These all bore the name of Tascher. For the young men situations were found, and the young lady was lodged in the Tuileries. She was by no means deficient in beauty, but the change of climate affected her health, and rendered impossible all the plans which the Emperor had formed for a brilliant marriage for her. At first he thought of marrying her to the Prince of Baden; then for some time he destined her for a prince of the house of Spain. At last, however, she was married to the son of the Duke of Arenberg, who was of a Belgian family. This marriage, so much desired by this family, who hoped from it to gain great advantages, was in no degree a success. The husband and wife never suited each other, and after a time their misunderstandings and incompatibilities culminated in a separation which was without scandal. After the divorce the Arenbergs, disappointed in their ambitious hopes and plans, openly evinced their discontent at this alliance, and after the King's return the marriage was completely broken. Mme. de —— lives to-day very obscurely in Paris.

The eldest of her brothers, after residing in France some two or three years without being in the least dazzled by the honor of having an aunt who was an Empress, began to grow very weary of the Court; and, having no taste for military life, he yielded to his homesickness, and asked and obtained permission to return to the colonies. He took some money back with him, and, leading a calm life there, has probably more than once congratulated himself on this philosophical departure. Another brother was attached to Joseph Bonaparte, and remained in Spain in his military service. He married Mlle. Clary, daughter of a merchant at Marseilles, and niece of Mme. Joseph Bonaparte. A third brother married the daughter of the Princess of Leyen. He is now with her in Germany. The fourth brother was infirm, and lived with his sister. I do not know what became of him.

The Beauharnais have also profited by the elevation of Mme. Bonaparte, and continued to crowd about her. I have told how she married the daughter of the Marquis de Beauharnais to M. de la Valette. The Marquis was for a long time Ambassador to Spain; he is in France to-day. The Comte de Beauharnais, the son of the lady who wrote poetry and novels, had married early in life Mlle. de Lesay-Marnesia. From this marriage sprang a daughter, who resided after her mother's death with an old aunt, who was very religious. The Comte de Beauharnais, marrying again, never seemed to think of this young girl. Bonaparte made him Senator. M. de Lesay-Marnesia, uncle to the young Stéphanie, suddenly recalled her from Languedoc; she was fourteen or fifteen. He presented her to Mme. Bonaparte, who found her very pretty and refined in all her little ways. She placed her in Mme. Campan's boarding-school, from which she emerged in 1806 to find herself suddenly adopted by the Emperor, called Princess Imperial, and married shortly after to the hereditary Prince of Baden. She was then seventeen, with a most agreeable face, great natural cleverness and vivacity, a certain childishness in her manner which suited her well, a charming voice, lovely complexion, and clear, blue eyes. Her hair was exquisitely blonde.

The Prince of Baden was not long in falling in love with her, but at first his affection was not returned. He was young, but very stout; his face was commonplace and inexpressive; he talked little, seemed always out of place and bored, and generally fell asleep

wherever he might be. The youthful Stéphanie, gay,
piquante, dazzled by her lot, and proud of being
adopted by the Emperor, whom she then regarded
with some reason as the first sovereign in the world,
gave the Prince of Baden to understand that he was
greatly honored by her bestowing her hand upon him.
In vain did they seek to correct her ideas in this respect. She made no objection to the marriage, and
was quite ready to consent to its taking place whenever the Emperor wished it; but she persisted in saying that Napoleon's daughter should marry a king or
the son of a king. This little vanity, accompanied by
many piquant jests, to which her seventeen years
gave a charm, did not displease the Emperor, and in
fact rather amused him. He became more interested
than before in his adopted daughter, and precisely at
the time he married her to the Prince he became, with
considerable publicity, her lover. This conquest finished turning the head of the new Princess, and confirmed her in her haughtiness toward her future husband, who sought in vain to please her.

As soon as the Emperor had announced to the Senate the news of this marriage, the youthful Stéphanie
was installed in the Tuileries, in an apartment especially arranged for her, and there she received the
deputations from the governmental bodies. Of that
from the Senate her father was one. Her situation
was certainly a little odd, but she received all the addresses and feliciations without any embarrassment,
and replied extremely well. Having become the
daughter of the sovereign, and being a favorite in
addition, the Emperor ordered that she should everywhere follow next to the Empress, thus taking precedence of the whole Bonaparte family. Mme. Murat
was extremely displeased, who hated her with a cor-
dial hatred, and could not conceal her pride and jeal-

ousy. Mademoiselle thought this very amusing, and laughed at it as she did at everything else, and succeeded in making the Emperor laugh also, as he was inclined to be amused at all she said. The Empress was much displeased at this new fancy of her husband's. She spoke seriously to her niece, and showed her how wrong it would be for her not to resist the efforts which Bonaparte was making to complete her seduction. Mlle. de Beauharnais listened to her aunt's counsels with some docility. She confided to her certain attempts, sometimes extremely bold, made by her adopted father, and promised to conduct herself with caution and reserve. These confidences renewed all the former discord of the Imperial household. Bonaparte, unchanged, did not take the trouble to conceal his inclination from his wife, and, too sure of his power, thought it extremely unhandsome in the Prince of Baden that he should be wounded by what was going on under his very eyes. Nevertheless, the fear of an outburst and the number of eyes fixed upon all the persons concerned rendered him prudent. On the other side, the young girl, who only wished to amuse herself, showed more resistance than he had at first anticipated. But she hated her husband. The evening of her marriage it was impossible to persuade her to receive him in her apartment. A little later the Court went to Saint Cloud, and with it the young pair. Nothing, however, could induce the Princess to permit her husband to approach her. He complained to the Empress, who scolded her niece. The Emperor, however, upheld her, and his own hopes revived. All this had a very bad effect, which at last the Emperor realized; and at the end of some little time—occupied with grave affairs, fatigued by the importunity of his wife, struck by the discontent of the young Prince, and persuaded that he had to do with a young person who only wished to amuse herself by coquetting with him—he consented to the departure of the Prince of Baden, who took his wife away with him. She shed many tears at leaving France, regarding the principality of Baden as a land of exile. When she arrived there she was received somewhat coldly by the reigning Prince. She lived for a long time on bad terms with her husband. Secret negotiations were sent from France to make her understand how important it was to her that she should become the mother of a Prince—an hereditary Prince in his turn. She submitted; but the Prince, rendered frigid by so much resistance, now showed very little tenderness toward her, and this marriage seemed destined to make them both very unhappy. It was not eventually so, however; and we shall see later that the Princess of Baden, having acquired a little more sense with years, began at last to recognize her duty, and by her good conduct succeeded finally in regaining the affection of the Prince, and enjoyed the advantages of a union which she at first had so entirely under-estimated.

I have not as yet mentioned the fact that among the amusements of this Court was an occasional theatrical representation—a comedy played at Malmaison— which was no uncommon thing during the first year of the Consulate. Prince Eugène and his sister had real talent in this direction, and found great amusement in exercising it. At this time Bonaparte too was greatly interested in these representations, which were given before a limited audience. A pretty hall was built at Malmaison, and we played there very often. But by degrees the rank of the family became too exalted for this kind of pleasure, and finally it was permitted only on certain occasions, like that of the birthday of the Empress. When the Emperor came back from Vienna, Mme. Louis Bonaparte took it into her head to have an appropriate little vaudeville arranged in which we all played, and each sang a verse. A number of persons had been invited, and Malmaison was illuminated in a charming manner. It was somewhat of a trying ordeal to appear on the stage before an audience like this, but the Emperor showed himself particularly well disposed. We played well. Mme. Louis had, and was entitled to have, a great triumph. The verses were pretty, the flattery delicate, and the evening a complete success. It was really curious to observe the tone in which each said in the evening, " The Emperor laughed, the Emperor applauded! " and how we congratulated each other. I particularly, who accosted him always with a certain reserve, found myself all at once in a better position toward him, in consequence of the manner in which I had fulfilled the part of an old peasant-woman who dreamed continually that her hero did the most incredible things, and who saw events surpass her wildest dreams. After the play was over, he paid me a few compliments. We had played with our whole hearts, and he seemed somewhat touched. When I saw him in this mood thus suddenly and unexpectedly moved by emotion, I was tempted to exclaim, " Why will you not allow yourself occasionally to feel and think like other men? " I felt a sensation of intense relief on these rare occasions, for it seemed to me that hope once more revived within me. Ah! how easily the great master us, and how little trouble they need take to make themselves beloved! Perhaps this last reflection has already escaped me, but I have made it so often during the last twelve years of my life, and it presses so heavily upon me whenever I look back upon the past, that it is by no means extraordinary that I should express it more than once.

CHAPTER XIX

BEFORE resuming the succession of events, I have a strong desire to dwell a little on the names of those persons who at this time composed the Court, and who occupied a distinguished position in the Government. I shall not be able, however, to draw a series of portraits which can vary enough, one from the other, to be piquant. We know very well that despotism is the greatest of levelers. It regulates the thoughts, it determines both actions and words; and the regulations to which all submit are often so strictly observed that the exteriors are assimilated, and perhaps even some of the impressions received.

I remember that during the winter of 1814 the Empress Maria Louisa received a large number of persons every evening. They came to obtain news of the army, in whose movements and plans every one was deeply interested. At the moment when the Emperor, in his pursuit of the Prussian General Blücher, left to the Austrian army leisure to advance as far as Fontainebleau, Paris believed itself about to fall into the power of strangers. Many persons met in the saloons of the Empress and questioned each other with great anxiety. Toward the end of this evening M. de Talleyrand came to call on me after leaving the Tuileries. He told me of the anxiety which he had witnessed, and then said: " What a man, madame, this must be, who can cause the Comte de Montesquiou and the Councilor of State Boulay (de la Meurthe) to experience the same anxiety, and to evince it in the same words!" He had found these two persons with the Empress. They had both struck him by their pallor, and both expressed their dread of the events which they began to foresee in the future.

With few exceptions—either because chance did not gather round the Emperor persons of any marked individuality, or because of the uniformity of conduct of which I have just spoken—I can not recall many purely personal peculiarities which deserve to be commemorated. Setting the principal figures aside, as well as the events which I propose to relate, I have but the names of the others to recount, the costumes which they wore, and the duties with which they were intrusted. It is a hard thing for men to feel that the sovereign to whom they are attached has a thorough and universal contempt for human nature. Such a consciousness saddens the spirits, discourages the soul, and compels each man to confine himself to the purely material duties of his position, which he ends by regarding as mere business. Each one of these men who composed the Court and the Government of the Emperor had undoubtedly a mind of his own, and especial feelings and opinions. Some among them silently practiced certain virtues, others concealed their faults and even their vices. But both appeared on the surface only at the word of command, and, unfortunately for the men of that time, Bonaparte believed that more was to be made out of the bad side of human nature than from the good, and therefore looked for vices rather than for virtues. He liked to discover weaknesses, and profited by them; and, where there were no vices, he encouraged these weaknesses, or, if he could do no better, he worked on their fears— anything to prove himself always and constantly the strongest. Thus he was by no means ill pleased that Cambacérès, though possessing estimable and distinguished qualities, allowed his foolish pride to be seen, and gave himself the reputation of a certain license of morals and habits which counterbalanced the just admiration rendered to his cultivation and to his natural probity. Nor did the Emperor ever deplore the indolent immorality of M. de Talleyrand, his careless indifference, nor the small value he placed on the esteem of the public. He was infinitely amused by what he saw fit to call the silliness of the Prince de Neuchâtel, and the servile flattery of M. Maret.

He took advantage of the avarice which he himself had developed in Savary, and of the callousness of Duroc's disposition. He never shrank from the remembrance that Fouché had once been a Jacobin; indeed, he said with a smile: " The only difference is that he is now a *rich* Jacobin; but that's all I want."

His Ministers he regarded and treated as more or less efficient clerks, and he used to say, " I should not know what to do with them if they were not men of mere ordinary abilities and character."

If any one had been conscious of real superiority of any kind, he must needs have endeavored to hide it; and it is probable that, warned by an instinctive sense of danger, everybody affected dullness or vacuity when those qualities were not real.

Memoirs of this period will suffer from this remarkable feature of it, which will give rise to a plausible, though unmerited, accusation against the writers of being malevolent in their views, partial toward themselves, and extremely severe toward others. Each writer will in reality be able to tell his own secret only, but will have been unable to penetrate that of his neighbor.

Ecclesiastical influence in the Emperor's household

was insignificant. Mass was celebrated in his presence every Sunday, and that was all. I have already spoken of Cardinal Fesch. In 1807 M. de Pradt, Bishop of Poitiers, and subsequently Archbishop of Mechlin, made his appearance at Court. He was clever and scheming, verbose but amusing, and fond of gossip; he held liberal opinions, but he expressed them in cynical language. He attempted many things without perfectly succeeding in any one of them. He could, indeed, talk over the Emperor himself, and he may perhaps have given him good advice; but, when he was appointed to put his own counsels into action, nothing came of the attempt, for he possessed neither the confidence nor the esteem of the public.

The Abbé de Broglie, Bishop of Ghent, was cunning, but also imprudent; he obtained at a cheap rate the honor of persecution.

The Abbé de Boulogne, Bishop of Troyes, proved himself in those days as eager to extol despotism as he now is to emerge from the obscurity to which he has happily been reduced by the constitutional government of the King.

Bonaparte made use of the clergy, but he disliked priests. He had both philosophical and revolutionary prejudices against them. I do not know whether he was a deist or an atheist, but he habitually ridiculed everything connected with religion in familiar conversation; and, besides, he was taken up too much with the affairs of this world to concern himself with the next. I may venture to say, that the immortality of his name was to him of much greater importance than that of his soul. He had an antipathy to pious persons, and invariably accused them of hypocrisy. When the priesthood in Spain stirred up the people against him, when he met with opposition from the French Bishops which did them honor, when the Pope's cause was embraced by great numbers, he was quite confounded, and said more than once, " I thought men were more advanced than they really are."

The military household of the Emperor was numerous, but, except in times of war, its members had to discharge duties of a civil nature. Dreading the recollections of the field of battle, he distributed the various functions on another footing at the palace of the Tuileries. He made chamberlains of the generals, and subsequently he obliged them to wear embroidered uniforms, and to exchange their swords for court rapiers. This transformation was displeasing to many of them, but they had to submit, and, having been wolves, to become shepherds. There was, however, a good reason for this. A display of military renown would, to a certain extent, have eclipsed other classes whom it was necessary to conciliate; military manners were by this expedient refined perforce, and certain recalcitrant marshals lost some of their prestige while acquiring the polish of court manners. They became, indeed, slightly ridiculous by this apprenticeship—a fact which Bonaparte knew how to turn to advantage.

I believe I may confidently state that the Emperor did not like any of his marshals. He frequently found fault with them, sometimes in very serious respects. He accused them all of covetousness, which he deliberately encouraged by his gifts. One day he passed them all in review before me. On Davoust he pronounced the verdict which I think I have already mentioned: " Davoust is a man on whom I may bestow glory; he will never know how to wear it." Of Marshal Ney he said: " He is ungrateful and factious. If I were destined to die by the hand of a marshal, I would lay a wager that hand would be his." I recollect that he said he regarded Moncey, Brune,

Bessières, Victor and Oudinot as men of middling abilities, who would never be more than titled soldiers. Masséna he looked upon as effete, but it was evident he had formerly been jealous of him. Soult sometimes gave him trouble; he was clever, rough, and vain, and he would argue with his master and dispute his conditions. Bonaparte could rule Augereau, who was rather unpolished in manner than obstinate. He was aware of Marmont's vanity, which he might wound with impunity, and of Macdonald's habitual ill humor. Lannes had been his comrade, and the Marshal would sometimes remind him of this: on such occasions he would be gently called to order. Bernadotte had more spirit than the others: he was continually complaining, and, indeed, he often had cause for complaint.

The way in which the Emperor curbed, rewarded, or snubbed with impunity men so proud and puffed up with military fame was very remarkable. Other writers can relate with what wonderful skill he made use of these men in war, and how he won fresh glory for himself by utilizing their fame, ever showing himself, in very truth, superior to all others.

I need not give the names of the chamberlains; the Imperial Almanac supplies them. By degrees their number became considerable. They were taken from all ranks and classes. Those who were most assiduous and least talkative got on best; their duties were troublesome and very tedious. In proportion as one's place was nearer to the Emperor, one's life became more burdensome. Persons who have had none but business relations with him can have no adequate idea of the unpleasantness of any that were closer; it was always easier to deal with his intellect than with his temper.

Nor shall I have much to relate concerning the

ladies of the period. Bonaparte frequently said: "Women shall have no influence at my Court; they may dislike me, but I shall have peace and quietness." He kept his word. We were ornamental at the fêtes, and that was about all. Nevertheless, as it is the privilege of beauty never to be forgotten, some of the ladies-in-waiting deserve a passing notice here. In Mme. de Mottevelle's Memoirs, she pauses to describe the beauties of her time, and I must pass over in silence those of our own.

At the head of the Empress's household was Mme. de la Rochefoucauld. She was short and deformed, not pretty, yet her face was not unattractive. Her large blue eyes, with black eyebrows, had a fine effect; she was lively, fearless, and a clever talker; a little satirical, but kind-hearted, and of a gay and independent spirit. She neither liked nor disliked any one at Court, lived on good terms with all, and looked at nothing very seriously. She considered she had done Bonaparte an honor by coming to his Court, and by dint of saying so she persuaded others of it, so that she was treated with consideration. She employed herself principally in repairing her shattered fortunes, obtaining several ambassadorships for her husband, and giving her daughter in marriage to the younger son of the princely house of Borghese. The Emperor thought her wanting in dignity, and he was right; but he was always embarrassed in her company, for he had no idea of the deference due to a woman, and she would answer him sharply. The Empress, too, was rather afraid of her, for in her easy manner there was no little imperiousness. She remained faithful to old friends who held opposite opinions to her own, or rather to what we may suppose to have been her own, judging by the post she occupied at Court. She was daughter-in-law to the Duc de Liancourt, and she left the Court when the divorce took place. She died in Paris, under the Restoration.

Mme. de la Valette, the Mistress of the Robes, was daughter to the Marquis de Beauharnais. Her complexion had been slightly spoiled by small-pox, but she had a pleasing though expressionless face. Her gentleness almost amounted to inanity, and small vanities chiefly occupied her thoughts. Her mind was narrow, her conduct was correct. Her post was a complete sinecure, for Mme. Bonaparte allowed no one to interfere with her dress. In vain did the Emperor insist that Mme. de la Valette should make up accounts, regulate expenditure, and superintend purchases; he was obliged to yield, and to give up the idea of maintaining any order on these points, for Mme. de la Valette was incapable of defending the rights of her place in opposition to her aunt. She confined herself, therefore, to taking Mme. de la Rochefoucauld's duties when the latter absented herself on account of illness. Everybody knows what courage and energy misfortune and conjugal love subsequently developed in this young lady.

Chief among the Ladies of the Palace was Mme. de Luçay, who had held that position longest. In 1806 she was no longer young. She was a gentle and quiet person. Her husband was Prefect of the Palace; their daughter married the younger son of the Count de Ségur, and has since died.

I come next on the list, and I feel inclined to make a little sketch of myself; I believe I can do this truthfully. I was twenty-three when I first came to Court; I was not pretty, yet not altogether devoid of attraction, and I looked well in full dress. My eyes were fine, my hair was black, and I had good teeth; my nose and face were too large in proportion to my figure, which was good, but small. I had the reputation of being a clever woman, which was almost a reproach at Court. In point of fact, I lack neither wit nor sense, but my warmth of feeling and of thought leads me to speak and act impulsively, and makes me commit errors which a cooler, even though less wise, person would avoid.

I was often misinterpreted at Bonaparte's Court. I was lively, and was supposed to be scheming. I liked to be acquainted with persons of importance, and I was accused of being ambitious. I am too much devoted to persons and to causes which appear to me to have right on their side, to deserve the first accusation; and my faithfulness to friends in misfortune is a sufficient answer to the second. Mme. Bonaparte trusted me more than others, and thereby put me into a difficult position; people soon perceived this, and no one envied me the onerous distinction of her friendship. The preference which the Emperor at first showed me was a cause of greater jealousy. I reaped little benefit from his favor, but I was flattered by it and grateful for it; and, so long as I felt a regard for him, I sought to please him. When my eyes were opened, I drew back; dissimulation is absolutely opposed to my character. I came to Court too full of inquisitiveness. It seemed to me so curious a scene that I watched it closely, and asked many questions that I might fully understand it. It was often thought that I did this from design. In palaces no action is supposed to be without a motive; " *Cui bono?* " is said on every occasion.

My impetuosity frequently brought me into trouble. Not that I acted altogether on impulse, but I was very young, very unaffected, because I had always been very happy; in nothing was I sufficiently sedate, and my qualities sometimes did me as much harm as my defects. But, amid all this, I have met with friends who loved me, and of whom, no matter how I may be circumstanced, I shall retain a loving recollection.

I soon began to suffer from disappointed hopes, betrayed affections, and mistaken beliefs. Moreover, my health failed, and I became tired of so arduous a life, and disenchanted both with men and things. I withdrew myself as far as possible, and found in my own home feelings and enjoyments that could not deceive. I loved my husband, my mother, my children, and my friends; I should have been unwilling to give up the peaceful pleasure I found in their society. I contrived to retain a kind of liberty amid the numerous trivial duties of my post. Lastly, when I approved of any one and when I ceased to do so, both states of mind too plainly showed. There could be no greater fault in the eyes of Bonaparte. He dreaded nothing in the world so much as that any one in his circle should use their critical faculty with regard to him.

Mme. de Canisy, a great-niece of M. de Brienne, the former Archbishop of Sens, was a beautiful woman when first she came to Court. She was tall and well made, with eyes and hair of raven-black, lovely teeth, an aquiline nose, and a rich brunette complexion.

Mme. Maret was a fine woman; her features were regular and handsome. She seemed to live on excellent terms with her husband, who imparted to her some of his own ambition. Seldom have I seen more unconcealed or more solicitous vanity in any one. She was jealous of every distinction, and tolerated superior rank in the Princesses only. Born in obscurity, she aimed at the highest distinctions. When the Emperor granted the title of countess to all the ladies-in-waiting, Mme. Maret felt annoyed at the equality it implied, and, obstinately refusing to bear it, she remained plain Mme. Maret until her husband obtained the title of Duc de Bassano. Mme. Savary and she were the most elegantly dressed women at Court. Their dress is said to have cost more than fifty thousand francs a year. Mme. Maret thought that the Empress did not sufficiently distinguish her from the others; she therefore made common cause with the Bonapartes against her. She was feared and distrusted with some reason, for she repeated things which reached the ear of the Emperor through her husband, and did a great deal of harm. She and M. Maret would have liked people to pay regular court to them, and many persons lent themselves to this pretension. As I showed a decided objection to doing so, Mme. Maret took an aversion to me, and contrived to inflict many petty annoyances upon me.

Any one who chose to speak evil of others to Bonaparte was pretty sure of gaining his ear; for he was always credulous of evil. He disliked Mme. Maret; he even judged her too severely; nevertheless he chose to believe all stories that came to him through her. I believe her to have been one of the greatest sufferers by the fall of that great Imperial scaffolding which brought us all to the ground.

During the King's first residence in Paris, from 1814 to 1815, the Duc de Bassano was accused, on sufficient grounds, of having carried on a secret correspondence with the Emperor in the island of Elba, and kept him informed of the state of feeling in France, so that he was induced to believe he might once more offer himself to the French as their ruler. Napoleon returned, and his sudden arrival clashed with and thwarted the revolution which Fouché and Carnot were preparing. Then these two, being obliged to accept Bonaparte, compelled him to reign during the Hundred Days according to their own system. The Emperor wished to take M. Maret, whom he had so many reasons for trusting, back into his service; but Fouché and Carnot strongly objected to Maret, as a man of no ability and only capable of blind devotion to his master's interest. Some idea of the state of bondage in which the men of the Revolution kept the netted lion at this period may be gathered from the answer that Carnot ventured to make when the Emperor proposed putting M. Maret into the Government. " No, certainly not; the French do not wish to see *two Blacas* in one year "—alluding to the Count de Blacas, whom the King had brought with him from England, and who had all the influence of a favorite.

On the second fall of Bonaparte, Maret and his wife hastened to leave Paris. M. Maret was exiled, and they repaired to Berlin. For the last few months Mme. Maret has been again in Paris, endeavoring to obtain the recall of her husband. It is not unlikely she may succeed, such is the kindness of the King.

Pride of rank was not confined to Mme. Maret alone. Mme. Ney also possessed it. She was niece to Mme. Campan, first dresser to Marie Antoinette, and daughter of Mme. Augué, also one of the Queen's dressers, and she had been tolerably well educated. She was a mild, kind-hearted woman, but her head was a little turned by the honors to which she attained. She occasionally displayed a pretentiousness which, after all, was not inexcusable, for she based it on the great military renown of her husband, whose own pride was sufficiently self-asserting. Mme. Ney, afterward Duchesse d'Elchingen, and later Princesse de la Moskowa, was in reality a very good, quiet woman, incapable of speaking or doing evil, and perhaps as incapable of saying or doing anything good. She enjoyed the privileges of her rank to the full, especially in the society of inferiors. She was much aggrieved at the Restoration by certain differences in her position, and by the disdain of the ladies of the royal Court. She complained to her husband, and may have contributed not a little to irritate him against the new state of things, which, though not altogether ousting him, laid them both open to little daily humiliations, quite unintentionally on the part of the King. On the death of her husband she took up her abode in Italy with three or four sons. Her means were much smaller than might have been supposed, and she had acquired habits of great luxury. I have seen her start for a watering-place, taking with her a whole household, so as to be waited on according to her liking. She took a bedstead, articles of furniture, a service of traveling-plate made expressly for her, a train of *fourgons,* and a number of couriers; and she would affirm that the wife of a marshal of France could not travel otherwise. Her house was magnificently appointed; the purchase and furnishing cost eleven hundred thousand francs. Mme. Ney was tall and slight; her features were rather large, her eyes fine. Her expression was mild and pleasant, and her voice very sweet.

Mme. Lannes, afterward Duchesse de Montebello, was another of our beauties. There was something virginal in her face; her features were pure and regular, her skin was of a delicate fairness. She was a good wife and an excellent mother, and was always cold, reserved, and silent in society. The Emperor appointed her Lady of Honor to the Archduchess, who became passionately fond of her, and whom she completely governed. She accompanied the Archduchess on her return to Vienna, and then came back to Paris, where she now lives in retirement, entirely devoted to her children.

The number of the ladies-in-waiting became by

degrees considerable, but, on the whole, there is little to be said about so many women, all playing so small a part. I have already spoken of Mmes. de Montmorency, de Mortemart, and de Chevreuse. There remains for me simply to name Mmes. de Talhouët, Lauriston, de Colbert, Marescot, etc. These were quiet, amiable persons, of ordinary appearance, no longer young. The same might be said of a number of Italians and Belgians who came to Paris for their two months of Court attendance, and who were all more or less silent and apparently out of their element. In general sufficient regard was paid to youth and beauty in the selection of the ladies-in-waiting; they were always placed with extreme care. Some of them lived in this Court silent and indifferent; others received its homages with more or less ease and pleasure. Everything was done quietly, because Bonaparte willed that such should be the case. He had prudish caprices at times either in regard to himself or others. He objected to any demonstrations of friendship or dislike. In a life that was so busy, so regulated and disciplined, there was not much chance for either the one or the other.

Among the persons of whom the Emperor had composed the various households of his family, there were also ladies of distinction; but at Court they were of still less importance than ourselves.

I am inclined to believe that life was rather dreary under his mother's roof. With Mme. Joseph Bonaparte it was simple and easy. Mme. Louis Bonaparte gathered about her her old school companions, and kept up with them, so far as lay in her power, the familiarity of their youth. At Mme. Murat's, although a trifle stiff and stilted, things were carefully regulated with order and discipline. Public opinion stigmatized the Princess Borghese; her conduct cast an unfortunate reflection upon the young and pretty women who formed her court.

It may not be useless to linger here for a little, to say a few words in regard to those persons who were at this time distinguished in literature and art, and to the works which appeared from the foundation of the Consulate up to this year, 1806. Among the former I find four of whom I can speak with some detail.

Jacques Delille, whom we more generally know under the title of the Abbé de Delille, had seen the best years of his life pass away in the times which preceded our Revolution. He united to brilliant talents the charms of sweetness of temper and agreeable manners. He acquired the title of Abbé because in those days it conferred a certain rank; he dropped it after the Revolution to marry a woman of good family, commonplace, and by no means agreeable, but whose ministrations had become essential to him. Always received in the best society of Paris, highly regarded by Queen Marie Antoinette, overwhelmed by kindness from the Comte d'Artois, he knew only the pleasant side of the life of a man of letters. He was petted and made much of; his grace and simplicity of soul were very remarkable; the magic of his diction was incomparable; when he recited verses every one was eager for the pleasure of hearing him. The bloody scenes of the Revolution appalled this young and tender nature; he emigrated, and met everywhere in Europe with a reception so warm that it consoled him for his exile. However, when Bonaparte had reëstablished order in France, M. Delille wished to return to his native land, and he came back to Paris with his wife. He had grown old and was nearly blind, but always delightful, and teeming with fine works which he meant to publish in his own country.

Again did all literary people crowd about him, and
Bonaparte himself made some advances. The professor's chair in which he had inculcated with so much
talent the principles of French literature was restored
to him, and pensions were offered him as the price of
a few laudatory verses. But M. Delille, desiring to
preserve the liberty of the recollections which attached
him irrevocably to the house of Bourbon, withdrew
to a retired part of the city, and thus escaped both
caresses and offers. He gave himself up exclusively
to work, and answered every one with his own lines
from " L'Homme des Champs ":

> " Auguste triomphant pour Virgile fut juste.
> J'imitai le poète, imitez-donc Auguste,
> Et laissez-moi sans nom, sans fortune, et sans fers,
> Rêver au bruit des eaux, de la lyre et des vers."

If Bonaparte was offended by this resistance, he
never showed it; esteem and general affection were the
ægis which protected the amiable poet. He lived,
therefore, a serene and tranquil life, and died too soon,
since, with the sentiments he had preserved, he would
have rejoiced at the return of the Princes whom he
had never ceased to love.

In the times when Bonaparte was still only Consul,
and when he amused himself in following up even less
conspicuous persons, he took it into his head that he
wished M. Delille to see him, hoping perhaps to gain
him over, or at all events to dazzle him. Mme. Bacciochi was bidden to invite the poet to pass an evening
at her house. Some few persons, of whom I was one,
were also invited. The First Consul arrived with
something of the air of Jupiter Tonans, for he was
surrounded by a great number of aides, who stood in
line and showed some surprise at seeing their General
take so much trouble for this frail old gentleman in a
black coat, who seemed, moreover, a little afraid of

them all. Bonaparte, by way of doing something,
took his seat at a card-table, and summoned me. I
was the only woman in the *salon* whose name was not
unknown to M. Delille, and I instantly understood
that Bonaparte had selected me as the connecting link
between the poet's time and that of the Consul. I
endeavored to establish a certain harmony between
them. Bonaparte consented to the conversation being
literary, and at first our poet seemed not insensible to
the courtesy extended him. Both men became animated, but each in his own way; and I very soon
realized that neither the one nor the other produced
the effect he desired and intended. Bonaparte liked to
talk; M. Delille was loquacious and told long stories;
they interrupted each other constantly; they did not
listen, and never replied; they were both accustomed
to praise; they each felt a conviction before many
minutes had expired that they were not making a
good impression on each other, and ended by separating with some fatigue, and perhaps discontented.
After this evening M. Delille said that the Consul's
conversation *smelled of gun-powder;* Bonaparte
declared that the old poet *was in his dotage.*

I know very little in regard to M. de Chateaubriand's
youth. Having emigrated with his family, he knew
in England M. de Fontanes, who saw his first manuscript, and encouraged him in his intention of writing.
On his return to France they kept up their relations,
and I believe Chateaubriand was presented by M. de
Fontanes to the First Consul. Having published the
" Génie du Christianisme " at the time of the Concordat of 1801, he concluded that he had best dedicate
his work to the *restorer of religion.* He was by no
means wealthy; his tastes, his somewhat disorderly
character, his ambition, which was boundless though
vague, and his excessive vanity, all inspired him with

sary for me to make an example in Brittany; it will
fall upon a man of very little interest, for this relation
of M. de Chateaubriand has a mediocre reputation. I
know that his cousin cares not one sou for him, and
this fact is proved to me by the very things he has
compelled you to do. He has had the childishness not
to write to me; his letter to the Empress is stiff and
even haughty in tone. He would like to impress me
with the importance of his talents; I answer him with
that of *my policy,* and in all conscience this ought not
to humiliate him. I have need of an example in
Brittany to avoid a crowd of petty political prosecu-
tions. This will give M. de Chateaubriand an opportunity of writing some pathetic pages, which he will
read aloud in the Faubourg Saint Germain. The fine
ladies will keep, and you will see that this will console
him! ''

It was impossible to shake a determination expressed
in this way. All means that the Empress and I
attempted were useless, and the sentence was executed.
That same day I received a note from M. de Chateaubriand, which in spite of myself recalled Bonaparte's
words. He wrote to me that he had thought it his
duty to be present at the death of his relative, and
that he had shuddered afterward on seeing dogs lap
up the blood. The whole note was written in a similar
tone. I had been touched, but this revolted me. I do
not know whether it was he or myself that was in
fault. A few days later M. de Chateaubriand, dressed
in full mourning, did not appear much afflicted, but
his irritation against the Emperor was greatly augmented.

This event brought me into connection with him.
His works pleased me, but his presence disturbed my
liking for them. He was, and is still, much spoiled by
society, particularly by women. He places his asso-

ciates in a most embarrassing position at times, because one sees immediately that one has nothing to teach him as to his own value. He invariably takes the first place, and, making himself comfortable there, becomes extremely amiable. But his conversation, which displays a vivid imagination, exhibits also a certain hardness of heart, and a selfishness that is but ill concealed. His works are religious, and indicate none but the noblest sentiments. He is in earnest when he writes, but he lacks gravity in his bearing. His face is handsome, his form somewhat awry, and he is careful and even affected in his toilet. It would seem that he prefers in love that which is generally known as *les bonnes fortunes*. It is plain that he prefers to have disciples rather than friends. In fine, I conclude from all that I have seen that it is better to read him than to know him. Later on, I will narrate what took place in regard to the decennial prizes.

I have hardly seen Mme. de Staël, but I have been surrounded by persons who have known her well. My mother and some of my relatives were intimate with her in their youth, and have told me that in her earliest years she displayed a character which promised to carry her beyond the restraints of nearly all social customs. At the age of fifteen she enjoyed the most abstract reading and the most impassioned works. The famous Franclieu of Geneva, finding her one day with a volume of J. J. Rousseau in her hand, and surrounded by books of all kinds, said to her mother, Mme. Necker: "Take care; you will make your daughter a lunatic or a fool." This severe judgment was not realized, and yet it is impossible not to feel that there was something very odd, something that looked like mental alienation, in the manner in which Mme. de Staël acted her part as a woman in the world. Surrounded in her father's house by a circle consisting of all the men in the city who were in any way distinguished, excited by the conversations that she heard as well as by her own nature, her intellectual faculties were perhaps developed to excess. She then acquired the taste for controversy which she has since practiced so much, and in which she has shown herself so *piquante* and so distinguished. She was animated even to agitation, perfectly true and natural, felt with force, and expressed herself with fire. Harassed by an imagination which consumed her, too eager for notoriety and success, hampered by those laws of society which keep women within narrow bounds, she braved everything, conquered everything, and suffered much from this stormy contest between the demon that pushed her on and the social proprieties which could not restrain her.

She had the misfortune to be excessively plain, and to be miserable on that account; for it seemed as if she felt within herself a craving for successes of all kinds. With a passably pretty face, she would probably have been happier, because she would have been calmer. Her nature was too passionate for her not to love strongly, and her imagination too vivid for her not to think that she loved often. The celebrity she acquired naturally brought to her much homage, by which her vanity was gratified. Although she had great kindness of heart, she excited both hatred and envy; she startled women, and she wounded many men whose superior she thought herself. Some of her friends, however, were always faithful, and her own loyalty to friendship never failed.

When Bonaparte was made Consul, Mme. de Staël had already become famous through her opinions, her conduct, and her works. A personage like Bonaparte excited the curiosity, and at first even the enthusiasm, of a woman who was always awake to all that was remarkable. She became deeply interested in him— sought him, pursued him everywhere. She believed that the happy combination of so many distinguished qualities and of so many favorable circumstances might be turned to the profit of her idol, Liberty; but she quickly startled Bonaparte, who did not wish to be either watched or divined. Mme. de Staël, after making him uneasy, displeased him. He received her advances coldly, and disconcerted her by his bluntness and sharp words. He offended many of her opinions; a certain distrust grew up between them, and, as they were both high-tempered, this distrust was not long in changing to hatred.

When in Paris, Mme. de Staël received many people, and all political subjects were freely discussed under her roof. Louis Bonaparte, then very young, visited her sometimes and enjoyed her conversation. His brother became uneasy at this, and forbade his frequenting the house, and even went so far as to have him watched. Men of letters, publicists, men of the Revolution, great lords, were all to be met there.

"This woman," said the First Consul, "teaches people to think who never thought before, or who had forgotten how to think." And there was much truth in this. The publication of certain works by M. Necker put the finishing touch to his irritation: he banished Mme. de Staël from France, and did himself great harm by this act of arbitrary persecution. In addition to this, as nothing excites one like a first injustice, he even pursued those persons who believed it their duty to show her kindness in her exile. Her works, with the exception of her novels, were mutilated before their appearance in France; all the journals were ordered to speak ill of them; no generosity was shown her. When she was driven from her own land, foreign countries welcomed her warmly.

Her talents fortified her against the annoyances of her life, and raised her to a height which many men might well have envied. If Mme. de Staël had known how to add to her goodness of heart and to her brilliant genius the advantages of a calm and quiet life, she would have avoided the greater part of her misfortunes, and seized while living the distinguished rank which will not long be refused her among the writers of her century. Her works indicate rapid and keen insight, and a warmth that comes from her soul. They are characterized by an imagination that is almost too vivid, but she lacks clearness and good taste. In reading her writings one sees at once that they are the results of an excitable nature, rebelling under order and regularity. Her life was not exactly that of a woman, nor could it be that of a man; it was utterly deficient in repose—a deprivation without remedy for happiness, and even for talent.

After the first restoration, Mme. de Staël returned to France, overwhelmed with joy at being once more in her own land, and at seeing the dawn of the constitutional *régime* for which she had so ardently longed. Bonaparte's return struck terror to her soul. Again she resumed her wanderings, but her exile this time lasted only *a hundred days*. She reappeared with the King. She was very happy. She had married her daughter to the Duc de Broglie, who unites to the distinction of his name a noble and elevated nature; the liberation of France satisfied her, her friends were near her, and the world crowded about her. This was the time when death claimed her, at the age of fifty. The last work on which she was engaged, and which she had not completed, was published after her death; this has made her thoroughly known to us. This work not only paints the times in which she lived, but gives a clear and exact idea of the century which gave her birth—which alone could have developed her, and of which she is not one of the least results.

I occasionally heard Bonaparte speak of Mme. de Staël. The hatred he bore her was unquestionably founded in some degree upon that jealousy with which he was inspired by any superiority which he could not control; and his words were often characterized by a bitterness which elevated her in spite of himself, and lowered him in the estimation of those who, in the full possession of their reasoning faculties, listened to him.

While Mme. de Staël could complain with so much justice of the persecution to which she was subjected, there was another woman, much her inferior and far less celebrated, who had had reason to rejoice in the protection accorded to her by the Emperor. This was Mme. de Genlis. He never found in her either talents or opinions in opposition to his own. She had loved and glorified the Revolution, and well understood how to profit by all its liberties. In her old age she became both a prude and a *dévote*. She attached herself to order and discipline, and for this reason, or under this pretext manifested a profound admiration for Bonaparte by which he was much flattered; he bestowed a pension upon her, and instituted a sort of correspondence with her, in the course of which she kept him informed of all that she felt would be useful to him, and taught him much regarding the ancient *régime* which he wished to know. She loved and protected M. Fiévée, then a very young writer; she drew him into this correspondence, and it was in this way that between himself and Bonaparte were established those relations of which Fiévée subsequently boasted so much. Although flattered by the admiration of Mme. de Genlis, Bonaparte understood her thoroughly. He once expressed himself openly in my presence in regard to her. He was speaking of that prudery which permeates all her works. " When Mme. de Genlis," he said, " wishes to define virtue, she speaks of it as of a discovery! "

The Restoration did not reëstablish relations between Mme. de Genlis and the house of Orleans. The Duke of Orleans did not choose to see her more than once, but contented himself with continuing the pension allowed her by the Emperor.

These two women were not the only ones who wrote and published their works under Bonaparte's rule. Of the others I will mention only a few, at the head of whom I will place Mme. Cottin, so distinguished for the warmth of an impassioned imagination which communicated itself to her style, and Mme. de Fla-hault, who married at the beginning of this century M. de Souza, then Ambassador from Portugal, and who wrote some very pretty novels. There were others still whose names are to be found in the news-papers of that day. Novels have multiplied greatly in France in the last thirty years, and merely by reading these one has a very clear idea of the progress of the French mind since the Revolution. The disorder of the first years of this Revolution turned the mind from all those pleasures which only interest when in repose. Young people generally were but half educated; the differences of parties destroyed public opinion. At the time when that great regulator had entirely disap-peared, mediocrity could show itself without fear. All sorts of attempts were made in literature, and imagi-native works, always easiest when most fantastic, were published with impunity. People, with their minds heated by the rapidity of events, yielded to a kind of excitement and enthusiasm which found a field in the invention of fables and in the style of our romances. Liberty alone, which men did not enjoy, can develop with grandeur those emotions which our great political storms had aroused. But in all times and under all governments women can write and talk of love, and works of this kind met with general approval. There was little or none of Mme. de la Fayette's elegance, nor of Mme. Riccoboni's delicate, refined wit: nor did they amuse themselves by describing the usages of courts, the habits of a state of society now nearly passed away; but they represented powerful scenes of passion and human nature in trying positions. The heart was often unveiled in these animated fables, and some men even, in order to give variety to their sensations, engaged in this style of composition.

After all, there is some truth and nature in the tone of the works published since the epoch of which we speak. Even in the romances, the enthusiasm is rather too strong than too affected, and, generally speaking, they are not perverted by a false taste. The wild errors of our Revolution upheaved French society, and later this society was unable to recreate itself on the same erroneous foundation. Each of the individuals who composed it was not only displaced, but was even entirely changed. Merely conventional customs have by degrees disappeared, and in all the relations of life the difference has been felt. Discourses written and spoken are no longer the same, nor are pictures. We have come to seek stronger sensations and emotions that are more real, because sorrow has developed the habit of keener feeling. Bonaparte caused nothing to move backward, but he restrained everything. The return of order to the Government brought back also what M. de Fontanes called *les bonnes lettres*. It now began to be felt that good taste, discretion, and moderation should count for something in the works of talent. If the good genius of France had permitted Bonaparte to bestow upon us some shadow of liberty at the same time that he brought us repose, it is probable that the recollections of a stormy period, combined with the comfort of a more settled state of things, would have led to more important productions. But the Emperor, desiring that all should turn to his advantage alone, while at the same time making enormous efforts to attach to his reign all celebrities, so hampered their minds and marked them with the seal of his despotism that he virtually interdicted all hearty efforts. The greater number of writers exhausted their inventive genius in varying the prescribed and well-recompensed praise. No political works were sanctioned, and in all imaginary creations every doubtful application was avoided with the utmost care. Comedy dared not depict the manners of the day. Tragedy only ventured to represent certain heroes. There was so much in the Emperor that could honestly be praised, that conscience was appeased; but true invention, repressed, soon becomes extinct.

Meanwhile time and progress, combined with the habitual good taste of France, which had such examples in the past, all had their effect. All that was produced had a certain amount of elegance, and those who engaged in authorship wrote more or less well. A prudent mediocrity was the order of the day. The first quality of genius is strength of thought, and when thought is restrained one limits one's self to the perfecting of one's diction. One can only conscientiously do the best that is permitted. And this explains the sameness of the works of the beginning of this century. But nowadays the liberty we have gained extends in all directions, and we have bequeathed to our children the habit of perfecting the details of execution, with the hope that they will enrich these details by their genius.

I have previously said that, while strength of expression was forbidden us, we were at least allowed to be natural, and this quality certainly makes itself felt in the greater number of the literary productions of our time. The stage, which was afraid to present the vices and the follies of each class, because all classes were recreated by Bonaparte, and it was necessary to respect his work, disembarrassed itself of the affectation and cant which preceded the Revolution. At the head of our comic authors Picard must be placed—Picard, who has so often, with so much originality and gayety, given us an idea of the manners and customs of Paris under the government of the Directory. After his name come those of Duval and several authors of comic opera.

We have seen the birth and death of many distinguished poets: Legouvé, who was made known to us by "La Mort d'Abel," which he followed by "La Mort d'Henri IV.," and who wrote fine fugitive poems; Arnault, author of "Marius à Minturnes"; Raynouard, who made a great success in "Les Templières"; Lemercier, who appeared before the public first with his "Agamemnon," the best of his works; Chénier, whose talents bore too revolutionary an imprint, but who had a strong perception of the tragic. Then follow a whole crowd of poets, all more or less pupils of M. Delille, and who, having acquired from him the art of rhyming elegantly, celebrated the charms of the country and simple pleasures and repose to the sound of Bonaparte's cannon echoing all through Europe. I will not enter on this long list, which may be found anywhere. There were excellent translations made. Very little history was written; the time had come when it was necessary to use a forcible pen in writing it, and no one was prepared to use such a pen.

Every one had fortunately become disgusted with the light and mocking tone of the philosophy of the last century, which, overthrowing all belief by the aid of ridicule, blighted and tarnished all that was best in life, and made of irreligion a jest and an intolerant dogma. Sorrowful experience had begun to teach the value of religious faith. Men were insensibly drawn into a better path, and followed it, though slowly.

Art, which stands not in so much need of liberty as letters, had not stood altogether still. It had made some progress, but at the same time it had suffered from the general restraint. Among our most famous painters was David, who most unfortunately marred his reputation by abandoning himself to the most disgusting errors of the Revolutionary madness. After refusing in 1792 to paint Louis XVI., because he said he did not choose that his brush should delineate a tyrant's features, he submitted with a very good grace to Bonaparte, and represented him in all ways. Then came Gérard, who painted so many historical portraits, an immortal "Battle of Austerlitz," and not long since an "Entry of Henry IV. into Paris," which stirred every French heart; Girodet, so admirable for the purity of his drawing and the boldness of his conceptions; Gros, an eminently dramatic artist; Guérin, whose brush stirs the souls of all who can feel; Isabey, so clever and so delicate in his miniatures; and a crowd of others of all kinds. The Emperor patronized and protected all. Everything was reproduced by the brush and the palette, and money was lavished on these artists. The Revolution had placed them in society, where they occupied an agreeable and often very useful position. They guided the development of luxury, and at the same time drew largely on the poetic and picturesque incidents of our Revolution and of the Imperial reign. Bonaparte was able indeed to chill the expression of strong thoughts; but he kindled men's imaginations, and that is enough for most poets and for all painters.

The progress of science was not interrupted, for it was useful to the Government and awakened no distrust. The Institute of France numbers many distinguished men. Bonaparte courted them all, and enriched some. He even bestowed some of his new dignities upon them. He summoned them to his Senate. It seems to me that this was an honor to that body, and that the idea was not without grandeur. *Savants* under his rule have been more independent than any other classes. Lagrange, whom Bonaparte made Senator, held himself aloof; but Laplace, Lacépède, Monge, Berthollet, Cuvier, and some others accepted his favors eagerly, and repaid them with unfailing admiration.

I can not conscientiously close this chapter without mentioning the great number of physicians who did honor to their profession. Music has attained to high perfection in France. Bonaparte had an especial liking for the Italian school. The expenditures he made in transplanting it to France were very useful to us, although he allowed his own caprices to govern him in the distribution of his favors. For example, he always repelled Cherubini, because that composer, displeased on one occasion by a criticism made by Bonaparte when he was only a general, had answered him somewhat rudely, that " a man might be skillful enough on a battle-field and yet know nothing of harmony. He took a fancy to Lessueur, and lost his temper at the time of the award of the decennial prizes because the Institute did not proclaim this musician worthy of the prize. But as a general thing he did his best to advance this art. I saw him receive at

Malmaison old M. Grétry, and treat him with remark-able distinction. Grétry, Dalayrac, Méhul, Berton, Lesueur, Spontini, and others still were distinguished under the Empire, and received recompenses for their works.

In like manner actors met with great favor. All that I have said of the tendency of our authors may apply with equal truth to the drama. The natural has acquired a great influence on our stage since the Revolution. Good taste has proscribed pompous gravity in tragedy and affectation in comedy. Talma and Mlle. Mars have done much toward strengthening the alliance between art and nature. Ease united to vigor has been introduced in dancing. In short, it may be said that simplicity, elegance, and harmony now characterize French taste, and that all the shams of phantasy and conventionality have disappeared.

CHAPTER XX

(1806.)

ON the suggestion of M. Portalis, the Minister of Public Worship, the Emperor issued a decree appointing his birthday to be kept on the Feast of the Assumption, the 15th of August, which was also the anniversary of the conclusion of the Concordat. The first Sunday of each December was also set apart as a holiday, in commemoration of Austerlitz.

On the 30th of March there was an important session of the Senate, which gave rise to much and various comment. The Emperor communicated to the Senators a long list of decrees, which were destined to affect Europe from one end to the other. It will not be amiss to give some details of these, as well as an extract from the speech of Cambacérès, the Arch-Chancellor, which affords an example of the obsequious skill with which the sudden resolves of a master who kept all things, even men's minds, in unceasing ferment, could be clothed in specious phrases.

" Gentlemen," said Cambacérès, " at the time when France, animated by the same spirit as ourselves, secured alike her happiness and her glory by an oath of obedience to our august sovereign, you foresaw in your wisdom the necessity of coördinating the system of hereditary government in all its parts, and likewise of strengthening it by institutions analogous to its nature.

" Your wishes have been partly fulfilled; they will

be still further accomplished by the various enactments which his Majesty the Emperor and King orders me to lay before you. You will receive with gratitude these fresh proofs of his confidence in the Senate, and his love for the people, and you will hasten, in conformity with his Majesty's intention, to inscribe them on your registers.

"The first of these decrees is a statute to regulate all things relating to the civil status of the Imperial family, and it also defines the duties of the princes and princesses toward the Emperor.

" The second decree unites the states of Venice to the kingdom of Italy.

" The third confers the throne of Naples on Prince Joseph." (Here follows an elaborate panegyric of the virtues of the new King, and of the measure, by which he retains the title of Grand Dignitary of the Empire.)

" The fourth contains the cession of the duchy of Cleves and the duchy of Berg to Prince Murat." (Similar panegyric.)

" The fifth bestows the principality of Guastalla on the Princess Borghese and her husband." (Praises of both.)

" The sixth transfers to Marshal Berthier the principality of Neufchâtel." (He is complimented like the rest. This touching proof of the solicitude of the Emperor for his companion in arms, for his brave and intelligent fellow soldier, will not fail to touch every loyal heart, and to gladden every loyal spirit.)

" The seventh erects in the states of Parma and Piacenza three great titles, which will be suitably supported by considerable sums to be raised in those states by order of his Majesty.

" By similar provisions, contained in decrees relating to the states of Venice, the kingdom of Naples, and the principality of Lucca, his Majesty has created rewards worthy of himself for several of his subjects who have performed great services in war, or who, in the discharge of important functions, have contributed in a signal manner to the welfare of the state. These dignities and titles become the property of those invested with them, and will descend in the male line to their legitimate heirs. This grand conception, while it proclaims to Europe the price attached by his Majesty to acts of valor in his soldiers, and to faithfulness in those employed by him in important affairs, is also of political advantage. The brilliant position of eminent men gives to their example and their counsels an influence with the people which a monarch may sometimes substitute, with advantage, for the authority of public officials. At the same time, such men are intercessors between the people and the throne."

It must be admitted that a good deal of progress had been made since the still recent time when the decrees of the Government were dated " Year 14 of the Republic."

" It is, therefore, on these bases that the Emperor wishes to build the great political system with the idea of which Providence has inspired him, and by which he increases the love and admiration for his person which you share with all the French nation."

After this speech, the various decrees were read aloud. The following are the most important articles:

By the decree regulating the civil status of the Imperial family, the princes and princesses could not marry without the consent of the Emperor. Children born of a marriage contracted without his consent would have no claim to the privileges which in certain countries attach to morganatic marriages.

Divorce was forbidden to the Imperial family, but separation, if authorized by the Emperor, was allowed.

The guardians of Imperial children were to be named by him.

Members of the Imperial family could not adopt children without his permission.

The Arch-Chancellor of the Empire was to fulfill toward the Imperial family all the functions assigned by law to the officers of the civil status. A Secretary for the status of the Imperial family was to be chosen among the Ministers or from among the State councilors.

The ceremonial for marriages and births was arranged.

The Arch-Chancellor was to receive the will of the Emperor, as dictated by him to the Secretary of the Imperial Family, in presence of two witnesses. The will was to be placed in the keeping of the Senate.

The Emperor was to regulate everything concerning the education of the princes and princesses of his family, appointing or removing those who had it in charge. All princes born in the order of succession were to be brought up together in a palace not more than twenty leagues from the residence of the Emperor.

The education of the princes was to begin at the age of seven, and end at that of sixteen. Children of certain persons distinguished by their services might be admitted by the Emperor to share in the advantages of this education.

If a prince in the order of succession should ascend a foreign throne, he would be bound, on his sons attaining the age of seven, to send them to the aforesaid palace.

The princes and princesses could not leave France, nor remove beyond a radius of thirty leagues, without permission of the Emperor.

If a member of the Imperial family were to misconduct himself, forgetting his high position and his duties, the Emperor might, for a space of time not exceeding one year, place him under arrest, forbid him his presence, or send him into exile. He might forbid any intercourse between members of his family and persons who seemed to him of doubtful character. In serious cases, he might order two years' seclusion in a state prison. This was to be done in the presence of the Arch-Chancellor and of a family council presided over by himself; the Secretary of the Imperial Family to be in attendance.

The great dignitaries and the dukes of the Empire were subject to the provisions of these latter articles.

After this first decree came the following:

"We have established and we establish as duchies and great fiefs of our Empire the provinces hereinafter to be named:

Dalmatia,	Tréviso,
Istria,	Feltre,
Friuli,	Bassano,
Cadore,	Vicenza,
Belluno,	Padua,
Conegliano,	Rovigo.

"We reserve to ourselves the investiture of the said fiefs, to descend in succession to male issue. In the event of extinction, the said fiefs shall revert to the Imperial Crown.

"It is our intention that a fifteenth part of the revenue that our kingdom of Italy draws, or may draw, from the said provinces shall be an appanage to the said fiefs, and be possessed by those whom we shall have invested with them. We reserve to ourselves for the same purpose the disposal of thirty millions of francs from national property situate in the said provinces. *Le Mont Napoléon* shall be charged with twelve hundred thousand francs as Government annuities, in favor of those generals, officers, and soldiers who have done good service to the country and to our Crown, but on the express condition that they shall not alienate the same within ten years, without our permission.

" Until the kingdom of Italy shall have an army, we grant to the said kingdom a French contingent, to be maintained by our Imperial Treasury. To this end, our Royal Treasury of Italy shall pay monthly to our Imperial Treasury the sum of two million five hundred thousand francs during the time that our army shall sojourn in Italy, that is, during six years. The heir presumptive of Italy shall be entitled Prince of Venice.

" The tranquillity of Europe requires that we should secure the safety of the peoples of Naples and Sicily, who have fallen into our power by the right of conquest, and who are part of the Grand Empire; we therefore declare our brother Joseph Napoleon, Grand Elector of France, King of Naples and Sicily. The crown shall be hereditary in the male line; failing this, we appoint it to our own legitimate children in the male line, and failing these, to the children of our brother Louis Napoleon; reserving to ourselves, in the event of our brother Joseph's dying without male children, the right of naming as successor to the said crown a prince of our own family, or an adopted son, according as we may deem it desirable in the interests of our people, and of that great system which Divine Providence has destined us to found.

" Six great fiefs are established in the said kingdom, with the title of duchy, and the same prerogatives as the others, to be in perpetuity appointed by us and our successors.

" We reserve to ourselves a revenue of one million on the kingdom of Naples, for distribution among the generals, officers, and privates of our army, on the same conditions as those set forth in the case of *le Mont Napoléon.*

" The King of Naples shall be in perpetuity a grand dignitary of the Empire, we reserving to ourselves the right of creating him a Prince instead of Grand Elector.

" We declare that the crown of Naples, which we place on the head of Prince Joseph and his heirs, shall in no way bar their right to the succession to the throne of France. But it is our will also that the crowns of France, Italy, and Naples and Sicily shall never be united on the same head.

" We give the duchies of Cleves and of Berg to our brother-in-law Prince Joachim, and to his heirs male; failing whom, they shall devolve on our brother Joseph, and if he have no male issue, on our brother Louis; but they are never to be united to the crown of France. The Duke of Cleves and Berg will continue to be Grand Admiral, and we shall have power to create a Vice-Admiral."

Lastly, the principality of Guastalla was bestowed on Princess Borghese. The Prince was to bear the title of Prince of Guastalla. Should they have no issue, the Emperor was to dispose of the principality at his pleasure. The same conditions were to hold good in the case of the principality of Neufchâtel.

The principality of Lucca was augmented by the addition of some lands detached from the kingdom of Italy, and in return was to pay an annual sum of two hundred thousand francs, which was likewise destined for military rewards. A portion of the national property situate in the duchies of Parma and Piacenza was reserved for the same object.

I have deemed it well to give almost the entire text of the different decrees which seem to me to call for comment. This act of Bonaparte's revealed to some extent the preponderance which he intended to give the French Empire over the conquered states of Europe, and also that which he reserved to himself personally. It may easily be conceived that these decrees excited such disquiet throughout Europe as forbade us to cherish the hope of a long peace. It is also plain from them that Italy, which had been eager to seize on the independence which unity of government seemed to promise her, soon found her hopes betrayed by the secondary position in which she was placed by the bonds which subjected her to the Emperor.

No matter how careful Prince Eugène was, or how mild and just his government, the Italians soon perceived that conquest had placed them in the power of a master, who made use of the resources of their beautiful land for his own advantage only. They maintained on their territory, and at their cost, a foreign army. The largest part of their revenue served to enrich Frenchmen. In everything that was exacted of them, much less regard was paid to their interests than to the advantage of the Grand Empire, and this soon became synonymous with the ambitious projects of one man, who did not hesitate to claim from Italy sacrifices he would scarcely have dared to ask of France. The Viceroy endeavored to obtain some alleviation for the Italians, but in vain. They learned, however, to do justice to the character of Eugène, and to distinguish between him and the rigorous measures which he was forced to carry out; they were grateful to him for what he tried to do, and for his good intentions. This, however, did not last; the too much oppressed people lost the power of being just, and included all Frenchmen, Prince Eugène at their head, in the hatred they bore to the Emperor.

The Viceroy himself, who was a faithful servant to Bonaparte, though he was under no delusion regarding him, told his mother in my presence that the Emperor, jealous of the affection Eugène had won, had imposed useless and oppressive measures upon him, in order to alienate the good will of the Italians.

The Vice-Queen contributed also, at first, to the popularity of her husband. She was beautiful, very kind-hearted, pious, and benevolent, and she charmed every one who approached her. Toward Bonaparte her manner was dignified and cold. He disliked to hear her praised. She never passed much time in Paris.

Several of the articles of these decrees were never carried out. Change of circumstances led to change of purpose; new passions brought forth new fancies, or sudden suspicion altered former resolves. In many respects the government of Bonaparte resembled the Palace of the Legislature, in which the Chamber of Deputies is now installed. The former building remains unaltered; but, in order to render it more imposing, a façade has been erected, which seen from the river-side is undoubtedly a grand object, but, if we walk round the building, we find that it does not harmonize with the architecture of the front. Bonaparte frequently erected façades only, political, legislative, or administrative.

After the reception of these messages the Senate passed a vote of thanks to the Emperor, and deputations were sent to the new Queen of Naples, who received them with her usual simple grace, and to the two princesses. Murat had already departed to take possession of his duchy. The newspapers assured us he was received with acclamations, and gave a similar account of the delight of the Neapolitans; but from private letters we learned that the war was to be continued, and that Calabria would make a stout resistance. Joseph has a mild disposition, and in no place has he made himself personally disliked; but he is wanting in tact, and he has always shown himself unequal to the position in which he was placed. To tell the truth, the business of kingship, as established by Bonaparte, has been a difficult one.

Having settled these important points, the Emperor turned to occupations of a lighter kind. On the 7th of April the betrothal of the young couple of whom I have already spoken in a preceding chapter took place at the Tuileries. The ceremony was performed in the Diana Gallery in the evening; there was a numerous and brilliant Court. The bride elect wore a silver-embroidered gown ornamented with roses. The witnesses on her side were MM. de Talleyrand, de Champagny, and de Ségur; and for the bridegroom, the Hereditary Prince of Bavaria, the Grand Chamberlain of the Elector of Baden, and Baron Dalberg, Minister Plenipotentiary of Baden.

On the following evening the marriage was celebrated in state. The Tuileries were illuminated; fireworks were exhibited on the Place Louis XV., then called Place de la Concorde.

The Court displayed a special splendor for the occasion, even beyond its usual extravagant luxury. The Empress wore a gown entirely covered with gold embroidery of different shades, and wore, besides the Imperial crown, pearls in her hair to the value of a million francs. Princess Borghese shone with all the

Borghese diamonds added to her own, which were priceless; Mme. Murat wore rubies; Mme. Louis was almost covered with turquoises set in brilliants; the new Queen of Naples, slight and delicate-looking, seemed to bend beneath the weight of precious stones. I remember that I had a Court dress made for the occasion, although I was not usually among the most brilliantly dressed ladies of the Court. It was of pink crape, spangled with silver, and looped up with wreaths of jasmine; on my hair was a crown of jasmine and diamond wheat-ears. My jewels were worth from forty thousand to fifty thousand francs —far less than those of most of our Court ladies.

Princess Stéphanie had received magnificent gifts from her husband, and still more splendid ones from the Emperor. She wore a circlet of diamonds surmounted with orange-blossom. Her court dress was of white tulle, with silver stars and sprays of orange-blossom. She approached the altar with much gracefulness, and made her deep courtesies so as to charm the Emperor and every one else. Her father, who stood among the Senators, was moved to tears. His position in this ceremony was curious, and his feelings must have been rather complex. The Order of Baden was conferred on him.

The Cardinal Legate, Caprara, solemnized the marriage. At the conclusion of the ceremony, we returned from the chapel to the state apartments in the same order as that in which we had come down: the princes and princesses heading the procession, the Empress followed by all her ladies, with the Prince of Baden at her side, and the Emperor leading the bride. He wore his state costume. I have already said that it became him well. Nothing was wanting to the pageantry of the procession but a more deliberate step; but Bonaparte always would walk fast, and he hurried us more than was dignified or desirable.

The trains of the princesses and queens and that of the Empress were borne by pages. As for the rest of us, although letting our trains fall would have greatly improved our appearance, we were obliged to carry them over one arm, because their excessive length would have caused far too much delay for the Emperor's quick pace.

It frequently happened in state ceremonials, and rendered them less imposing, that the chamberlains preceding him would repeat in a low tone, as they trod on our heels, " Now then, ladies, please to get on." The Countess d'Arberg, who had been at the Court of the Archduchess in the Netherlands, and was accustomed to German etiquette, was always so visibly annoyed by this intimation, that we who were used to it could not but laugh at her. She used to say, with some humor, that we ought to be called " postillions-in-waiting," and that we had better have had short skirts given to us than the long train, which was of no use.

M. de Talleyrand also was much annoyed by this habit, as, in his capacity of Grand Chamberlain, he had to precede the Emperor, and he, on account of a weakness of the lower limbs, found even slow walking difficult. The aides-de-camp used to be amused at his vexation. As for the Empress, this was one of the points on which she would not yield to her husband. She had a very graceful manner of walking, and was averse to hiding any of her accomplishments; therefore nothing could induce her to hurry. The pressure began among those who were following her.

When we were starting for the chapel, I recollect that the Emperor, who was little used to giving his hand to ladies, was puzzled, not knowing whether to offer his right or his left hand to the bride. It was she who had to make the decision.

A great reception was held that day in the state apartments; there was a concert, then a ballet and supper, as I have before described. The Queen of Naples having passed next after the Empress, Bonaparte placed his adopted daughter at his right hand, above his mother. On that evening again Mme. Murat had to endure the great mortification of passing through the doorways after the young Princess of Baden.

The Court removed next day to Malmaison, and shortly afterward to Saint Cloud. I have already related what occurred there. On the 20th we came back to Paris, to be present at a splendid fête given in honor of the marriage.

The Emperor, wishing to display his Court to the Parisians, allowed a considerable number of invitations to be sent to men and women of every class. The state apartments were filled by an immense crowd. Two quadrilles were danced. One, in which I took part, was Mme. Louis Bonaparte's, and was performed with dance-steps in the Salle des Maréchaux. Sixteen ladies, in groups of four, dressed in white, their heads wreathed with flowers of different colors, their dresses ornamented with flowers, and with diamond wheat-ears in their hair, danced with sixteen gentlemen wearing white satin coats, and scarfs corresponding in color to their partners' flowers. When our dance was concluded, the Empress and the Imperial family entered the Diana Gallery, where Mme. Murat was at the head of another quadrille—the persons composing it being costumed as Spaniards, with hats and feathers.

After this, every one was allowed to dance—city

and Court together. Ices and refreshments were distributed in profusion. The Emperor returned to Saint Cloud, having remained about an hour, and spoken to a great number of persons; that is to say, having asked each one his or her name. Dancing was kept up after his departure until morning.

Perhaps I have lingered too long on these details, but they are a relief from the serious narrative I have undertaken, and of which my woman's pen becomes at times a little weary.

While making and unmaking kings, according to the expression of M. de Fontanes, while giving his adopted daughter in marriage, and joining in the festivities of which I have spoken, the Emperor assiduously attended the state councils, hastened on their work, and forwarded daily a great number of laws to the Legislature. State Councilor Treilhard was the bearer of the code of procedure, completed during this year; many regulations were agreed to concerning trade, and the session was closed by a statement which conveyed grand ideas of the flourishing state of our finances. Not an extra sou was demanded from the nation; public works had been accomplished, and others were in contemplation; there was a formidable army, as was well known, and only a fixed debt of 48,000,000; a civil list of 35,000,000 against 8,000,000 of revenue.

Meanwhile the Emperor's resentment against the English Government was growing deeper. The Cabinet, which, however changed in its individual members, had not changed in its policy toward us, declared war on the King of Prussia, to punish him for his neutrality in the last war, and for his conquest of Hanover, which he had just taken.

A long article on European politics appeared in the "Moniteur." The author tried to prove that by this

rupture England would accelerate the policy which
must close the northern ports against her (the ports
of the south being already closed), and that she would
strengthen the union between France and the Continent. The position of Holland was next fully discussed. The Grand Pensionary Schimmelpenninck
had, it was reported, become blind. What would be
the course taken by the Dutch? It was known that
the Emperor had not directly authorized the recent
changes in the organization of that country, and that
he had said on the occasion that " the prosperity and
liberty of nations could only be assured by one of two
systems of government—a constitutional monarchy
or a republic, constituted according to the principles
of liberty. In Holland the Grand Pensionary exercises an important influence on the elections of the
representatives of the legislative body; this is a rad-
ical vice in the Constitution. Nevertheless all nations
can not with impunity leave the choice of their representatives to the public, and, when there is danger to
be apprehended from assembling the people, recourse
must be had to the principles of a good and wise
monarchy. This, perhaps, is what will occur to the
Dutch. It is for them to appreciate their situation,
and to choose between the two systems that one which
is most likely to establish public prosperity and public liberty on a solid basis." These words were sufficiently indicative of what was in store for Holland.
The writer next pointed out the advantages which
must result to France from the duchies of Cleves and
Berg being occupied by a Frenchman, inasmuch as
our relations with Holland would be better, and that
all the countries on the right bank of the Rhine would
be occupied by allies of the Imperial family.

The Prince of Neufchâtel was about to close Switzerland against English traders. The Emperor of

Austria was said to be engaged in tending his wounds, and resolved on a long peace. The Russians, still agitated by English policy, had had fresh contests in Dalmatia, being unwilling to give up the country situated near the mouth of the Cattaro, which was in their occupation; but the presence of the Grand Army, whose return had been suspended, had compelled them at length to fulfill the conditions of the last treaty.

The Pope was dismissing from Rome all persons, whether English, Russians, or Sardinians, suspected of intriguing, and whose presence gave umbrage to the French Government.

The kingdom of Naples was almost entirely subjugated; Sicily was defended by a mere handful of English. France was in close alliance with the Porte; the Turkish Government was less mercenary and less ignorant than had been supposed, and understood that the presence of the French in Dalmatia might be most useful in protecting Turkey from Russian invasion. Lastly, our army was more formidable than ever, and well able to resist the attacks of a fourth coalition, to form which, after all, Europe was not disposed.

This sketch of our position with regard to Europe could only be reassuring to those who took plausible phrases emanating from the highest quarters in their literal sense. It was easy enough for any one who read them without absolute credulity to perceive that the populations were not so docile as we tried to make out; that we were beginning to sacrifice their interests to our own policy; that England, angered by failure, was bent on raising up new enemies for us; that the King of Prussia was selling us his friendship; and that Russia was still threatening us. Men no longer believed in the pacific intentions which the

Emperor announced in all his speeches. But there was something so impressive in his plans, his military talent was so abundantly proved, he bestowed such greatness on France, that, duped by her own glory, forced as she was to bend beneath the yoke, she consented also to be beguiled by the enchanter. Moreover, the internal prosperity of the country had apparently increased; there was no augmentation of taxes; everything contributed to dazzle us, and not one of us, acted upon as we were by the impulsion which Bonaparte had given us all, had either the leisure or the will for serious reflection. The Emperor used to say, " Luxury and glory have never failed to turn the heads of the French."

Shortly after, we were told that a great council had been held at the Hague by the representatives of the Batavian people, at which affairs of the highest importance had been discussed; and a rumor was allowed to spread that a new Dutch monarchy was about to be founded.

Meanwhile, the English newspapers were full of criticisms on the progress which the Imperial power was making in Europe. " If Bonaparte," they said, " succeeds in accomplishing his system of a Federal Empire, France will become the sovereign arbiter of almost the whole continent." He was delighted at this prediction, and resolutely strove to realize it.

M. de Talleyrand, at that time in great repute, used his influence in Europe to gain over the foreign Ministers. He asked for and obtained from the sovereigns exactly those ambassadors whom he knew he could make amenable. For instance, he obtained from Prussia the Marquis de Lucchesini, who subsequently acted in the French interest, against his own master. He was a clever man, of a somewhat scheming disposition. He was born at Lucca, but a taste for traveling took him in his youth to Berlin, where he was received by Frederick the Great, who, liking his conversation and his philosophical principles, kept him near his own person, gave him a place at Court, and founded his fortunes. He was subsequently intrusted with Prussian affairs, became a person of importance, and had sufficient luck and ability to remain long in high repute. He married a Prussian lady, and both he and his wife, when they came to France, devoted themselves to M. de Talleyrand, who made use of them to further his own ends. It was long before the King of Prussia found out that his ambassador had joined in the plots against him, and Lucchesini did not fall into disgrace until some years later. The Marquis then repaired to Italy, and found a fresh field for his ambition in the influence he obtained over the sovereign of Lucca, who had become Grand Duchess of Tuscany. The events of 1814 caused his downfail to follow on that of his mistress. The Marchesa de Lucchesini, who was rather addicted to coquetry, was while in Paris one of the most obsequious of Madame de Talleyrand's friends.

On the 5th of June the Emperor received an Ambassador Extraordinary from the Porte, with messages of congratulation and friendship from the Sultan. These messages were accompanied by magnificent presents of diamonds, a pearl necklace worth eighty thousand francs, perfumes, innumerable shawls, and Arab horses, with housings adorned with precious stones. The Emperor gave the necklace to his wife, and distributed the diamonds and the shawls among the ladies-in-waiting. Some were given also to the wives of ministers and marshals, and to a few others. The Empress reserved the finest for herself, and there yet remained enough to be used afterward for the decoration of a boudoir at Compiègne, which Josephine had arranged for herself with special care, but which was never used except by the Empress Marie Louise.

On the same day the Envoy from Holland came to announce that it had been decided at the Hague, upon mature deliberation, that a constitutional monarchy was the only form of government that would thenceforth be suitable for Holland, because such a monarchy would harmonize with the principles now spreading in Europe; and that, in order to consolidate it, they solicited Louis Napoleon, the Emperor's brother, to become their first King.

Bonaparte replied that such a monarchy would doubtless be profitable to the general policy of Europe, and that, by removing anxieties of his own, it would enable him to deliver important places into the hands of the Dutch, which hitherto he had felt it his duty to retain. Then, turning toward his brother, he enjoined him to have a care of the people intrusted to him.

This scene was well acted. Louis made a fitting reply. On the audience coming to an end, the doors were flung open, as on the occasion when Louis XIV. accepted the succession to Spain, and the new King of Holland was announced to the assembled Court.

Immediately on this, the Arch-Chancellor carried to the Senate, according to custom, the new Imperial message, and made the usual speech.

The Emperor guaranteed to his brother the integrity of his states, and that his children should succeed him; but the crowns of France and of Holland were never to be united on one head.

In the case of a minority, the Queen was to be regent, and failing her, the Emperor of the French, in right of his position as perpetual head of the Imperial family, was to appoint a regent, whom he was to select from among the princes of the royal family or among the Dutch nation.

The King of Holland was to remain Constable of the Empire, a Vice-Constable to be created at the Emperor's pleasure.

The message also contained an announcement to the Senate that the Arch-Chancellor of the German Empire had asked of the Pope that Cardinal Fesch might be designated as his coadjutor and successor; and that his Holiness had informed the Emperor of this request, who had approved of it.

"Lastly, the duchies of Benevento and of Ponte Corvo being a subject of litigation between the Courts of Naples and Rome, in order to put an end to these difficulties, and reserving to ourselves the indemnification of these Courts, we erect them," says the decree, " into duchies and fiefs of the Empire, and we bestow them on our Grand Chamberlain Talleyrand, and on our cousin Marshal Bernadotte, to reward them for services rendered to the country. They will bear the titles of these duchies, they will take an oath to serve us as faithful and loyal subjects, and, if their issue should fail, we reserve to ourselves the right of disposing of those principalities." Bonaparte had no great liking for Marshal Bernadotte; he probably felt bound to promote him because he had married the sister of Joseph Bonaparte's wife, and it seemed fitting that the sister of a Queen should be at least a Princess.

It is unnecessary for me to add that the Senate approved of all these proceedings.

On the day following the ceremonial which introduced another King into Bonaparte's family circle, we were at breakfast with the Empress, when her husband entered the room, looking extremely pleased, and holding little Napoleon by the hand. He addressed us all in these terms: " Mesdames, here is a little boy who is going to recite to you one of La Fontaine's fables. I made him learn it this morning, and you shall hear how well he knows it." On this the child began to repeat the fable of the frogs who asked for a king, and the Emperor laughed loudly at each allusion that seemed applicable to the circumstances. He stood behind Mme. Louis's arm-chair— she was seated at table opposite her mother—and pinched her ears as he asked her over and over again, " What do you say to that, Hortense? " No one said much in reply. I was smiling to myself as I ate my breakfast, and the Emperor, in high good humor, said to me, laughing also, " I see that Mme. de Rémusat thinks I am giving Napoleon a good education."

Louis's acquisition of a kingdom revealed to his brother the deplorable state of his domestic affairs. Mme. Louis could not contemplate her accession to a throne without bitter weeping. The ungenial climate to which she was about to remove, which must needs aggravate the wretched state of her health; the dread she felt of living alone with her tyrannical husband; his increasing dislike of her, which did not lessen his jealousy, although it deprived it of rational excuse—all these things made her resolve to open her heart to the Emperor. She confided her sorrows to him, and prepared him for the fresh troubles that no doubt awaited her. She entreated his protection in the future, and exacted from him a promise never to judge her unheard. She went so far as to tell him that, foreseeing the persecution she would have to endure in the isolation to which she would be subjected, her mind was made up that when she should have endured up to a certain point she would leave the world and retire to a convent, relinquishing a crown of which she could already feel the thorns.

The Emperor entreated her to have courage and patience; he promised to protect her, and directed her to advise with him before taking any decisive step.

I can bear witness that this unhappy lady ascended the throne in the spirit of a victim resigning herself to sacrifice.

CHAPTER XXI

(1806.)

IN the June of this year I went to take the waters at Cauterets, and remained away three months. I was in very delicate health, and needed a respite from Court life and from the daily anxieties which were wearing alike to mind and body. My family—that is to say, my husband, my mother, and my children—were settled at Auteuil, whence M. de Rémusat could easily get to Saint Cloud, and there they passed a happy and peaceful summer. Our Court was then in solitude; the sovereigns of Holland had taken their departure, and the members of Bonaparte's family had separate establishments. The Emperor was engrossed by the gathering clouds in Europe, and was constantly at work; his wife employed her leisure in beautifying her estate of Malmaison.

The "Moniteur" contained glowing accounts of the triumphal entries of the princes created by Bonaparte into their respective states. Enthusiasm was said to be at the highest at Naples, at Berg, at Baden, and in Holland, and the populace was delighted everywhere. The speeches of the new kings or princes, in which they treated their subjects to a pompous panegyric of the great man whose envoys they were, were published for our edification. It is certain that, at first, Louis Bonaparte found favor with the Dutch. His wife shared his popularity in it, and displayed such affability that very soon, as I heard from some French people who accompanied them, her strange husband became jealous of the affection she inspired.

Like his brother, Louis was intolerant of the least independence in others. After exacting that the Queen should hold a brilliant Court, he suddenly changed his mind, and reduced her by degrees to a very solitary life, thus isolating her from the people over whom she too had been appointed to reign. If I may believe the accounts I have received from persons who could have had no motive for inventing them, he resumed his distrustful jealousy and his system of spying, and the Queen was constantly subjected to insult. The poor young creature, in a state of chronic ill health and profound melancholy, perceived that it was not her husband's pleasure that she should share the affection he hoped to inspire in his Dutch subjects. Sorrow had made her indifferent to such things; she withdrew into the solitude of her palace, where she lived almost as a prisoner, devoting herself to the arts she loved, and indulging her excessive affection for her eldest boy. The child, who was forward for his age, greatly loved his mother, to the extreme jealousy of Louis. The latter would sometimes try to obtain his preference by indulgence carried to excess; sometimes he would alarm him by outbreaks of passion, and the boy clung the more to her, who always loved and never frightened him. Men were found—and such as are always to be found in courts—who, for hire, undertook to watch the Queen and report her every action. The letters she wrote were opened, lest they might contain any allusion to events in her husband's dominions. She has assured me that more than once she found her desk open and her papers upset, and that, if she had chosen, she might have detected the King's spies in the act of carrying out his instructions. It was soon perceived at the Dutch Court that to appear to be influenced in any way by the Queen was to lose one's own chances of favor, and on this she was immediately forsaken. Any unfortunate person addressing himself to her, in order to solicit a favor, would be immediately suspected; any minister conversing with her on the most trifling matter would fall under the King's displeasure. The damp climate of Holland aggravated her ailments; she fell into a state of atrophy perceptible to every one, but which the King did not choose at first to notice. She has told me that her life at this time was so hard and seemed so hopeless, that frequently, when residing at one of her country-houses not far from the sea, and gazing at the ocean stretched out before her, and English vessels blockading the harbors, she ardently wished that some chance would bring one of them to the coast, and that some partial invasion might be attempted, in which she would have been made a prisoner. At last her physicians ordered her to Aix-la-Chapelle, and the King himself, who was out of health, resolved on taking the waters there with her.

From this time Holland began to suffer from the prohibitive system which the Emperor imposed on everything appertaining to the Empire. It must be conceded to Louis Bonaparte that he promptly defended the interests of the people confided to him, and opposed the tyrannical measures forced on him by the Imperial policy as strongly as was in his power. He bore with firmness the Emperor's reproaches on the subject, and resisted him in such a manner as to gain the affection of the Dutch. In this they did him justice.

Switzerland also was compelled to decline all trade with England, and English goods were seized everywhere. These measures served to strengthen the party in London who were anxious to force France into fresh European wars at any price. Mr. Fox, who was then Prime Minister, seemed, however, to lean toward peace, and to be willing to receive overtures of negotiation. During the summer he was attacked by the illness which subsequently proved fatal to him, and his influence declined. The Russians were still contending with our troops for the possession of certain parts of Dalmatia. The Grand Army showed no sign of returning to France; the promised fêtes were constantly deferred.

The King of Prussia was inclined to peace, but his young and lovely consort, as well as Prince Louis of Prussia and a part of the Court, did all they could to incite him to war. They pointed out to him that the future had in store the liberation of Poland, the aggrandizement of Saxony, the danger of the Confederation of the Rhine being organized; and it must be admitted that the Emperor's line of conduct was a justification for the disquiet of Europe.

English policy was by degrees regaining its influence over the Emperor of Russia. Count Woronzoff had been sent to London, and he fell so completely under the influence exerted over him that the Continent was again disturbed. The Czar had sent Baron d'Oubril to Paris, to negotiate with us, and a treaty of peace was in fact signed by him and M. de Talleyrand on the 20th of July, but as will be seen hereafter, it was never ratified at St. Petersburg.

About this time General Junot was made Governor of Paris.

France was in a state of profound tranquillity. Day by day the Emperor met with less opposition. A firm, equable, and strict administration, which was just, inasmuch as it was equal for all, regulated both the exercise of authority and the mode of supporting it. Conscription was rigorously enforced, but as yet the murmurs of the people were but faint; the French had not then exhausted the sentiment of glory, as they have done since that time, and, moreover, the brilliant possibilities of a military career fascinated the youth of France, and they all espoused the cause of Bonaparte. Even in the families of the nobility, who were, on principle or from habit, in opposition, the political creed of the fathers was less firmly held by the children, and parents were perhaps, in their secret heart, not sorry to relax somewhat of their severity on the plea of paternal concession. Nor was any opportunity overlooked of indicating that the nation had returned to the natural course and order of things.

The feast of the 15th of August having become that of St. Napoleon, the Minister of the Interior wrote a circular letter to all the prefects, recommending them to combine in the solemnization of the fête rejoicings for both the birthday of the Emperor and the reëstablishment of religion. " No holiday," said the letter, " can inspire deeper feelings than that in which a great people, in the pride of victory and the consciousness of happiness, celebrates the birthday of the sovereign to whom all its felicity and glory are to be ascribed."

It ought to be constantly repeated, as well for the sake of nations to come as for the sake of those who are called to reign over them, that both peoples and kings who allow themselves to be deceived by an appearance of calm, after the storm of a revolution, are in the wrong. If this time of peace has not called into existence an order of things indicated by national needs, then it is fallacious calm, a respite resulting from circumstances—of which a clever man will indeed avail himself, but which he will not really utilize unless he prudently regulates the advance of those who have trusted him. Far from so acting, Bonaparte, powerful and headstrong, opened, as it were, a long parenthesis in the French Revolution. He always had a conviction that this parenthesis would be closed at his death, which to him seemed the only possible limit to his fortune.

He seized the reins of France when Frenchmen were wandering bewildered in every direction, and were fearful that they should never reach the goal to which they aspired. Their energies, which were vague because they no longer ventured to undertake any kind of enterprise boldly, were then turned into military ardor, which is the most dangerous of any, because the most opposed to the true citizen spirit. For a long while Bonaparte reaped the advantage of this, but he did not foresee that, in order to rule after his fashion a nation which for a time had become distrustful of its own strength, and which yet felt the need of a great restoration, it was imperative that victory should always follow on war, and that reverses must inevitably make man reflect in a direction dangerous for himself.

He was, I believe, hurried along by the force of circumstances, resulting from the events of every day. But he was determined to check the growth of liberty at any cost, and to this end he directed all his efforts. It has been frequently said, both during the Empire and after his fall, that he understood the science of governing better than any other man. This is the case, doubtless, if it be only understood as the knowledge of means whereby to enforce obedience; but if the word " science " includes " the clear and certain knowledge of a thing founded on principles either self-evident or proved to demonstration," then it is certain that in Bonaparte's system of government there was no place for those elements which manifest the esteem of the sovereign for his subjects. He by no means recognized the concession of certain rights which every man who intends to rule other men for any length of time must begin by making to them, lest, weary of their mental inaction, they should one day claim these rights for themselves. He did not know how to stir generous passion, or to appreciate and evoke moral virtues, and thus to elevate himself in proportion as he aggrandized human nature.

Singular in every respect, he believed himself to be vastly superior to the rest of the world, and nevertheless he was afraid of superiority in others. Is there one among those who knew him well who has not heard him say that he preferred men of second-rate abilities? Is there one who has not remarked that when he made use of a man of talent, of whatever kind, he would, before he felt he could trust him, find out his weak point, and in most cases hasten to divulge it? Did he not always depreciate, and often falsely, those whose services he employed? The truth is, Bonaparte's gifts, whether to the world, to nations, or to individuals, were all bargains. These bargains, which were enforced rather than offered, flattered the vanity of human nature, and thus for a long time beguiled men's minds, so that it is now hard to reduce them to bounds of possibility and reason. Such a policy as this may certainly avail to purchase service of every kind, but it follows that it must be based on unvarying success. Are we to conclude from this that the French were unpardonably guilty, because they fell into the power of such a man? Will posterity condemn them for their imprudent trust in him? I think not.

Bonaparte, who employed good or evil things indifferently, according as they served his purpose, understood thoroughly that no secure foundations can be laid in times of trouble. He therefore began by restoring order, and it was thus he won us, poor tired wayfarers that we were, battered by many a storm! That which he created for his own profit only we accepted gratefully; the social order which was restored by him, that it might become the groundwork of his despotic sway, we regarded as the greatest of his gifts, and as the pledge of other benefits. We believed that the man who reëstablished public morality, religion, and civilization, who patronized art and literature, and who undertook to reduce society to order, must have a soul capable of true greatness; and perhaps, after all, our error, which was deplorable because it served his purposes so long, proves the generosity of our sentiments rather than our imprudence.

Until Prussia declared war, no event of any importance took place. In the course of the summer Count Metternich, the Austrian Ambassador, arrived in Paris. He occupied an important position in Europe, took part in events of the highest importance, and finally made an enormous fortune; but his abilities did not rise above the schemes of a second-rate policy. At the period of which I am speaking he was young, good-looking, and popular with women. A little later he formed an attachment to Mme. Murat, and he retained a feeling toward her which for a long time aided to keep her husband on the throne of Naples, and which probably is still of service to her in her retirement.

In the month of August a decree which settled the new catechism of the Gallican Church was promulgated. It was entitled " Bossuet's Catechism," and it contained, together with doctrines taken from the works of the Bishop of Meaux, some remarkable utterances on the duties of French people toward their Emperor.

Page 55: " *Question.* What are the duties of Christians toward their rulers; and what, in particular, are our duties toward Napoleon I., our Emperor?

"*Answer*. Christians owe to the princes who govern them, and we, in particular, owe to Napoleon I., our Emperor, love, respect, obedience, fidelity, military, service, and the tributes ordained for the preservation and defense of the Empire and of his throne. To honor and serve our Emperor is, therefore, to honor and to serve God.

"*Q*. Are there any special reasons which should more strongly attach us to our Emperor Napoleon I.?

"*A*. Yes; for it is he whom God raised up in difficult circumstances to restore the public profession of the holy religion of our forefathers, and to be its protector. He has restored public order by his profound and active wisdom; he defends the state by his powerful arm, and he has become the anointed of the Lord through the consecration of the Sovereign Pontiff, the Head of the Universal Church.

"*Q*. What ought we to think of such persons as may fail in their duties toward our Emperor?

"*A*. According to the Apostle St. Paul, they would thereby be resisting the orders of God Himself, and would become worthy of eternal damnation."

During Mr. Fox's tenure of office, Bonaparte, either from private information, or because he perceived the policy of the Prime Minister to be opposed to that of his predecessor, flattered himself that he should be able to conclude a treaty of peace with England. Besides the advantages to be gained from this, his pride was always singularly mortified that the English Government did not acknowledge him as a sovereign. The title of "General," which the English newspapers gave him, always annoyed him extremely. Notwithstanding his greatness, he had some of the weaknesses of a *parvenu*. When Fox fell ill, the "Moniteur" announced that there was reason to fear that the gravity of his malady might throw English policy back once more into its ordinary complications.

Meanwhile, the design of the Confederation of the Rhine was suddenly disclosed. In the Emperor's grand feudal plan this was comprised: it would increase the number of the feudatories of the French Empire, and spread the European revolution. But if it be true that the old institutions of the Continent have reached a point at which their decrepitude gives irresistible warning of the necessity of their fall, it is also true that the time has come when their fall is not to be for the advantage of despotism. Bonaparte never ceased trying to make a counter-revolution, solely in his own interests, against those ideas which emerged into the light of day thirty years ago. Such an undertaking is, happily, beyond the power of man; and we owe it to him, at least, that his failure to accomplish that reaction settled for ever this important question.

The grand duchies of Germany were therefore separated from the Germanic Empire, and the Emperor of France was declared to be their protector. The contracting parties—that is to say, the Empire and the confederated states—engaged to take up arms in the case of war being declared on one or the other. The contingent of the Confederation was named at 63,000 men, that of France at 200,000. The Elector Arch-Chancellor of the Germanic Empire became Prince Primate of the Confederation; on his death the Emperor was to nominate his successor. Moreover, the Emperor renewed the declaration by which he bound himself not to extend the frontiers of France above the Rhine; but, at the same time, he declared that he would use every means to procure the freedom of the seas. This appeared in the " Moniteur " of the 25th of July.

M. de Talleyrand had a large share in the honor of forming this Confederation. He was in very high repute at this time. He seemed destined to reduce the wide and ambitious projects of the Emperor to a definite system; but, at the same time, he did not neglect the increase to his own fortune which was to be got out of them. The German princes paid, as a matter of course, for slight advantages obtained by them in the arrangement; and the name of M. de Talleyrand, being always connected with such important negotiations, became more and more renowned throughout Europe.

One of his favorite theories, and it is one which has always seemed just and reasonable, is that the policy of France ought to tend to the release of Poland from a foreign yoke, and to the use of that country as a barrier against Russia and a counterpoise to Austria. He always exerted his influence in this direction. I have often heard him say that the repose of all Europe depended on Poland. It would appear that the Emperor was of the same opinion, but that he did not persevere sufficiently in endeavoring to realize this project. Accidental circumstances also interfered with it. He often complained of the passionate, yet shallow, character of the Poles. " It was impossible," he said, " to guide them on any system." They required special and exclusive attention, and Bonaparte could only think of Poland occasionally. Moreover, as it was the Emperor Alexander's interest to obstruct French policy in this particular, he would not have remained a quiet spectator of efforts in any such direction; and so it happened that only a half-hearted course was taken with respect to Poland, and all the advantages that might have been gained were

lost. However, after some slight differences between
the Russians and ourselves about the cession of the
mouths of the Cattaro, the two Emperors apparently
came to terms, and Baron d'Oubril was sent to Paris
from St. Petersburg to sign a treaty of peace.

Although the return of our army was constantly
announced to us, yet it did not take place, either
because Bonaparte had already become aware of the
difficulty of keeping so large a number of soldiers in
France, a burden upon the citizens, or that he foresaw
fresh disturbances in Europe, and that the peace would
be of no long duration. A kind of bazaar for the
exhibition of French industrial produce was opened
on the Place des Invalides; but the fêtes promised to
the Grand Army were no longer spoken of. This
exhibition took place, and profitably occupied the
minds of the people.

In the beginning of September Jérôme Bonaparte
arrived in Paris. Every attempt which had been made
on the colonies had failed, and the Emperor gave up
naval enterprise for ever. He began to plan a marriage for his young brother with one of the European
princesses, having insisted that his first marriage
should be regarded as null and void.

On creating the Confederation of the Rhine, Bonaparte had declared that the Hanseatic towns should
retain their liberty; but, whenever there was a question
of liberty, it was natural enough to believe that the
Emperor's gift of it was in reality but a temporary
loan, and his resolutions on the subject caused great
agitation in Prussian politics. The Queen and the
nobility urged the King of Prussia to war. Consequently, during the campaign which was very shortly
begun, the former was made an object of vituperation
in the bulletins, frequently of a coarse kind. At first
she was compared to Armida, who, torch in hand,

tried to raise up enemies against us. As a contrast to this poetical comparison, a few lines farther on we find a phrase in an utterly different style: "What a pity! for they say that the King of Prussia is a very well-meaning man." Bonaparte frequently said that there is but one step from the sublime to the ridiculous; this is true, both of actions and words, when true art is neglected, and it must be owned that he made little account of it.

Mr. Fox died in September, and the war party resumed power. The Russian Ministry was changed; a national movement was set on foot among the Russian nobility; the people were beginning to respond; the storm was gathering, and it suddenly burst when the Czar refused to ratify the treaty signed in Paris by his plenipotentiary, Baron d'Oubril. From that moment war was inevitable. No official intimation was made, but the matter was openly discussed.

At the beginning of the month I returned from Cauterets, and I was enjoying the happiness of my home circle when M. de Rémusat received a sudden order to proceed to Mayence, whither the Emperor was going a few days later. I was deeply grieved by this fresh separation. As I enjoyed none of those honors which offer compensation to some women even for the sufferings of a soldier's wife, I found it hard to resign myself to these constantly recurring separations. I remember the Emperor asking me, after M. de Rémusat was gone, why I looked so sad, and, when I answered that it was because my husband had left me, he laughed at me. "Sire," I added, "I know nothing of the delights of heroism, and I always meant to take out my share of glory in happiness." He laughed again. "Happiness?" he said. "Ah, yes! much we think of happiness in this age."

Before the departure for Mayence I again met M.

de Talleyrand, who was very friendly. He assured me that nothing could be better for our prospects than that M. de Rémusat should be in attendance on the Emperor in all his journeys; but, as he saw tears in my eyes, he spoke seriously, and I was grateful to him for not jesting on a subject which to me only was a real grief, but which certainly must have appeared of slight consequence to the many wives and mothers whose husbands and sons were leaving them for real scenes of danger. M. de Talleyrand's natural tact and his admirable good taste lead him to adapt his tone perfectly to those whom he addresses; this is one of his most attractive characteristics.

The Emperor went away suddenly on the 25th of September, without sending any message to the Senate in explanation of his absence. The Empress, who always parted with him unwillingly, had not been able at first to obtain permission to accompany him, though she hoped to rejoin him later. She, however, used such persuasion, during the last day of his stay at Saint Cloud, that toward midnight he yielded, and she entered his traveling carriage with him and only one attendant. The Imperial suite did not join her until a few days later. I was no longer included in these journeys; my health forbade. I may affirm that the Empress, who had become accustomed to the gratification to her vanity afforded her by ladies of a higher rank than mine seeking to join her Court, had returned in her heart to her former friendship, and now felt real regret at my absence. As for the Emperor, I counted for little in his eyes, and he was right. At his Court a woman was nothing, and a woman in ill health less than nothing.

Mme. Bonaparte told me that her husband entered upon this Prussian campaign with some reluctance. Luxury and ease had had their natural effect upon him, and the hardships of camp-life now affected his imagination unpleasantly. Nor was he devoid of solicitude. The Prussian troops were renowned; their cavalry was recognized as first-rate, while ours as yet inspired no confidence, and our military men expected a formidable resistance.

The prompt and unparalleled result of the battle of Jena is one of those miracles which upset all human calculations. The victory astonished and confounded all Europe, proved the good fortune as well as the genius of Bonaparte, and bore witness to French valor.

He did not remain long at Mayence; the Prussians had marched into Saxony, and it was imperative to follow them. At the opening of this campaign the Emperor formed two new companies of gendarmes; the command of one was given to the Vicomte de Montmorency. This was an appeal to the nobility to take their share of glory, to nibble at the bait of a semblance of privilege; and, in fact, a few gentlemen did join that regiment.

During the preparations for the important coming events, it was decided that the Empress, with those members of the Court who had accompanied her, should remain at Mayence. M. de Rémusat was in waiting, having the superintendence of her entire household, and M. de Talleyrand was also to remain until further orders.

Just before the Emperor's departure, my husband was present at a scene which made a great impression on him. M. de Talleyrand was in the Emperor's cabinet, where M. de Rémusat was receiving final instructions; it was evening, and the traveling-carriages were waiting. The Emperor sent my husband to summon the Empress; he returned with her in a few moments. She was weeping. Agitated by her tears, the Emperor held her for a long time in his arms, and seemed almost unable to bid her farewell. He was strongly moved, and M. de Talleyrand was also much affected. The Emperor, still holding his wife to his heart, approached M. de Talleyrand with outstretched hand; then, throwing his arms round both at once, he said to M. de Rémusat, " It is very hard to leave the two persons one loves best." As he uttered these words, he was overcome by a sort of nervous emotion, which increased to such a degree that he wept uncontrollably, and almost immediately an attack of convulsions ensued, which brought on vomiting. He was placed in a chair, and drank some orange-flower water, but continued to weep for fully a quarter of an hour. At length he mastered himself, and, rising suddenly, shook M. de Talleyrand by the hand, gave a last embrace to his wife, and said to M. de Rémusat: " Are the carriages ready? Call the suite, and let us go."

When, on his return, my husband described this scene to me, it made me feel glad. The fact that natural feeling had got the mastery over Bonaparte always seemed to me a victory in which we were all interested. He left Mayence on the 22d of October, at 9 P. M.

No announcement had as yet been made to the Senate, but every one expected a formidable war. It was a national war on the part of the Prussians, for in declaring it the King had yielded to the ardent desire of all the nobility and a majority of the people.

Moreover, the rumors regarding the foundation of a kingdom of Poland were disquieting to reigning sovereigns. A Northern League was in contemplation, which was to embrace all the states not comprised in the Confederation of the Rhine.

The young Queen had much influence with her husband, and great confidence in Prince Louis of Prussia, who longed for an opportunity to distinguish himself. He was brave, amiable, had great taste for the fine arts, and had fired the youthful nobility with his own ardor. The Prussian army, full of life and spirit, inspired complete confidence in the new coalition; its cavalry was considered the finest in Europe. When we remember how easily all this was dispersed, we must believe that the leaders were very incompetent, and that the old Prince of Brunswick must once more have misdirected the courageous soldiers confided to him.

Even at the opening of this campaign, it was easy to see that France was weary of the uncertainty which was brought into both public and private affairs. Discontent was visible in the expression of men's countenances, and it was evident that the Emperor must indeed do wonders to rekindle feelings that were beginning to chill. In vain did the newspapers contain articles describing the zeal with which the new conscripts came to be enrolled in all the departments; no one was deceived by these accounts—no one even tried to appear to be deceived. Paris fell into the gloomy condition which war always produces in capital cities while it lasts. The progress of our industrial pursuits was admired at the Exhibition of which I have spoken, but curiosity alone will not stir the heart of a nation; and, when citizens may not take the least part in their own government, they regard the improvements in civilization which are due to that government merely as a spectacle. We began to feel in France that there was something mysterious in Bonaparte's conduct toward us. We perceived that it was not for us that he lived and acted; that what he wanted from us was an appearance of prosperity, brilliant rather than solid, which should surround him with fresh lustre. I recollect writing to my husband during the campaign in the following terms: " The situation is greatly changed; so are men's minds: the military miracles of this year do not produce half the effect of former ones. The enthusiasm excitéd by the battle of Austerlitz is not to be aroused now." The Emperor himself perceived it; for, when he had returned to Paris after the treaty of Tilsit, he said: " Military glory soon palls upon modern nations. Fifty battles produce little more sensation than five or six. To the French I shall always be the man of Marengo, rather than of Jena or Friedland."

As the Emperor's designs on Europe increased in magnitude, it became more and more needful for him to centralize his administration, in order that his commands, all emanating from the same point, might be rapidly transmitted to the proper quarters. The submission of the Senate might be taken for granted; the importance of the Corps Législatif was lessening every day. Bonaparte had doubtless resolved on seizing the first pretext for ridding himself of the Tribunate, and he extended the powers of the Council of State, which consisted of men of ability, on whom he exercised a direct pressure. By a new decree he now appointed a Committee for Petitions in the Council of State, which consisted of councilors, masters of requests, and auditors. They met three times a week, and reported to Bonaparte. MM. Molé and Pasquier, both of them " Masters of Requests," were members of this committee. They had entered public life at the same period; both, although widely differing in age, bore names well known in the magistracy; they had the same social connections, equal zeal, and similar ambition, and they were beginning to make themselves felt in the new Government. Meanwhile, the Emperor already displayed a preference for M. Molé. He exercised an ascendency over this young man, who, although naturally of a grave disposition, was yet capable of enthusiasm. He thought he could mold his opinions in his own way, and he partly succeeded, while he made use of the parliamentary tendencies of M. Pasquier. " I use one," he said sometimes, " but I *create* the other." I quote these words of his to show how he was accustomed to analyze his own conduct toward every one.

Horse-races, which had been decreed by the Emperor himself when he was as yet only First Consul, took place in Paris in the autumn of this year. In fact, France had come to resemble a great audience at a theatre, before whom performances of all kinds were given on the sole condition that hands should be raised only to applaud.

On the 4th of October the Senate was convoked. The Arch-Chancellor, as he had done in the past, and as he was to do in the future, announced the war in an insignificant and pompous speech. After this, he read a letter from the Emperor, dated from headquarters, in which he stated that the King of Prussia was the aggressor, and deplored the evil influence that constantly disturbed the repose of France, while he announced that the invasion of Saxony had obliged him to march rapidly forward. This letter was accompanied by the official report of the Minister of Foreign Affairs. He could discover no valid cause for war; he expressed surprise that the freedom granted to the Hanseatic towns could have given umbrage to the Prussian Government, and quoted a note from M. de Knobelsdorff, the new envoy from Prussia.

A rumor arose that, some time previously, M. de Lucchesini, who was devoted, it was said, to England, had alarmed the Court by *unfounded* reports of a universal monarchy planned by the French Government. On being informed of this, the Emperor had requested that M. de Lucchesini should be recalled. M. de Knobelsdorff succeeded him, but no good result ensued. The coolness between the two Cabinets increased. The Emperor departed. The Prussian Minister received a final note from his sovereign, demanding the immediate evacuation of the whole of Germany by the French troops, and requiring that the ratification of this demand should be sent to the King of Prussia's headquarters by the 8th of October. M. de Knobelsdorff dispatched this note to M. de Talleyrand, then at Mayence, and it was forwarded by him to the Emperor, who had already reached Bamberg.

The first bulletin on the opening of the campaign gives the following account of what had taken place: "On the 7th the Emperor received dispatches from Mayence, consisting of M. de Knobelsdorff's note and a letter from the King of Prussia, twenty pages long —a pamphlet, in fact, in the style of those written to order for the English Government, by authors hired for £500 a year. The Emperor did not read it through, and remarked to the persons about him: 'I am sorry for my brother, the King of Prussia; he does not understand French. He has certainly not read this rhapsody.' Then he turned to Marshal Berthier: 'Marshal, they give us a rendezvous for the 8th; never has a Frenchman failed to keep such an appointment. But, as it seems that a lovely Queen wishes to be a spectator at our contest, let us be courteous, and march without delay toward Saxony.'"

And, in fact, hostilities began on the 8th of October, 1806.

The Emperor's proclamation to his soldiers was, like the former ones, in a style peculiar to himself and belonging to no particular epoch.

"Let us march," he said, "since our moderation has failed to cure them of their astounding folly. Let the Prussian army meet the same fate as that which befell it fourteen years ago. Let them learn that if it is easy to acquire an increase of territory and of power by means of the friendship of a great nation, so its enmity, which can only be incurred by forsaking all wisdom and reason, is more terrible than the storms of ocean."

At the same time, the King of Holland returned to the Hague, in order to assemble the States, and to ask them to pass a law enacting the payment in advance of one year's land-tax. Having obtained this, he moved his headquarters to the frontier. Thus, the Dutch, to whom a long continuation of prosperity, in return for the surrender of their liberty, had been promised, were from the very first threatened with war, and had to endure a double taxation and a blockade of the continent, which destroyed their trade.

Mme. Louis Bonaparte joined her brother at Mayence, and seemed to breathe freely when once more among her own people. The young Princess of Baden also came to Mayence; there was still, at this time, a great coolness between her husband and herself. The Empress received a visit from the Prince Primate and from some of the sovereigns belonging to the Confederation. Her life at Mayence was very bright and stirring; many distinguished personages came thither to pay their respects to her. She would have preferred to follow the Emperor, but, when she wrote asking leave to join him, he answered: " I am not able to send for you here. I am the slave of the nature of things and the force of circumstances; we must wait until they decide."

The Empress, who was very anxious now that her husband was about to incur fresh risks, had no friend among her court circle to sympathize affectionately with her. In her suite were several ladies who belonged by their very names to memories which they claimed a right to retain at the new Court; and they took leave to disapprove of the war, and especially to express an interest which was natural enough in the beautiful Queen. She soon became an object of attack in each successive bulletin. The death of Prince Louis of Prussia, with whom some of the ladies-in-waiting during the time of their emigration had been acquainted, was also much lamented by them, and a sort of disdainful opposition formed itself around our Empress, of which Mme. de la Rochefoucauld took the lead.

M. de Rémusat, who had the superintendence of this miniature Court, became the recipient of the complaints of the Empress, who, having nothing serious to occupy her, was annoyed by foolish and vain speeches which she ought to have despised. He advised her to pay no attention to these vexations, and by no means to mention them to the Emperor, who would make them of more importance than was at all desirable. Mme. Bonaparte, however, wrote all the history to her husband, and subsequently M. de Talleyrand, who was present during these little storms which might have been so easily dispersed, thought to amuse the Emperor with a description of them. Bonaparte did not regard the matter in a harmless light. I have dwelt on this in order, later on, to explain what came of it to ourselves personally.

Meanwhile, a life so trivial and so empty was wearisome to my husband. He amused himself by learning German, in order, as he wrote to me, " at least to occupy a portion of each day usefully." He took increasing pleasure in the society of M. de Talleyrand, who treated him with confidence and warm friendship. Whenever the slightest appearance of feeling is attributed to M. de Talleyrand, one is obliged to put the statement with strong affirmation, because it will inevitably be received with doubt. The world judges him with severity, or at least too sweepingly. I know him to be capable of affection, and I venture to say that, had he been altogether deceitful, I could not have become so sincerely attached to him.

During this time I was living very quietly in Paris with my mother, my sister, and my children. Some distinguished people came to my house; also a number of literary men, who were attracted thither by my husband's authority over the theatres. Princess Caroline only (Duchess of Berg) required any court to be paid to her. She lived at the Elysée with a certain amount of state; people waited on her as they did on the Arch-Chancellor Cambacérès. Occasional visits had to be paid to the ministers, but the remainder of one's time was one's own. News from the seat of war was received without enthusiasm, but not without interest, because every family was more or less connected with the army.

The knowledge that every drawing-room was watched by the police prevented all serious conversation; every one was engrossed by secret anxieties and a sort of isolation, which was just what the Emperor wished, was the result.

Nevertheless, a little incident happened during the campaign which amused all Paris for several weeks. On the 23d of October Cardinal Maury was chosen— by that class of the Institute which has received the name of the French Academy—to succeed M. Target. When the day for his reception drew near, some one raised the question whether he should be addressed as *Monseigneur*, and a great commotion ensued. Before the Revolution a similar discussion had occurred on the same subject. D'Alembert and the three members of the Academy had pleaded for the rights of equality in the sanctuary of letters; but the Academy, having in 1806 become "the Right," was disposed to grant the title of *Monseigneur,* in opposition to the party headed by Regnault de St. Jean d'Angely, his brother-in-law Arnault, Chénier, etc. The discussion ran so high, the Cardinal declared so positively that he would not present himself unless he were to be addressed according to his rank, the difficulty of arriving with due freedom at any decision was so great, that it was determined to refer the matter to the Emperor himself, and this foolish dispute was actually brought before him on the battle-field. Meanwhile, whenever the Cardinal met any of the members of the Institute who were hostile to him, he attacked them. On one occasion he met M. Regnault dining at Mme. Murat's, and an amusing passage-at-arms, at which I was present, took place between them. Almost at the very beginning of the conversation, the Cardinal requested M. Regnault to go into another room, to which M. Regnault consented, provided that some of the other guests would accompany him. The Cardinal, who was annoyed, began to get excited. "You do not recollect, then, sir," he said, "that at the Constituent Assembly I called you *little boy*." "That is no reason," replied M. Regnault, "why we should give you a token of respect at the present day." "If my name were Montmorency," returned the Cardinal, "I could afford to laugh at you; but I owe to my abilities only my elevation to the Academy, and, if I yielded the point of *Monseigneur,* the next day you would treat me as an equal." M. Regnault reminded us that once only had the French Academy consented to use the title of *Monseigneur*, and that then it was in favor of Cardinal Dubois, who was received by Fontenelle. "But," he added, "times are greatly changed." I must own that, looking at Cardinal Maury, I ventured to think men were not so much altered. Finally the discussion became hot; it was reported to the Emperor, who sent orders to the academicians to address the Cardinal as *Monseigneur*. On this everybody immediately submitted, and we heard no more about it.

CHAPTER XXII
(1806-1807.)

THE Emperor had left Bamberg, and was hastening to the assistance of the King of Saxony. Our armies, which had been gathered
together with the surprising rapidity that always
defeated the plans of the enemy, were marching onward. The first skirmishes took place at Salfield,
between Marshal Lannes and the vanguard of Prince
Hohenlohe, commanded by Prince Louis of Prussia.
The latter, who was brave to rashness, fought in the
ranks until, coming to a hand-to-hand conflict with a
quartermaster and refusing to surrender, he fell covered with wounds. His death disheartened the Prussians, while it increased the ardor of our troops.
"If," says the Imperial bulletin, "his last moments
were those of a bad citizen, his death was glorious
and deserving of regret. He died as every good soldier must wish to die."

I am ignorant whether, in Prussia, Prince Louis
was considered to have preferred his own glory to the
interests of his country by promoting the war. It
may have been imprudent to commence it when he
did; doubtless the right moment for declaring would
have been at the formation of the coalition in the
preceding year; yet the feelings of the Prince were,
even at this time, shared by a great number of his
countrymen.

For some days the bulletins gave accounts of several partial engagements which were but the prelude

to the great battle of the 14th of October. The Prussian Court was described as being in great confusion, and despotic advice was given to those princes who are led into hesitation by consulting the multitude on great political interests above its comprehension! As if nations, having reached their present degree of enlightenment, could continue to intrust the money taken from their coffers, and the men levied from among their ranks, to their rulers, without ascertaining the uses to which the gold and the soldiers are to be put!

On the 14th of October the two armies met at Jena, and in a few hours this important battle decided the fate of the King of Prussia. The renowned Prussian cavalry could not resist our infantry; confused orders caused confusion in the ranks; a great number of Prussians were killed or taken prisoners; several general officers lay dead on the field of battle; the Prince of Brunswick was severely wounded, and the King was forced to fly. In fact, the rout was complete. Our bulletins were full of the praises of Marshal Davoust, who had in truth greatly contributed to the success of the day, and the Emperor willingly acknowledged this. He was not usually so ready to render justice to his generals. When the Empress questioned him on his return about the eulogiums he had allowed to be lavished on Davoust on this occasion, he answered her, laughingly: "I can heap upon him as much glory as I please; he will never be strong enough to carry it."

On the evening of the battle a whimsical adventure happened to M. Eugène de Montesquiou. He was an orderly officer, and was sent by the Emperor to the King of Prussia with a letter, to which I shall presently allude. He was detained all day at the Prussian headquarters, where the defeat of the French was considered certain, and they wished him to witness it. He remained, therefore, an agitated but inactive spectator of the course of events. The generals, and Blücher in particular, affected to give alarming orders in his presence. Toward evening the young man, involved in the flight of the Prussians, was endeavoring to rejoin our camp. On his way he met with two Frenchmen, who joined him, and the three together contrived to get hold of eighteen disbanded Prussians, whom they brought in triumph to the Emperor. This capture greatly diverted him.

The battle of Jena was followed by one of the rapid marches which Bonaparte was wont to impose on his army in the hour of victory. No one ever knew better how to profit by victory than he; he bewildered the enemy, leaving him not a moment's repose.

The town of Erfurt capitulated on the 16th. The King of Saxony was slightly reprimanded for having yielded to the King of Prussia, by giving him the entry of his states and taking part in the beginning of the war, but his prisoners were restored to him. General Clarke was made Governor of Erfurt.

' The bulletins of this period are especially remarkable. Bonaparte was angry at having been deceived by the Emperor Alexander. He had calculated on the unchanging neutrality of Prussia; he was mortified at English influence on the Continent; and his ill humor was perceptible in every word dictated by him. He attacked in turn the English Government, the Prussian nobility, whom he wished to denounce to the people, the young Queen, women, etc. Grand and noble expressions, often of a poetical nature, were strangely contrasted with abusive terms. He gratified his resentment and anger, but he lowered himself by giving such expression to his own feelings, and, above all, he sinned against Parisian good taste. We were beginning to grow accustomed to military wonders, and the form in which intelligence of them was transmitted to us was freely criticised. After all, the attention that nations pay to the words of kings is not so foolish as it may appear. The words of sovereigns, even more than their actions, reveal their dispositions, and the disposition of their ruler is of primary importance to subjects. The King of Prussia, who was now pushed to extremity, asked for an armistice: it was refused, and Leipsic was taken.

The French marched across the battle-field of Rossbach, and the column erected there in commemoration of our former defeat was removed and sent to Paris.

On the 22d of October M. de Lucchesini came to our headquarters. He brought a letter from the King of Prussia, the publication of which, said the "Moniteur," was forbidden by the secrecy necessary in diplomatic affairs. "But," it continued, "the Emperor's reply was considered so admirable that a few copies of it have been made; we have procured one, and we hasten to lay the letter before our readers."

Every determination taken by the Emperor, from the greatest to the least, seems partly founded on the lion's reason in La Fontaine's fable—"*Because my name is Lion.*"

"The Prussians are surprised at the briskness of our pursuit; they are probably accustomed to the manœuvres of the Seven Years' War." And when they asked for three days' truce, in order to bury their dead—"Think of the living," replied the Emperor, "and leave to us the care of burying the dead. That needs no truce."

The Emperor reached Potsdam on the 24th of October. As may be supposed, he visited Sans-Souci, and reminiscences of Frederick the Great are to be found in the bulletins. "The handsome Emperor (the Czar) and the lovely Queen" received fresh insults in these documents, from which we gathered that a war with Russia would follow the Prussian war. Paris was thrown into consternation; the news from the seat of war was read publicly at the theatres, but the only applause that greeted it was hired. "War, nothing but war, is all that is left to us." Such words as these, uttered with more or less of wrath or grief, struck ominously on the ear of the adherents of the Emperor, yet they could not contradict them.

On the same day, the 25th of October, the fortress of Spandau capitulated.

To all these accounts of the war was added a letter supposed to be written by a private soldier from a town in the duchy of Brunswick. It contained enthusiastic praise of French valor, which it attributed to the military system adopted in our army. "It is also certain," continues the writer, "that any soldier who can say to himself, 'It is not impossible for me to become a Marshal of the Empire, a Prince, or a Duke, as it has happened to others, must be greatly encouraged by that thought. It was quite another thing at Rossbach. The French army was commanded then by gentlemen who owed their military rank only to their birth, or to the patronage of a Pompadour; and the troops were of so-called soldiers, on whose track, after their defeat, were found nothing but pigtails and powdering-bags."

When the Emperor made his entry into Berlin on the 26th of October, in the midst of acclamations, he vented his displeasure on those among the Prussian nobles who were presented to him. "My brother the King of Prussia," he said, "ceased to be King from the day on which he failed to have Prince Louis hanged, when he dared to go and break his Minister's windows." And to Count Nesch he said roughly, "I will bring the nobles of this Court down so low that they shall be obliged to beg their bread."

By violent speeches of this kind, which were published, the Emperor not only gratified his anger against the instigators of the war, but imagined that he fulfilled obligations toward our Revolution. Although he was a determined counter-revolutionist, he was obliged from time to time to render some homage to the ideas which, by a fatal deviation, had produced his own accession. A mistaken longing for equality, a noble desire for liberty, were the causes of our civil discord; but in his thirst for power he gave us no encouragement toward that freedom which, if we succeed in obtaining it, will be the most glorious conquest of our times, but limited himself, in his bargain with the age, to advancing equality only. The love of liberty is an unselfish sentiment, which a generous ruler ought at the present day to foster in his people; but Bonaparte only sought to aggrandize his own power. Sometimes, with entire forgetfulness of his own origin, he spoke and acted as if he were a king by the grace of God, and then every word of his became, as it were, feudal; while at other times he affected a sort of Jacobinism, and then he would abuse legitimate royalty, treat our old memories with disdain, and denounce the nobility to the plebeians of every country. Never did he seek to establish the true rights of nations; and the unostentatious aristocracy of letters and of a noble civilization was far more displeasing to him, in reality, than that of titles and privileges, which he could make use of as he pleased.

On the 29th of October M. de Talleyrand left

Mayence to join the Emperor, who had sent for him. M. de Rémusat felt much regret at his departure. He had found his society a great resource; the somewhat solemn idleness of court life made them necessary to each other. M. de Talleyrand, having recognized both the trustworthiness and the superior abilities of my husband, would throw aside this habitual reserve in his company, and would confide to him his views on passing events and his opinion of their common master. An aristocrat by taste, by conviction, and by birth, M. de Talleyrand approved of Bonaparte's repression of what he regarded as the excesses of the Revolution; but he would have wished that a headstrong temper and a determined will had not led the Emperor aside from a course in which his own prudent counsels might have guided him aright. He was thoroughly conversant with the European political situation, and better versed in the law of nations than in their true rights, and he propounded with accuracy the diplomatic course that he would have had the Emperor follow. He was alarmed at the possible preponderance of Russia in Europe, and was in favor of founding an independent power between us and the Russians. For this reason he encouraged the ardent, though vague, desires of the Poles. "A kingdom of Poland," he used to say, "ought to be established. It would be the bulwark of our independence; but it ought not to be done by halves." With his head full of this plan, he started to join the Emperor, resolving on advising him to turn his brilliant success to good account.

After M. de Talleyrand's departure, M. de Rémusat wrote me that the dullness of his life was extreme. The Court at Mayence was monotonously regular. There, as elsewhere and in all places, the Empress was gentle, quiet, idle, and averse to take anything on herself, because, whether far or near, she dreaded the displeasure of her husband. Her daughter, who was delighted to escape from her wretched home, spent her time in diversions of a nature somewhat too childish for her rank and position. Hortense rejoiced with her mother over the promising qualities of her little son, then full of life and beauty, and very forward for his years.

The German princes came to pay their court at Mayence; great banquets were given; elegant costumes were worn; there was much walking and driving about, and great eagerness for news. The Court wanted to return to Paris; the Empress wanted to go to Berlin; and there, as elsewhere, all was dependent on the will of one man.

In Paris life was dull, but tranquil. The absence of the Emperor was always a relief: if people did not speak more freely, they seemed better able to breathe, and this sense of alleviation was especially to be observed in persons connected with his Government. The impression produced by the Emperor's victories became weaker every day; and a tangible proof was thus afforded to the world that lasting national enthusiasm could no longer be kindled by success in war.

Prince Eugène's army was marching onward in Albania, and Marshal Marmont was holding in check the Russians, who were moving on that side. A fresh proclamation was issued by the Emperor to his soldiers: it announced a rupture with Russia and an onward march, promised fresh triumphs, and alluded to the " love " of Bonaparte for his army. Marshal Brune, commanding the reserves stationed at Boulogne, issued on this occasion a curious order of the day, which was published by command in the " Moniteur ":

" SOLDIERS: You will read at mess, every day for a fortnight, the sublime proclamation of his Majesty the Emperor and King to the Grand Army. You will learn it by heart; each one of you will shed tears of courage, and will be filled with the irresistible enthusiasm inspired by heroism."

In Paris, no one was moved to tears, and the prolongation of the war filled us with dismay.

Meanwhile, the Emperor remained at Berlin, where he had established his headquarters. He announced in his bulletins that the great Prussian army had vanished like an autumnal mist, and he ordered his lieutenants to complete the conquest of all the Prussian states. At the same time a war-tax of one hundred and fifty millions was raised; the towns surrendered one by one—Küstrin and Stettin first, Magdeburg a little later. Lübeck, which had offered resistance, was stormed and horribly pillaged; there was fighting in every street; and I remember that Prince Borghese, who took part in the assault, gave us some particulars of the cruelty practiced by the soldiers in that unfortunate town. " What I then saw," he told us, " gave me an idea of the bloodthirsty intoxication which resistance at first, and victory afterward, can produce in soldiers." He added: " At such a moment every officer is a mere soldier. I was beyond all self-control; I felt, like everybody else, a sort of passionate longing to exert my strength against people and things. I should be ashamed to recall some absurdly horrible acts which I committed. In the midst of imminent danger, when one must cut one's way with the sword, with everything around in flames, when the thunder of cannon or the rattle of musketry mingles with the cries of a dense crowd, in which are people pressing in every direction, either seeking others or trying to escape from them, and all this in the narrow space of a street, then a man loses his head completely. There is no act of atrocity or of folly that he will not commit. He will wantonly destroy without profit to anybody, and will give himself up to an uncontrollable delirium of evil passions."

After the fall of Lübeck, Marshal Bernadotte remained there some time as governor of the town, and it was then that he began to lay the foundation of his future greatness. He behaved with perfect equity, and did his best to assuage the evils that had been caused by war. Strict discipline was maintained among his troops; the gentleness of his bearing attracted and consoled, and he won the admiration and sincere affection of the people.

During the Emperor's stay at Berlin, the Prince of Hatzfeld, who had remained there, and who, said the bulletins, " had accepted the post of governor," kept up a secret correspondence with the King of Prussia, in which he gave full accounts of the movements of our army. One of his letters was intercepted, and the Emperor gave orders for his arrest and trial before a military court. His wife, who was with child, was in despair; she obtained an audience of the Emperor, and threw herself at his feet. He showed her the Prince's letter, and when the poor young wife gave way to her sorrow, the Emperor, moved with pity, bade her rise, and said to her: " You have the original document, on which your husband may be condemned, in your own hand. Take my advice; profit by this moment to burn it, and then there will be no evidence to condemn him." The Princess, without a moment's delay, threw the paper in the fire, and bathed the Emperor's hands with her tears. This anecdote made a greater impression on Paris than all our victories.

Our Senate sent a deputation to Berlin with congratulations on so triumphant a campaign. The Emperor intrusted the envoys, on their return to Paris, with the sword of Frederick the Great, the ribbon of the Black Eagle worn by him, and several flags, among which, says the "Moniteur," "there are several embroidered by the hands of that fair Queen whose beauty has been as fatal to the people of Prussia as was the beauty of Helen to the Trojans."

Every day our generals invaded some new district. The King of Holland had advanced into Hanover, which was again being attacked by us; but all at once we heard that he had returned to his own states, either because he disliked acting merely as one of his brother's lieutenants, or because Bonaparte preferred that his conquests should be made by his own generals. Marshal Mortier took possession of the city of Hamburg on the 19th of November, and an enormous quantity of English merchandise was confiscated. A number of auditors belonging to the Council of State were sent from Paris; among them were M. d'Houdetot and M. de Tournon. These auditors were made Intendants of Berlin, Bayreuth, and other towns. By these young and active proconsuls the conquered states were governed in the interests of the conqueror, and victory was immediately followed by an administration which turned it to the best advantage.

The Emperor gained the affections of the young of every rank, by giving them opportunities for action, for self-assertion, and for exercising an absolute authority. Thus, he often said, "There is no conquest I could not undertake, for with the help of my soldiers and my auditors I could conquer and rule the whole world." We may suppose that the habits and the despotic notions that these young men brought back into their own country were rather perilous when the government of French provinces was confided to them. Most of them found it difficult not to rule those provinces like a conquered country. These young men, who were raised early in life to such important posts, are at the present time idle and without prospects, owing to the straitening of our territory. They fret under their enforced idleness, and form one of the most serious difficulties with which the King's Government is confronted.

The conquest of Prussia was completed, and our troops marched into Poland. The season was far advanced; they had not seen the Russians, but it was known that they were approaching; a severe and difficult campaign was anticipated. The cold was not severe, but the march of our soldiers was impeded by the marshy soil, in which men, guns, and carriages were continually sinking. The accounts of the sufferings endured by the army are terrible. Whole squadrons often sank up to the middle of the men's bodies in the marsh, and it was impossible to save them from a lingering death. Although the Emperor was determined to make the most of his victories, he felt the necessity of giving some repose to his troops, and he eagerly accepted the King of Prussia's offer of a suspension of hostilities, during which he was to remain on one bank of the Vistula, and the Prussians on the other. But it is probable that the conditions he annexed to this armistice were too severe, or perhaps it was only proposed by Prussia in order to gain time and effect a junction with the Russians; for the negotiations dragged slowly along, and the Emperor, on learning the movements of the Russian general, Benningsen, suddenly left Berlin on the 25th of November. He announced fresh danger and fresh success to his troops by the following spirited words, with which he closed his proclamation: "How should the Russians overthrow such designs? Are not they and we alike the soldiers of Austerlitz?"

A famous decree, dated from Berlin and preceded by a lengthy preamble, appeared at the same time, in which sundry grievances were set forth. This decree proclaimed the British Isles to be in a state of blockade, and it was only a reprisal on the usage of England, who, when she enters upon a war, declares a universal blockade, and in virtue thereof authorizes her ships to take possession of all other vessels in whatsoever seas. The Berlin decree divided the empire of the world in two, opposing the power of the Continent to the power of the seas. Every Englishman who should be found either in France or in any state occupied by us, or under our influence, was to become a prisoner of war, and this hard enactment was notified to all our sovereign allies. Thenceforth it was manifest that the struggle which was beginning, between despotic power in all its ramifications and the strength of such a constitution as that which rules and vivifies the English nation, could end only by the complete destruction of one of the assailants. Despotism has fallen, and, notwithstanding the terrible cost to ourselves, we ought to be grateful to Providence for the salvation of nations and the lessons taught to posterity.

On the 28th of November Murat made his entry into Warsaw. The French were enthusiastically received by those among the Poles who hoped that the liberty of their country would result from our conquests. In the bulletin which announced the entry these words occur: "Will the kingdom of Poland be restored? God alone, who holds in His hand the direction of events, can be the arbiter of this great political problem." Thenceforth Bonaparte's family began to covet the throne of Poland. His brother Jérôme had some hopes of obtaining it. Murat, who had displayed brilliant valor throughout all the campaign, was the first to be sent to Warsaw, and made his appearance there in the theatrical costume that he affected—plumed bonnet, colored boots, and richly laced cloak. His dress resembled that of the Polish nobles, and he flattered himself that one day that great country would be committed to his rule. His wife received many congratulations in Paris, and this, perhaps, made the Emperor, who disliked to be forestalled on any point, change his mind. I know that the Empress also had hopes of the Polish crown for her son. When the Emperor, at a later date, became father of a natural son, of whose fate I am at present uninformed, the Poles fixed their hopes on that child.

Writers better acquainted with the secrets of diplomacy than I, may explain why Bonaparte did not carry out, but merely sketched his plans for Poland, notwithstanding his own personal proclivities and M. de Talleyrand's influence and opinions on the subject. It may be that events succeeded each other with such rapidity, and clashed so rudely, that due care could not be bestowed on the projected enterprise. Subsequently to the Prussian campaign and the treaty of Tilsit, the Emperor often regretted that he had not pushed his innovations in Europe to the extent of changing every existing dynasty. "There is nothing to be gained," he used to say, "by leaving any power in the hands of people whom we have made discontented. There is no use in half measures; old works will not drive new machines. I ought to have made all other kings accessory to my own greatness, and, so that they should owe everything to me, they ought not to have had any greatness in the past to point to. Not that in my eyes this was of much value—certainly

not of value equal to that of founding a new race;
but nevertheless it has a certain influence over mankind. My sympathy with certain sovereigns, my
compassion toward suffering nations, my fear, I know
not why, of causing an utter overthrow of all things,
withheld me. I have been greatly in the wrong, and
perhaps I may have to pay for it dearly."

When the Emperor spoke in this sense, he took
pains to dwell on the necessity imposed by the Revolution of the renewal of all things. But, as I have
already said, he in his secret heart thought he had
done enough for the Revolution in changing the frontiers of states and the sovereigns who ruled them. A
citizen King, chosen either from among his own
kinsfolk, or from the ranks of the army, ought, he
considered, to satisfy all the citizen classes of modern
society by his sudden elevation; and, provided the
despotism of the new sovereign could be turned to
the advantage of his own projects, he should not be
interfered with. It must be owned, however, that if
" the spirit of the age," as Bonaparte called it, had
resulted only in nations being governed by men whom
a lucky chance had drawn from their native obscurity,
it was scarcely worth while to make such a fuss about
it. If we are to be ruled by a despot, surely the despot who can point to the greatness of his ancestors,
and who exercises his authority in virtue of ancient
rights made sacred by ancient glory, or even in virtue
of rights whose origin is lost in the obscurity of ages,
is the least mortifying to human pride.

At the close of the war Poland found that she was
free only in that portion of the country which had
been seized by Prussia. His treaties with the Emperor of Russia, the temporary need of repose, the
fear of displeasing Austria by interfering with her
possessions, cramped Bonaparte's plans. It may be

that they could not have been carried out; but, being only half attempted, they bore within them the elements of their own destruction.

The advantages and disadvantages of the continental policy with regard to the English nation have often been discussed. I am not competent either to state the objections raised to this system or the reasons for which many disinterested persons approve of it; still less would I venture to draw hasty conclusions. The system in question imposed conditions on the allies of France which were too much in opposition to their interests to be long endured by them; for, although it encouraged continental industry, it interfered with the luxuries of life, and with some few of its daily necessaries. It was also felt to be an act of tyranny. Moreover, it caused every Englishman to share the aversion of the British Government toward Bonaparte, because an attack upon trade is an attack on the fountain-head of every Englishman's existence. Thus the war with us became a national one for our enemies, and from that time was vigorously carried on by the English.

Meanwhile I have heard it said by well-informed persons that the consequence of this rigorous policy would in the end strike a fatal blow at the English Constitution, and that on this account especially it was advantageous to pursue it. The English Government was obliged, in order to act with the same rapidity as the enemy, to encroach little by little on the rights of the people. The people made no opposition, because they felt the necessity of resistance. Parliament, less jealous of its liberties, would not venture on any opposition; and by degrees the English were becoming a military people. The national debt was increased, in order to afford supplies to the coalition and the army; the executive was becoming

One shudders even now at the description of that terrible day. For twelve hours they fought without either side being able to claim the victory.

—p. 573

From the painting by F. Schommer.

accustomed to encroachments which had been tolerated in the beginning, and it would willingly have maintained them as an acquired right. Thus, the strained situation into which every Government was forced by the Emperor was changing the Constitution of Great Britain, and possibly, had the continental system lasted for a length of time, the English could only have recovered their liberties through violence or sedition. This was the Emperor's secret hope. He fomented rebellion in Ireland; supported as he was by every absolute sovereign on the Continent, he helped and protected the Opposition in England by all the means in his power, while the London newspapers in his pay stirred up the people to claim their liberties.

At a later period I heard M. de Talleyrand, who was greatly alarmed at this contest, express himself with more warmth than he usually displays in stating his opinions. "Tremble, foolish people that you are," said he, " at the Emperor's success over the English; for, if the English Constitution is destroyed, understand clearly that the civilization of the world will be shaken to its very foundations."

Before leaving Berlin the Emperor issued several decrees, dated thence, showing that, although he was at the camp, he had both leisure and will to attend to other pursuits besides those of war. Such were the appointment of certain prefects, a decree for the organization of the Naval Office, and one designating the site of the Madeleine, on the Boulevard, for the monument to be erected to the glory of the French army. Competition for designs for this monument was invited by circulars from the Minister of the Interior, which were distributed in every direction. Numerous promotions were made in the army, and there was a general distribution of crosses.

On the 25th of November the Emperor departed for Posen. The bad state of the roads obliged him to exchange his traveling-carriage for a country wagon. The Grand Marshal of the Palace was over-turned in his *calèche,* and dislocated his collar bone. The same accident happened to M. de Talleyrand's carriage, but he escaped without hurt; on account of his lameness, he had to remain four and twenty hours on the road in his overturned carriage, until means could be found to enable him to continue his journey. About this time he took occasion to answer a letter I had written to him. " I reply to your letter," he writes, " in the midst of the mud of Poland; next year, perhaps, I may address you from the sandy deserts of I know not what country. I beg you to remember me in your prayers." The Emperor was only too much inclined to despise the obstacles that destroyed part of his army. Moreover, it was imperative to march onward. The Russians were advancing, and he did not choose to await them in Prussia.

On the 2d of December the Senate was convoked in Paris. The Arch-Chancellor read a letter from the Emperor, giving an account of his victories, promis-ing others in the future, and requesting a *senatus con-sultum* which should order an immediate levy of the conscripts of 1807. This levy, in ordinary times, was made in September only. A commission was ap-pointed for form's sake. This commission sat in con-sultation upon the request for one morning only, and the next day but one—that is, on the 4th—the *sen-atus consultum* was reported.

It was also about this epoch that the dispute be-tween the Academy and Cardinal Maury was settled. The Emperor decided the question, and a long article appeared anonymously in the " Moniteur," which ended with these words: " The Academy, doubtless, has no wish to deprive a man, whose great abilities were conspicuous during a time of civil discord, of a right which custom confers upon him. His admission to the Academy was another step toward the entire oblivion of past events which can alone insure the duration of the tranquillity that has been restored to us. This is a long article on a subject which is apparently of very small importance; nevertheless, the light in which some persons have endeavored to place it gives rise to serious consideration. We perceive to what fluctuations we should once more be exposed, into what uncertainty we should again be thrown, only that fortunately for us the helm of the state is in the hands of a pilot whose arm is strong, whose steering is steady, and who has but one aim in view—the happiness of the country."

While Bonaparte forced his soldiers to endure terrible hardships of all kinds in the prosecution of the war, he lost no opportunity of proving that nothing interfered with the interest he, in the midst of camps, took in the progress of civilization.

An order of the day, dated from headquarters of the Grand Army, is as follows: " In the name of the Emperor. The University of Jena, its professors, teachers, and students, its possessions, revenues, and other prerogatives whatsoever, are placed under the special protection of the commanders of the French and allied troops. The course of study will be continued. Students are consequently authorized to return to Jena, and it is the Emperor's intention to favor that town as much as possible."

The King of Saxony, subdued by the power of the conqueror, broke off his alliance with Prussia and concluded a treaty with the Emperor. During a long reign this prince had enjoyed the blessings of peace and order. Venerated by his subjects, and occupied solely with their welfare, nothing but the hurricane of Bonaparte's success could have brought the horrors of war among the peaceful valleys of his kingdom. He was too weak to resist the shock; he submitted, and tried to save his people by accepting the victor's terms. But his fidelity to treaties could not save him, because Saxony subsequently became of necessity the battle-field on which the neighboring sovereigns contended more than once for victory.

Meanwhile, Paris and its inhabitants became every day more gloomy. The bulletins contained only vague accounts of bloody conflicts, with small results. It was easy to infer, from occasional allusions to the severity of the season and the ruggedness of the country, that our soldiers had great obstacles to surmount and much suffering to bear. Private letters, although cautiously written, or they would not have reached their destination, betrayed general anxiety and distress. The least movements of our army were represented as victories, but the Emperor's very triumphs involved him in difficulty.

The distinct advantage with which the campaign had opened made the Parisians hard to please as the war went on. Much trouble was taken to keep up the enthusiasm. The bulletins were solemnly read at the theatres; guns were fired from the Invalides immediately on receipt of news from the army; poets were paid for hastily written odes, chants of victory, and interludes, which were splendidly represented at the Opéra, and on the following day articles written to order commented on the heartiness of the applause.

The Empress, who was restless, idle, and tired of Mayence, wrote continually, begging to be allowed to go to Berlin. The Emperor was on the point of yield-

.ing to her, and I learned from M. de Rémusat with
fresh sorrow that in all probability his absence would
be prolonged. But the arrival of the Russians, and
the obligation he was under of marching into Poland,
made Bonaparte change his mind. Moreover, he was
informed that Paris was dull, and that the tradespeople were complaining of the harm done them by
the general uneasiness. He sent orders to his wife
to return to the Tuileries, there to keep up the accustomed splendor of her Court, and we all received commands to amuse ourselves ostentatiously.

Meanwhile, after a few partial engagements, the
Emperor determined on going into winter quarters;
but the Russians, who were better used to the severity
of the climate and the rudeness of the country, would
not allow of this, and after measuring their strength
in some bloody encounters, where our success was
dearly bought, the two armies met face to face near
the village of Preussisch Eylau, which has given its
name to a sanguinary battle. One shudders even now
at the description of that terrible day. The cold was
piercing, and the snow falling fast; but the opposition
of the elements only increased the ferocity of both
armies. For twelve hours they fought, without either
side being able to claim the victory. The loss of men
was immense. Toward evening the Russians retreated in good order, leaving a considerable number
of their wounded on the field of battle. Both sovereigns, Russian and French, ordered the *Te Deum* to
be sung. The fact is, this horrible butchery was to
no purpose, and the Emperor afterward said that, if
the Russian army had attacked him on the following
day, it is probable he would have been beaten. But
this was an additional reason for him to exult over
the victory loudly. He wrote to the bishops, informed
the Senate of his alleged success, contradicted in his

own journals the foreign versions of the event, and concealed as much as possible the losses that we had sustained. It is said that he visited the battle-field, and that the awful spectacle made a great impression on him. This would seem to be true, because the bulletin in which the fact is stated is written in a very simple style, unlike that of the others, in which he generally figures in a theatrical attitude.

On his return, he ordered a very fine painting from Gros the artist, in which he is represented among the dead and dying, lifting his eyes to heaven, as if praying for resignation. The expression given to him by the painter is extremely beautiful. I have often gazed at the picture with emotion, hoping with all my heart —for it still desired to cling to him—that such had really been the expression of his countenance on that occasion.

M. Denon, Director of the Museum, and one of the most obsequious servants of the Emperor, always followed him in his campaigns, in order to select objects of value in every conquered city, to add to the treasures of that magnificent collection. He fulfilled his task with exactness, which, people said, resembled rapacity, and he was accused of appropriating a share of the plunder. Our soldiers knew him only by the name of " The Auctioneer." After the battle of Eylau, and while at Warsaw, he received orders to have a monument erected in commemoration of the day. The more doubtful it was, the more the Emperor insisted on its being held to be a victory. Denon sent to Paris a poetical account of the Emperor's visit to the wounded. Many persons have declared that the painting by Gros represented a fiction, like that of the visit to the pest-stricken at Jaffa. But why should it be denied that Bonaparte could sometimes feel?

The subject was open to competition among our principal painters. A considerable number of sketches were sent in. Gros obtained every vote, and the choice fell upon him.

The battle of Eylau was fought on the 10th of February, 1807.

CHAPTER XXIII

(1807.)

AFTER the battle of Eylau, both armies were forced to come to a halt, in consequence of the confusion produced by a thaw, and both went into winter quarters. Our troops were in cantonments near Marienwerder, and the Emperor established himself in a country-house near Osterode.

The Empress had returned to Paris at the end of January. She was out of spirits, vaguely anxious, and not overpleased with those members of the Court who had accompanied her to Mayence. Besides this, she was in a state of nervousness, as she always was during the Emperor's absence, for she dreaded his disapproval of her actions. She was most gracious, and showed all her former friendship for me. It was said by some members of the Court that her low spirits were partly caused by tender feelings which she entertained toward a certain young equerry, then absent with the Emperor. I never inquired into the truth of this story, nor did she ever mention it to me; but, on the contrary, she was distressed by the stories she was told by some Polish ladies then in Paris, concerning the Emperor and a young countrywoman of theirs. Her affection for her husband was always dashed with the dread of divorce; and, of all her feelings, this was, I believe, the strongest. She would occasionally introduce a few words on the subject in her letters to Bonaparte, but he never made the least reply to them.

She tried to conform to the Emperor's wishes. She gave and accepted invitations, and could at any time find relief from her cares in the delight of displaying a magnificent dress. She behaved to her sisters-in-law coldly, but with prudence; she received a great number of persons, and always graciously, and she never said a word that was not studiously insignificant.

I once suggested to her that she might divert her mind by going to the theatre; but she told me that she did not derive enough amusement from the plays to go *incognito,* and that she could not venture to go publicly. "Why, madame?" I asked her. "I think the applause you would receive would be pleasing to the Emperor." "You do not know him, then," was her reply. "If I was received with much cordiality, I am sure he would be jealous of any little triumph which he would not have shared. When I am applauded he likes to take part in my success; and I should only mortify him by seeking any when he can not be present."

The uneasiness of the Empress Josephine was increased by any appearance of mutual understanding between several persons about her; she always imagined they were conspiring to injure her. Bonaparte had infected her with his habitual suspicion. She felt no fear of Mme. Joseph Bonaparte, who, although at that time Queen of Naples, was residing quietly at the Luxembourg Palace, being reluctant to exchange her peaceful life for that of a sovereign. The two Princes—one the Arch-Chancellor, the other the Arch-Treasurer of the Empire—were timorous and reserved; they paid her an assiduous court, and inspired her with no distrust.

Princess Borghese, who combined constant ill health with a life of intrigue, joined in no political

schemes, excepting such as were common to the whole
family. But the Grand Duchess of Berg caused her
sister-in-law constant jealousy and apprehension.
She lived in great splendor at the Elysée-Bourbon
Palace. Her beauty was set off by the most exquisite
dress; her pretensions were great, her manners affable
when she thought it prudent, and more than affable
to men whom she wished to fascinate. She was unscrupulous when intent on injuring, and she hated
the Empress, yet never lost her self-control. Of such
a woman Josephine might well be afraid. At this
time, as I have said, Caroline was desirous of obtaining the crown of Poland, and she endeavored to make
friends among the influential members of the Government who might be useful to her. General Junot,
Governor of Paris, became one of her ardent admirers, and, either from a reciprocal feeling or from
interested motives, she contrived to make his tender
sentiments serve her purpose; so that the Governor
of Paris, in his reports to the Emperor—a certain branch of police being in his charge—always
gave favorable accounts of the Grand Duchess of
Berg.

Another intimacy, in which there was no question
of love, but which was of great use to her, was that
between Fouché and herself. Fouché was on bad
terms with M. de Talleyrand, who was no favorite
of Mme. Murat's. She wanted to secure her present
position, and especially to elevate her husband in
spite of himself. She hinted to the Minister of Police that M. de Talleyrand would contrive to have
him removed, and she tried to gain his affection by a
number of other little confidential communications.
This intimacy gave daily recurring distress to the poor
frightened Empress, who narrowly watched all her
words and actions. Parisian society concerned itself

little with these Court secrets, and took no interest in the members of the Court circle. We had the appearance of being, and we were in fact, merely a living puppet-show, set up to surround the Emperor with what seemed to him necessary state. The conviction that no one had any influence over him led people to concern themselves little with his surroundings. Every one knew beforehand that his will only would finally determine all things.

Meanwhile, the sovereigns who were either related or allied to the Emperor sent deputations to Poland, to congratulate him on his victories. From Naples, Amsterdam, and Milan came envoys to Warsaw, offering homage from the various states. The kingdom of Naples was disquieted by disturbances in Calabria only, but this was enough to keep it in agitation. The new King, a lover of pleasure, did not carry out with sufficient firmness the plan which the Emperor had laid down for the kingdoms he had called into existence. The Emperor also found fault with his brother Louis; but those reproaches did honor to the latter.

Louis's domestic affairs became every day more deplorable. Mme. Louis, who had enjoyed some liberty at Mayence, no doubt found it hard to return to the dreary bondage in which she was held by her husband; and the depression, which she did not sufficiently conceal, embittered him, perhaps, still more. The division between them increased until they lived apart in the palace—she in retirement with two or three of her ladies, and he immersed in affairs, and making no secret of his dissatisfaction with his wife. He would not allow the Dutch to impute all the blame of the notorious domestic troubles to him. Who can say to what such a position of affairs might have led, but for the common misfortune which shortly fell

upon the unhappy pair, and which drew them together in a common sorrow?

Toward the end of the winter an order from the
Emperor reached Paris, to the effect that the newspapers were to remind persons distinguished either
in art or science that the decree, dated from Aix-la-
Chapelle, 24th Fructidor, year 12, concerning the decennial prizes, was to come into effect at the expira-
tion of one year and eight months from the then date.
This decree promised considerable rewards to every
author of an important work, of any kind whatsoever. The prizes were to be assigned at intervals of
ten years, dating from the 18th Brumaire, and the
jury which was to allot them was to consist of members of the Institute. This project has real greatness
in it; we shall see, hereafter, how it fell to pieces in
consequence of a fit of ill humor on the part of the
Emperor.

In March the Vice-Queen of Italy gave birth to a
daughter, and the Empress was much pleased at being
grandmother to a little princess related to all the
greatest powers in Europe.

During the suspension of war on both sides, from
the inclemency of the season, the Emperor took every
means to insure that in the spring his army should
be more formidable than ever. The kingdoms of
Italy and Naples had to furnish further contingents.
Men born under the smiling skies of those beautiful
lands were suddenly transported to the wild banks
of the Vistula; and they might wonder at the change,
until others were seen marching from Cadiz, to per-
ish beneath the walls of Moscow, thus affording a
proof of the courage and strength of which men are
capable, and also of what can be done by the strength
of the human will. The army was reorganized; our
newspapers were filled with columns of promotions,

and it is curious, among these military decrees, to come upon one dated, like the rest, from Osterode, appointing bishops to vacant sees both in France and in Italy.

But, notwithstanding our victories, or perhaps because of them, our army had suffered considerable loss. The extreme humidity of the climate caused sickness among the troops. Russia was evidently about to make an immense effort. The Emperor felt that this campaign must be decisive; and, not feeling satisfied that the numerous troops furnished to him were sufficient to insure victory, he put his own power and our submission to the test. After having, at the end of December, 1806, levied the conscription for 1807, he demanded from the Senate in April the levy for 1808. The Prince of Neufchâtel's report, which was published in the " Moniteur," announced that during the year the army had been augmented by one hundred and sixty thousand men, levied by the conscriptions of 1806 and 1807; sixteen thousand men were non-combatants either from sickness or superannuation, and, without troubling himself with calculations, which it was too certain no one would venture to make, because it was our system to conceal our losses, he put down the " casualties " of the campaign at fourteen thousand men. As our army had been increased by only a hundred and thirty thousand efficient soldiers, prudence required that the eighty thousand men of the conscription of 1808 should be raised, and drilled, each in his own department. " Were this delayed," said the report, " the men would have to march at once to the seat of war; but, by making the levy six months in advance, they will acquire strength and knowledge, and will be better able to defend themselves."

State Councilor Regnault de St. Jean d'Angely,

who was the bearer of the Imperial message to the
Senate, paused when he came to this portion of the
report, and called the attention of the Senators to
the paternal goodness of the Emperor, who would not
allow the new conscripts to brave the dangers of war
without some previous preparation. The Emperor's
letter announced that the whole of Europe was again
in arms—that two hundred thousand recruits had
been raised in England; and declared his own desire
for peace, on condition that the English were not
prompted by passion to seek their own prosperity in
our abasement.

The Senate passed the required decree, and voted
an address of congratulation and thanks to the Emperor. He must have smiled on receiving it.

The minds of men who wield absolute power need
to be very generous, in order to resist the temptation
to despise the human species—a temptation which is
only too well justified by the submission that is accorded to them. When Bonaparte beheld a whole nation giving him its life-blood and its treasure in order
to satisfy his insatiable ambition, when educated men
of that nation consented to veil his acts of invasion
on the human will in plausible phrases, how could
he fail to regard the whole world as a vast field, open
to the first person who would undertake to occupy
and till it? Heroic greatness of soul alone could have
discerned that the adulatory words and the blind obedience of the citizens who were isolated by the tyranny of his institutions, and then decimated at his
command, were dictated by constraint only.

And yet, although Bonaparte had none of those
generous feelings, reasonable observation might have
shown him that the alert obedience with which the
French marched to the battle-field was but a misdirec-
tion of that national spirit which a great Revolution

had aroused in a great people. The cry of liberty had awakened generous enthusiasm, but the confusion that ensued had rendered men afraid to complete their work. The Emperor skillfully seized on this moment of hesitation, and turned it to his own advantage. For the last thirty years the French character has been so developed that the bulk of our citizens of every class have been possessed by the desire to live, or, if to live were impossible, by the desire to die, for some particular object. Bonaparte did not, however, invariably mistake the bent of the genius of the people whom he had undertaken to rule, but he felt within himself the strength to control it, and he directed it, or rather misdirected it, to his own advantage.

It was becoming hard to serve him; feelings which seemed instinctively to warn us of what was to come were not to be repressed. Many were the sad reflections of my husband and myself—I remember them well—in the midst of the splendor and luxury of a position for which we were no doubt envied. As I have said, our means were small when we joined the First Consul's Court. His gifts, which were sold rather than freely bestowed, had surrounded us with luxury on which he insisted. I was still young, and I found myself enabled to gratify the tastes of youth and to enjoy the pleasures of a brilliant position. I had a beautiful house; I had fine diamonds; every day I might vary my elegant dress; a chosen circle of friends dined at my table; every theatre was open to me; there was no fête given in Paris to which I was not invited; and yet even then an inexplicable cloud hung over me. Often on our return from a splendid entertainment at the Tuileries, and while still wearing our garb of state—or shall I say, of servitude?—my husband and I would seriously discuss all that was passing around us. A secret anxiety as to the future, an ever-growing distrust of our master, oppressed us both. Without distinctly knowing what we dreaded, we were aware that there was something to dread. " I am unfitted," my husband used to say, " for the narrow and idle life of a Court." " I can not admire," I would say to him, " that which costs so much blood and misery." We were weary of military glory, and shocked at the fierce severity it often inspires in those who have gained it; and perhaps the repugnance we felt for it was a presentiment of the price which Bonaparte was to make France pay for the greatness that he forced upon her.

To these painful feelings was added the fear of being unable to feel any affection for him whom we must still continue to serve. This was one of my secret troubles. I clung with the enthusiasm of youth and imagination to the admiration for the Emperor that I desired to retain; I sincerely tried to deceive myself with regard to him; I eagerly recalled cases when he had acted up to my hopes. The struggle was painful and vain, but I suffered more after I had relinquished it. In 1814 numbers of people wondered at my ardent desire for the fall of the founder of our fortune, and for the return of those who would ruin it; they accused us of ingratitude in so promptly forsaking the cause of the Emperor, and honored us with their surprise because of the patience with which we endured our heavy loss. They were unable to read our hearts; they were ignorant of the impressions that had been made on us long before. The return of the King ruined us, but it set our hearts and minds at liberty. It promised a future in which our child might freely yield to the noble inspirations of his youth. " My son," said his father, " will perhaps be poor, but he will not be shackled and hampered as we have been." It is not sufficiently known in the world—that is, in the regulated and factitious society of a great city—that there is happiness in a position which allows of the complete development of one's feelings and of freedom in all one's thoughts.

On the feast of St. Joseph, Princess Borghese and Princess Caroline gave a little fête in honor of the Empress. A large party was invited. A comedy or vaudeville was acted, full of verses in honor of the Emperor and in praise of Josephine. The two Princesses represented shepherdesses, and looked exquisitely lovely. General Junot took the part of a soldier just returned from the army, and in love with one of the young girls. The position seemed to suit them perfectly, whether on the stage or elsewhere. But Bonaparte's two sisters, although Princesses, sang out of tune; and, as each could detect this in the other, she ridiculed her sister's performance. Both my sister and I took part in the piece. I was greatly amused at the rehearsals by the mutual spitefulness of the two sisters, who had little love for each other, and the vexation of the author and the composer. Both thought a good deal of the production; they were annoyed at hearing their verses and songs badly rendered; they dared not complain, and, when they ventured on timid remonstrance, every one hastened to silence them.

The play was ill performed. The Empress cared little for the insincere homage of her sisters-in-law, and remembered that on this same stage, a few years before, she had seen her own children, young, gay, and loving, touch even Bonaparte's heart by offering him flowers. She told me that during the whole evening this recollection had been present with her. She was now away from her husband, anxious about him, uneasy about herself, far from her son and daughter. Ever since the day she ascended the throne she had regretted her happier past.

On the occasion of her fête-day the Emperor wrote affectionately to her: " I dislike very much being so far away from you. The chill of the climate seems to lay hold of my heart. We are all longing for Paris, that Paris which one regrets in every place, and for whose sake we are always in pursuit of glory, and after all, Josephine, only that we may be applauded on our return by the crowd at the Opéra. When spring comes, I hope to beat the Russians thoroughly, and then, mesdames, we will go home, and you shall crown us with laurel."

During the winter the siege of Dantzic was begun. Bonaparte took it into his head to give some glory (as he called it) to Savary. The military reputation of the latter did not stand very high with the army; but he was useful to the Emperor in other ways, and covetous of reward. The Emperor foresaw that some day he would be obliged to give him a decoration, in order to be able to use him as occasion might arise; so he chose to say that Savary had obtained an advantage of some kind over the Russians, and bestowed on him the grand cordon of the Legion of Honor. Military men disapproved, but Bonaparte cared as little for them as for others, and to bestow reward independently of merit or desert was a favorite exercise of his independence.

He seldom left his headquarters at Osterode, except for the purpose of inspecting the various cantonments. He issued decrees on a great number of subjects. He wrote a letter to M. de Champagny, the Minister of the Interior, which was mentioned in the " Moniteur," ordering him to announce to the Institute that a statue would be presented to it in honor of D'Alembert, the French mathematician, who, more than any other, had contributed to the advancement of science.

The bulletins contained statements of the position of the army only, and of the Emperor's health, which continued to be excellent. He often rode forty leagues in a day. He continued to make numerous promotions in his army, which were published in the " Moniteur " indiscriminately, and under the same date with the appointment of certain bishops.

The Empress of Austria's death occurred at this time. She was only thirty-four years of age. She left four sons and five daughters. The Princes of Bavaria and Baden, and some others belonging to the Confederation of the Rhine, were staying with the army and paying court to the Emperor. When the day's work was over, he attended concerts, given for him by Paër the musician, whom he had met at Berlin, and whom he engaged in his service and brought back with him to Paris. M. de Talleyrand's society was no doubt a great resource to the Emperor, but he frequently left him, in order to pass some days in great state at Warsaw, where he conversed with the nobles, and kept up the hopes which it was thought desirable they should not abandon. It was at Warsaw that M. de Talleyrand negotiated on the Emperor's behalf with ambassadors from the Porte and from Persia. Bonaparte permitted them to witness some manœuvres by a part of his army. At Warsaw also a suspension of arms between France and Sweden was signed.

The difficulty about the *Monseigneur* having been settled, Cardinal Maury was admitted to the Institute, and delivered a panegyric on the Abbé de Radovilliers as the usual reception speech. An immense crowd was present, but the Cardinal disappointed public expectation. His discourse was long and tedious, and it was justly inferred that his abilities were absolutely worn out. His pastorals and some Lenten sermons which he preached subsequently confirm that impression.

The death of her little grandson, Napoleon, on the 5th of May, was a severe blow to the Empress. The child, after a few days' illness, died of croup. The despair of the Queen of Holland surpassed description. She clung to the body of her son, and had to be removed by force. Louis Bonaparte, who was terrified as well as grieved at the state of his wife, treated her with great tenderness, and their loss brought about a sincere, though only temporary, reconciliation between them. At intervals the Queen became completely delirious, shrieking, calling on her son, and invoking death; and she was unable to recognize those who approached her. When reason partly returned, she remained buried in profound silence, and was indifferent to all around. At times, however, she would gently thank her husband for his care, in a manner which showed her deep regret that such a misfortune had been needed to change their mutual feelings. On one of these occasions, Louis, true to his strange and jealous temper, while standing beside his wife's bed, and promising her that in future he would do all he could to make her happy, insisted on her confessing the faults he imagined she had committed. " Confide your errors to me," he said; " I will forgive them all. We are about to begin a new life which will for ever efface the past." With all the solemnity of grief, and in the hope of death, the Queen assured him that, ready as she was to appear before the throne of God, she had not even the semblance of a guilty thought of which to accuse herself. The King, still unconvinced, asked her to swear this; but, even after she had taken an oath of her truth, he could not believe her, but recommenced his importunities, until his wife, exhausted by her grief, by the answers she had made, and by this dreadful persecution, felt herself about to faint, and said: "Leave me in peace; I shall not escape from you. We will resume the subject to-morrow." And with these words she again lost consciousness.

When the young Prince's death was made known in Paris, a courier was dispatched to the Emperor, Mme. Murat started for the Hague, and a few days later the Empress went to Brussels, whither Louis himself brought his wife and their surviving little son, in order to place them under the care of the Empress. He seemed to be in great grief, and to be very anxious about Queen Hortense, who remained in a state approaching delirium. It was settled that, after a few days' repose at Malmaison, she was to pass several months in the Pyrenees, where her husband would subsequently join her. After staying one day at the palace of Lacken, near Brussels, the King returned to Holland, and the Empress, her daughter, the latter's second son, thenceforth of necessity called Napoleon, and the Grand Duchess of Berg, who was ill calculated to console two persons whom she so greatly disliked, came back to Paris. M. de Rémusat, who was in attendance on the Empress on this melancholy journey, told me on his return of the attention with which Louis had treated his wife, and that he had observed that Mme. Murat was displeased by it.

Mme. Louis Bonaparte remained at Malmaison for a fortnight in profound retirement and deep dejection. Toward the end of May she left for Cauterets. She was indifferent to all things, tearless, sleepless, speechless. She would press the hand of any one who spoke to her, and every day, at the hour of her son's death, she had a violent hysterical attack. I never beheld grief so painful to witness. She was pale, motionless, her eyes rigidly fixed—one could not but weep on approaching her; then she would utter these few words: " Why do you weep? He is dead—I know it well; but I do not suffer. I assure you I feel nothing."

During her journey to the south, a tremendous storm roused her from this state of lethargy. There had been a storm on the day that her son died. When the thunder roared this time, she listened to it attentively; as it increased in violence, she was seized with a terrible nervous attack, followed by a flood of tears; and from that instant she regained the power of feeling and of suffering, and gave herself up to a profound grief which never completely subsided. Although I can not continue her history without anticipating dates, I will nevertheless conclude this episode in her life at once. She took up her abode among the mountains with a small suite, and tried to escape from herself by continually walking, so as to exhaust her strength. In a state of constant painful excitement, she wandered through the valleys of the Pyrenees, or climbed the rocks, attempting the most difficult ascents, and seemed, I have been told by others, as if only bent on wearing herself out.

At Cauterets she met by chance with M. Decazes, who was then young, unknown to fame, and, like the Queen, in deep grief. He had lost his young wife, and was in bad health. These two met and understood each other's grief. It is extremely probable that Mme. Louis, who was too unhappy to restrict herself to the conventionalities of her rank, and refused to receive unsympathetic persons, was more accessible to a man suffering from a sorrow like her own. M. Decazes was young and handsome; the idle sojourners at a watering-place and the inconsiderate tongue of

scandal pretended there was something more than
friendship in this. The Queen was too much absorbed
in her sorrow to take notice of anything that was
going on around her. Her only companions were
young friends devoted to her, anxious about her
health, and eager to procure her the least alleviation.
Meanwhile letters were written to Paris full of gossip about the Queen and M. Decazes.

At the end of the summer King Louis rejoined his
wife in the south of France. It would seem that the
sight of the sorrowing mother and of his only surviving son softened his heart. The interview was
affectionate on both sides, and the married pair, who
for long had lived in estrangement, were once more
reconciled. Had Louis returned immediately to the
Hague, it is probable that the reconciliation would
have been lasting; but he accompanied his wife to
Paris, and their domestic union displeased Mme.
Murat. I was told by the Empress that at first, on
their return to Paris, her daughter was deeply
touched by the grief of her husband, and said that,
through suffering, a new bond had been formed between them, and that she felt she could forgive the
past. But Mme. Murat—or so the Empress believed
on what appeared to be good grounds—began once
more to disturb her brother's mind. She related to
him, without appearing to believe them herself, the
stories told of the Queen's meetings with M. Decazes.
Less than this would have sufficed to rekindle Louis's
jealousy and suspicion. I can not now remember
whether he had himself met M. Decazes in the Pyrenees, or whether he had merely heard him spoken
of by his wife; for, as she attached not the least importance to her acquaintance with him, she often said,
before other persons, how much she had been touched
by the similarity of their sorrows, and how deeply

she felt, in her own grief, for the desolation of the bereaved husband.

The Empress, who was alarmed at the emaciated condition of her daughter, and who feared for her the fatigue of another journey, as well as the climate of Holland, entreated the Emperor, who had then returned to Paris, to persuade Louis to allow his wife to remain in Paris for her confinement. The Emperor obtained permission for her by commanding Louis to grant it. The latter, who was angry, embittered, and no doubt ill pleased at being forced to return alone to the gloomy mists of his kingdom, and who was beset by his own bad temper, resumed his suspicions and his ill humor, and once more vented both on his wife. At first she could hardly believe him to be in earnest; but, when she found herself again being insulted, when she began to understand that even in her sorrow she was not respected, and that she had been thought capable of an intrigue at a time when she had been only longing for death, she fell into a state of utter dejection. Indifferent to the present, to the future, to every tie she felt contempt for her husband, which perhaps she allowed to be too plainly perceptible, and she thought only of how she might contrive to live apart from him. All this took place in the autumn of 1807. When I shall have reached that date, I may have more to say about this unhappy woman.

The Empress shed many tears over the death of her grandson. Besides the ardent affection she had cherished for this child, who was of a lovable disposition, her own position was, she felt, endangered by his death. She had hoped that Louis's children would make up to the Emperor for her lack of offspring, and the terrible divorce, which cost her so often such agonizing dread, seemed after this sad loss once more to threaten her. She spoke to me at the time of her secret fears, and I had much difficulty in soothing her.

Even at the present day the impression produced by M. de Fontanes' fine speech on this misfortune, into which he contrived to introduce a remarkable description of Bonaparte's prosperity, is not yet forgotten. The Emperor had ordered that the colors taken from the enemy in this last campaign and the sword of Frederick the Great should be borne in state to the Invalides. A *Te Deum* was to be sung, and an oration delivered in the presence of the great dignitaries, the Ministers, the Senate, and the pensioners themselves. The ceremony, which took place on the 17th of May, 1807, was very imposing, and the speech of M. de Fontanes will perpetuate for us the remembrance of those sacred spoils, which have since been restored to their former owners. The orator was admired for aggrandizing his hero, and yet for refraining from insult to the vanquished, and for reserving his praise for what was really heroic. It was added that, strictly speaking, his praise might be taken for advice; and such was the state of submission and fear in those days that M. de Fontanes was held to have displayed remarkable courage.

In his peroration he described his hero surrounded with the pomp of victory, but turning from it to weep over a child. But the hero did not weep. He was at first painfully affected by the boy's death, then shook off the feeling as soon as possible. M. de Talleyrand told me afterward that the very next day after hearing the news the Emperor was conversing freely and just as usual with those around him, and that when he was about to grant an audience to some of the great nobles from the Court of Warsaw, who came to offer their condolence, he (M. de Talleyrand) thought himself obliged to remind him to assume a serious expression, and ventured to offer a remark on his apparent indifference, to which the Emperor replied that " he had no time to amuse himself with feelings and regrets like other men."

CHAPTER XXIV
(1807.)

MEANWHILE the severity of winter gradually lessened in Poland, and everything indicated a renewal of hostilities. The bulletin of the 16th of May informed us that the Emperor of Russia had rejoined his army; and the temperate language in which the sovereigns were spoken of, together with the epithet of "brave soldiers" applied to the Russians, made us understand that a vigorous resistance was expected. The siege of Dantzic was intrusted to Marshal Lefebvre; some skirmishing took place, and finally, on the 24th of May, Dantzic capitulated. The Emperor immediately removed thither. To reward the Marshal, he made him Duke of Dantzic, and, together with the title, granted him a considerable sum of money. This was the first creation of the kind. He pointed out its advantages, in his own way, in a letter which he wrote to the Senate on the occasion; and he endeavored to lay particular stress on those reasons for this step which would be least unwelcome to lovers of equality, whose opinions he was always careful to respect. I have often heard him speak of the motives which led him to create an intermediate caste, as he called it, between himself and the vast democracy of France. His reasons were, the necessity of rewarding important services in a way not onerous to the state, and of contenting French vanity, and also that he might have a court about him, like the other sovereigns of Europe. "Liberty," he used to say, "is

needed by a small and privileged class, who are gifted
by nature with abilities greater than those of the bulk
of mankind. It can therefore be restricted with impunity. Equality, on the other hand, delights the
multitude. I do not hurt that principle by giving
titles to certain men, without respect of birth, which
is now an exploded notion. I act monarchically in
creating hereditary rank, but I remain within the
principles of the Revolution, because my nobility is
not exclusive. The titles I bestow are a kind of civic
crown; they may be won by good actions. Besides,
it is a sign of ability when rulers communicate to those
they govern the same impulses they have themselves.
Now, I move by ascending, and the nation must rise
in the same way."

On one occasion, after laying down this system in
his wife's presence and mine, he suddenly paused—
he had been walking up and down the room, as was
his habit—and said: " It is not that I do not perceive
that all these nobles whom I create, and especially the
dukes whom I endow with enormous sums of money,
will become partially independent of me. Their
honors and riches will tempt them to get loose, and
they will acquire probably what they will call the
spirit of their class." On this he resumed his walk
and was silent for a few minutes; then, turning to us
abruptly, he added, with a smile of which I can not
attempt to analyze the expression, " Ah, but they
won't run so fast but that I shall be able to catch
them! "

Although Lefebvre's military services were a sufficient reason for the gifts which the Emperor assigned
to him from the battle-field, yet the mocking humor
of the Parisians, unaffected by even justly won glory,
exercised itself upon the dignity of the new Duke.
There was something of the barrack-room about him

which partly encouraged this, and his wife, who was old and excessively homely in her manners, became the object of general ridicule. She openly expressed her preference for the pecuniary part of the Emperor's gifts, and when she made this admission in the drawing-room at Saint Cloud, and the simplicity of the speech made some of us laugh, she reddened with anger and said to the Empress, "Madame, I beg you to make your young hussies hold their tongues." It may be imagined that such a sally did not lessen our mirth.

The Emperor would willingly have put a stop to jesting on these points, but that was beyond his power; and, as it was known that he was sensitive on the subject, this was a favorite way of retaliating upon him for his tyranny.

Witty sayings and *calembourgs* were current in Paris, and written off to the army. The Emperor, in his vexation, rebuked the Minister of Police for his carelessness. The latter, affecting a certain disdainful liberality, replied that he thought he might as well leave idle people amusement of this kind. However, on learning that contemptuous or ill-natured remarks had been made in any Paris drawing-room, the Minister would send for the master or mistress of the house, advise them to keep a better watch over their guests, and dismiss them full of an undefined suspicion of their social circle.

Afterward the Emperor contrived to reconcile the old to the new nobility, by offering the former a share in his gifts; and they, feeling that every concession, however small in itself, was a recognition of their privileges, did not disdain favors which replaced them in their former position.

Meanwhile, the army was strongly reënforced. All our allies contributed to it. Spaniards hurried across France in order to fight against Russians on the Vis-

tula; not a sovereign ventured to disobey the orders
he received. The bulletin of the 12th of June
announced that hostilities had recommenced; it also
contained an account of the efforts that had been
made to bring about a peace. M. de Talleyrand
anxiously desired this; perhaps the Emperor himself
was not averse to it: but the English Government
refused to consent; the young Czar flattered himself
that Austerlitz would be forgotten; Prussia was weary
of us and wishing for the return of her King; Bonaparte, as conqueror, imposed severe conditions, and
war broke out again. Some partial engagements were
to our advantage, and our usual activity was resumed.
The two armies met at Friedland, and we gained
another great and hardly contested victory. Yet,
notwithstanding our success, the Emperor felt assured
that, whenever he should be pitted against the Russians, he must be prepared for a severe struggle, and
that on himself and Alexander depended the fate of
the Continent.

A considerable number of our general officers were
wounded at Friedland. M. de Nansouty, my brother-
in-law, behaved most gallantly: in order to support
the movements of the army, he endured the enemy's
fire for several hours at the head of his division of
heavy cavalry, maintaining his men, by his own
example, in a state of very trying inaction, which may
be said to have been as sanguinary as the thick of the
fight. Prince Borghese was sent from the battle-field
to Saint Cloud to convey the news of the victory to the
Empress; he held out at the same time the hope of an
early peace, and the rumor, which was soon spread,
was no little enhancement of the victory.

The battle of Friedland was followed by a rapid
march of our troops. The Emperor reached the
village of Tilsit, on the banks of the Niemen. The

river separated the two armies. An armistice was proposed by the Russian commander and accepted by us; negotiations were begun.

While these events were taking place, I had gone to Aix-la-Chapelle, where I was leading a quiet life, and waiting, like the rest of Europe, for the end of this terrible war. I met there M. Alexandre de Lameth, who was Prefect of the department. After taking a conspicuous part at the beginning of the Revolution, he had emigrated, and, after long years in an Austrian prison, had eventually returned to France at the same time as M. de la Fayette. Entering the Emperor's service, he attained the post of Prefect of the department of the Roer, as it was called, and managed it extremely well. The education I had received, the opinions I had heard expressed by my mother and her friends, had prejudiced me strongly against all who had aided the Revolution in 1789. I looked upon M. de Lameth as simply factious and ungrateful toward the Court, and as having thrown himself into opposition as a means of obtaining a celebrity flattering to his ambition. I was still more inclined to hold this opinion, because I found that he was a great admirer of Bonaparte, who certainly did not govern France on a system which emanated from the Constituent Assembly. But it may be that, like the majority of Frenchmen, our anarchy had sickened him of liberty so dearly bought, and that he sincerely welcomed a despotism which restored order to the country.

My acquaintance with him gave me the opportunity of hearing him discourse upon the rights of citizens, the balance of power, and liberty in a restricted sense. M. de Lameth defended the intentions of the Constituent Assembly, and I had no inclination to dispute the point with him; it seemed of little im-

portance at the date we had then reached. He
attempted to justify the conduct of the deputies in
1789; and, though I was unequal to arguing with him,
I felt confusedly that he was wrong, and that the Constituent Assembly had not fulfilled its mission with
due impartiality and conscientiousness. But I was
struck with the utility to a nation of less ephemeral
institutions, and the ardent words to which I listened,
together with the depression produced in me by our
endless wars, sowed in my mind the seeds of wholesome and generous thought, which subsequent events
have developed in full. But, whatever our ideas may
have been at that time, our reason or our instinct was
forced to bend before the triumphant fortune which
was then raising Napoleon to the zenith of his fame.
He could no longer be judged by ordinary rule;
fortune was so constantly at his side that, in rushing
onward to the most brilliant as well as the most
deplorable excesses, he seemed to be obeying destiny.

In the mean time the important political circumstances gave rise, at Aix-la-Chapelle as well as in
Paris, to rumors of every kind. The kingdom of
Poland was to be founded, and given to Jérôme Bonaparte, who was to marry a daughter of the Emperor
of Austria, and our Emperor was to carry out the old
project of the divorce. The public mind was excited
by the gigantic proportions of actual events, and
became more and more possessed by that longing for
the extraordinary which the Emperor so ably turned
to advantage. And, indeed, why should not the
country, seeing what was happening, expect that anything might happen? Mme. d'Houdetot, who was
then living, said of Bonaparte, "He diminishes history and enlarges imagination."

After the battle of Friedland the Emperor wrote a
really fine letter to the bishops. The following phrase

Queen Louise trying to win favour from Napoleon for Prussia. —p. 602

From the painting by R. Eichstadt.

occurs in it: " This victory has commemorated the anniversary of the battle of Marengo—of that day when, still covered with the dust of the battle-field, our first thought, our first care, were for the reëstablishment of order and peace in the Church of France." In Paris the *Te Deum* was sung and the city was illuminated.

On the 25th of June the two Emperors, having embarked one on each bank of the Niemen, in presence of a portion of the two armies, set foot at the same moment in the pavilion that had been erected for them on a raft in the middle of the river. They embraced on meeting, and remained together for two hours. The Emperor Napoleon was accompanied by Dumas, his Grand Marshal, and Caulaincourt, his Grand Equerry; the Czar, by his brother Constantine and two great personages of his Court. In that interview the peace was definitely settled. Bonaparte consented to restore a portion of his states to the King of Prussia, although his own inclination was toward a complete change of the form of the conquered countries, because an entire transformation would better suit his policy, which had universal dominion for its basis. He was, however, obliged to sacrifice some part of his projects during this final treaty. The Czar might still be a formidable enemy, and Napoleon knew that France was growing weary of the war and demanded his presence. A longer campaign would have led the army into enterprises of which none could foresee the issue. It was, therefore, necessary to postpone a portion of the great plan, and once more to call a halt. The Poles, who had reckoned upon complete liberation, beheld the portion of Poland that had belonged to Prussia turned into the duchy of Warsaw, and given to the King of Saxony as in pledge. Dantzic became a free town, and the King of Prussia undertook to

close his ports to the English.   The Emperor of
Russia offered to mediate with England for peace;
and Napoleon imagined that the great importance of
the mediator would terminate the quarrel. His vanity
was deeply concerned in bringing our insular neighbors to recognize his royalty. He frequently said
afterward that he felt at Tilsit that the question of
continental empire would one day be decided between
the Czar and himself; and that the magnanimity which
Alexander displayed, the young Prince's admiration
of him, and the genuine enthusiasm with which he
had been inspired in his presence, had captivated him,
and led him to desire that, instead of a total rupture,
a firm and lasting alliance should take place, which
might lead to the division of the Continent between
two great sovereigns.

On the 26th the King of Prussia joined the illustrious party on the raft, and after the conference the
three sovereigns repaired to Tilsit, where they remained while the negotiations lasted, exchanging
visits every day, dining together, holding reviews,
and appearing to be on the best possible terms. Bonaparte employed all the resources of his mind on this
occasion, and kept a close watch over himself. He
flattered the young Emperor, and completely captivated him. M. de Talleyrand completed the conquest
by the skill and grace with which he sustained and
colored his master's policy; so that Alexander conceived a great friendship for him, and trusted him
entirely. The Queen of Prussia came to Tilsit, and
Bonaparte did all he could to efface the impression of
his bulletins, by treating her with the utmost attention. Neither the Queen nor her husband could complain. They, the two dispossessed, were forced to
receive what was restored to them of their states
with gratitude. These illustrious conquered ones con-

cealed their pain, and the Emperor believed that he had gained them to his cause by reëstablishing them in the parceled-out kingdom from which he was unable to drive them altogether. He secured to himself in his treaty means of constant supervision, by leaving French garrisons in the states of certain second-rate princes; for instance, in Saxony, Coburg, Oldenburg, and Mecklenburg-Schwerin. A portion of his army still remained on the northern coast, because it appeared that the King of Sweden would not enter into the treaty. And, lastly, this war gave birth to a new kingdom, composed of Westphalia and a portion of the Prussian states. Jérôme Bonaparte was adorned with this new kingship, and his marriage with the Princess Catherine was arranged.

M. de Talleyrand and Prince Kourakine signed this treaty on the 9th of July, 1807, and the Emperor, wearing the decoration of the Russian Order of St. Andrew, immediately visited the Czar. He asked to see the Russian soldier who had conducted himself best during the campaign, and gave him the cross of the Legion with his own hand. The two sovereigns embraced anew, and parted, after having promised each other an eternal friendship. Decorations were distributed on both sides. Farewells were exchanged with great pomp between Bonaparte and the King of Prussia, and the Continent was once more pacified.

It was impossible to withhold admiration from glory such as this, but it is certain that the country took much less part in it than formerly. People began to perceive that it was of the nature of a yoke for us, though a brilliant one; and, as they were coming to know and distrust Bonaparte, they feared the consequences of the intoxication which his power might produce in him. Lastly, the predominance of the military element was exciting uneasiness; the foreseen vanities of the sword wounded individual pride. A secret trouble mingled with the general admiration, and the gloom which it produced was chiefly observable among those whose places or whose rank must bring them again into contact with Napoleon. We wondered whether the rude despotism of his manners would not be more than ever apparent in all his daily actions. We were still smaller than before in his sight, by all the difference of his added greatness, and we foresaw that he would make us feel this. Each of us made his examination of conscience with scrupulous care, seeking to discover on what point our hard master would manifest his displeasure on his return. Wife, family, great dignitaries, Ministers, the whole Court—in fact, everybody suffered from this apprehension; and the Empress, who knew him better than anybody else, expressed her uneasiness in the simplest way, saying, "The Emperor is so lucky that he will be sure to scold a great deal." The magnanimity of kings consists in elevating those around them by pouring out upon them a portion of their own moral greatness; but Bonaparte, who was naturally jealous always isolated himself, and dreaded anything like sharing. His gifts were immense after this campaign, but it was perceived that he paid for services in order that he might hear no more of them; and his recompenses were so evidently the closing of an account that they excited no gratitude, while they did, on the contrary, revive claims.

While the momentous interviews of Tilsit were taking place, nothing happened at Paris except the removal of the body of the young Napoleon from Saint Leu, in the valley of Montmorency (the residence of Prince Louis), to Notre Dame. The Arch-Chancellor received the coffin at the church, and it was committed to the care of the Cardinal Archbishop of Paris (De Belloy) until the termination of the repairs of Saint Denis, when it was to be placed in the ancient abbey. The vaults which had contained the ashes of our kings were then in course of reconstruction. The scattered remains, which had been outraged during the Reign of Terror, were now collected together, and the Emperor had given orders for the erection of expiatory altars in reparation of the sacrilege that had been perpetrated upon the illustrious dead. This fine and princely idea did him great honor, and was fitly extolled by some of the poets of the period.

When the Emperor returned to France, his wife was living at Saint Cloud with all possible precaution and the strictest prudence. His mother was living quietly in Paris; her brother, Cardinal Fesch, resided with her. Mme. Murat inhabited the Elysée, and was skillfully conducting a number of small schemes. The Princess Borghese was leading the only kind of life she understood or cared for. Louis and his wife were in the Pyrenees; they had left their child with the Empress. Joseph Bonaparte was reigning at Naples, benevolently but feebly, disputing Calabria with the rebels, and his ports with the English. Lucien was living at Rome, devoting himself to leisure and the fine arts. Jérôme brought back a crown; Murat, a strong desire to obtain one, and a deeply cherished animosity against M. de Talleyrand, whom he regarded as his enemy. He had formed an intimacy with Maret, the Secretary of State, who was secretly jealous of the Secretary for Foreign Affairs, and he highly approved of his wife's friendship with Fouché. These four persons were well aware that the Emperor had conceived, and was cherishing, the project of a divorce and an illustrious alliance; and they endeavored by every means to destroy the last links which still bound Josephine to Bonaparte, so that they might please the Emperor by aiding him to carry out this idea, and might also foil the Beauharnais and prevent M. de Talleyrand from acquiring a fresh claim to the confidence of his master. They wanted to have the direction of this affair in their own hands only.

M. de Talleyrand had been laboring for several years to acquire a European reputation, which, on the whole, he well deserved. No doubt he had more than once approached the subject of the divorce, but he was especially anxious that this step should lead to the Emperor's contracting a great alliance, of which he (M. de Talleyrand) should have the negotiation. So that, so long as he did not feel certain of succeeding in his objects, he contrived to restrain the Emperor in this matter by representing to him that it was of the utmost importance to select the fitting moment for action. When he returned from this campaign, the Emperor seemed to place more confidence than ever in M. de Talleyrand, who had been very useful to him in Poland and in each of his treaties. His new dignity gave M. de Talleyrand the right to replace Prince Joseph wherever the rank of Grand Elector called him; but it also obliged him to relinquish the Ministry of Foreign Affairs, which was beneath his present rank. He was, however, entirely in Napoleon's confidence with respect to foreign affairs, and was consulted by him in preference to the real Minister. Some would-be wise persons claimed afterward to have foreseen that M. de Talleyrand was exchanging a secure post for a brilliant but precarious position; and Bonaparte himself let it appear sometimes that he had not returned from Tilsit without feeling some displeasure at the preponderance of his Minister in Europe, and that he was annoyed at the generally prevalent belief that M. de Talleyrand was necessary to him. By changing his office, and availing himself of his services in consultation only, he made use of him just as he wished, while reserving the power of setting him aside or of not following his guidance whenever either course should suit him. I remember an anecdote which illustrates this position of affairs. M. de Champagny, a clever but narrow-minded man, was transferred from the Ministry of the Interior to that of Foreign Affairs, and M. de Talleyrand, on presenting to him the various persons who were to be under his authority, said: " Here, sir, are many highly commendable persons. They will give you every satisfaction. You will find them capable, punctual, exact, and trustworthy, but, thanks to my training, not at all zealous." At these words M. de Champagny expressed some surprise. " Yes," continued M. de Talleyrand, affecting the utmost seriousness; " with the exception of a few dispatching clerks, who fold up their covers with undue precipitation, every one here observes the greatest calmness, and all are totally unused to haste. When you have had to transact the business of the interests of Europe with the Emperor for a little while, you will see how important it is not to be in any hurry to seal and send off his decisions." M. de Talleyrand amused the Emperor by relating this incident, and describing the crestfallen and astonished air with which his successor received the useful hint. It will not be inappropriate to place here a statement of the cumulative income of which M. de Talleyrand was at this time in the receipt:

	Francs.
As Grand Elector	330,000
As Grand Chamberlain	40,000
From the Principality of Benevento	120,000
As Grand Cross of the Legion of Honor	5,000
Total	495,000

Certain endowments were afterward added to this sum. His personal fortune was estimated at three hundred thousand louis per annum; I never knew whether this was correct. The various treaties brought him immense sums of money and presents of enormous value. He lived in great style, and made very handsome allowances to his brothers. He bought the fine estate of Valençay, and furnished the house most luxuriously. At the time of which I am now speaking he had a fancy for books, and his library was superb. That year the Emperor ordered him to make a sumptuous display, and to purchase a house suitable to his dignity as a prince, promising that he himself would pay for it. M. de Talleyrand bought the Hôtel de Monaco, Rue de Varenne, enlarged it, and decorated it extensively. The Emperor, having quarreled with him, did not keep his word, but threw him into considerable embarrassment by obliging him to pay for this palace himself.

In concluding my sketch of the position of the Imperial family, I must add that Prince Eugène was then governing his fair realm of Italy with wisdom and prudence, happy in the affection of his wife, and rejoicing in the birth of their little daughter.

The Arch-Chancellor Cambacérès, who was cautious both by nature and training, remained in Paris, maintaining a certain state assigned to him by the Emperor, and which delighted his childish vanity. With equal prudence he presided over the State Council, conducting the debates with method and discernment, and contriving that the prescribed limits should never be exceeded. Le Brun, the Arch-Treasurer, interfered little with affairs; he kept up a certain state and managed his own revenues, giving no cause of offense and exerting no influence.

The Ministers confined themselves to their respective duties, preserving the attitude of attentive and docile clerks, and conducting the affairs with which they were intrusted on a uniform system, which had for its basis the will and the interests of their master. Each one's orders were the same: "*Promptitude* and *submission.*" The Minister of Police allowed himself a greater liberty of speech than the others. He was careful to keep on good terms with the Jacobins, for whose good behavior he made himself responsible to the Emperor. On this very account he was a little more independent, for he was at the head of a party. He had the direction of the various branches of police set over France, and was master of the details. Bonaparte and he may have often told each other falsehoods in their interviews, but probably neither of them was deceived.

M. de Champagny, subsequently Duc de Cadore, who had been Minister of the Interior, was placed at the head of foreign affairs, and was succeeded in his former post by State Councilor Crétet, who had been at first Director-General of Public Works (Ponts et Chaussées). He was not a clever man, but hard-working and assiduous, and that was all that the Emperor required.

Requier, the Chief Judge, subsequently Duc de Massa, of whom I have already spoken, administered justice with persevering mediocrity. The Emperor was anxious that neither the authority nor the independence of the law should increase.

The Prince de Neufchâtel made an able War Minister. General Dejean was at the head of the Commissariat Department. Both were under the personal superintendence of the Emperor.

M. Gaudin, the wise Minister of Finance, observed an order and regularity in the management of taxes and receipts which rendered him valuable to the Emperor. This was his sole employment. Afterward he was created Duc de Gaëta.

The Minister of the Treasury, M. Mollien, subsequently created a count, showed more talent and much financial sagacity.

M. Portalis, the Minister of Public Worship, was a man of talent and ability, and had maintained harmony between the clergy and the Government. It must be stated that the clergy, out of gratitude for the security and consideration which they owed to Bonaparte, submitted to him very willingly, and were partisans of a despotic authority conducive to universal order. When he demanded the levy of the conscripts of 1808, of which I have already spoken, he ordered the bishops, according to his usual custom, to exhort the peasantry to submit to the conscription. Their pastoral letters were very remarkable. In that of the Bishop of Quimper were these words: "What French heart will not ardently bless Divine Providence for having bestowed on this magnificent empire, when it was on the point of being for ever crushed beneath blood-stained ruins, the only man who, as Emperor and King, could repair its misfortunes and throw a veil of glory over the period of its dishonor?"

The death of M. Portalis occurred during this year, and he was succeeded by an excellent though less able man, M. Bigot de Préameneu, Councilor of State, who was subsequently made a count.

In conclusion, the Naval Minister had little occupation from the time that Bonaparte, giving up the hope of subduing England at sea, and vexed with the failure of all his maritime undertakings, had ceased to interest himself in naval affairs. M. Décrès, a man of real ability, was altogether pleasing to his master. His manners were rather rough, but he flattered Bonaparte after an unusual fashion. He cared little for public esteem, and was willing to bear the odium of the injustice with which the Emperor treated the French navy, so that it never appeared to emanate from Bonaparte himself. With unfaltering devotion, M. Décrès incurred and endured the resentment of all his former companions and friends. The Emperor afterward made him a duke.

At the time of which I am writing the Court atmosphere was cold and silent. There, especially, we were all impressed with the conviction that our privileges depended solely on the will of the master; and, as that will was apt to be capricious, the difficulty of providing against it led each individual to avoid taking needless action, and to restrict himself to the more or less narrow circle of the duties of his office. The ladies of the Court were still more cautious, and did not attempt anything beyond winning admiration either by their beauty or their attire. In Paris itself people were becoming more and more indifferent to the working of a mechanism of which they could see the results and feel the power, but in whose action they knew they could have no share. Social life was not wanting in attractions. French people, if they are but at peace, will immediately seek for pleasure. But credit was restricted, interest in national affairs was languid, and all the higher and nobler sentiments of public life were wellnigh paralyzed. Thoughtful minds were disturbed, and true citizens must have felt that they were leading useless lives. As a sort of compensation, they accepted the pleasures of an agreeable and varied social existence. Civilization was increased by luxury, which, while enervating the mind, makes social relations pleasanter. It procures for people of the world a number of little interests, which are almost always sufficient for them, and with which they do not feel ashamed of being satisfied, when for a length of time they have been suffering from the greater political disorders. The recollection of the latter was still fresh in our memory, and it made us prize this period of brilliant slavery and elegant idleness.

CHAPTER XXV

(1807.)

WHEN the Emperor reached Paris on the 27th of July, 1807, I was still at Aix-le-Chapelle, and was beginning to feel anxious as to the temper in which he had returned. I have already said that this was a prevailing uneasiness at Court whenever he was expected. I could make no inquiries, for none dared to write openly to their correspondents; thus it was only when I myself returned that I could learn any particulars.

The Emperor came back elated at his inconceivable good fortune, and it soon became evident that his imagination exaggerated the distance between himself and every other person. He showed, moreover, increased indignation at what he called the "gossip of the Faubourg Saint Germain." The first time that he saw M. de Rémusat, he rebuked him for not having given information respecting the persons in society in Paris, in some letters he wrote to Duroc, Grand Marshal of the Palace. "You are in a position," said he, "to know what is said in a number of drawing-rooms, and it is your duty to keep me informed. I can not accept the slight excuses on which you have withheld information from me." To this M. de Rémusat replied that there was very little to withhold, because people were naturally careful as to what they said before him, and that he would have been loath to attach any importance to idle words, which might have caused serious consequences to those who had uttered them, often without any really hostile feeling. On such an answer being made to him, the Emperor would shrug his shoulders, turn on his heel, and say to Duroc or to Savary: " I am very sorry, but Rémusat will not get on; he is not devoted to me as I understand devotion."

It may be thought, at least, that a man of honor, who was determined rather to mar his prospects than to purchase fortune by a sacrifice of his self-respect, would have been placed by that very resolution out of danger of those quarrels which result from what, alike in city and Court, is called tittle-tattle. But such was not the case; Bonaparte liked nobody to be at peace, and he knew admirably well how to compromise or embroil those who most desired to live in quiet.

It will be remembered that, during the stay of the Empress at Mayence, some ladies of the Court, of whom Mme. de la Rochefoucauld was the chief, had ventured to criticise the Prussian war with some severity, and to compassionate Prince Louis, and still more the beautiful and cruelly insulted Queen. The Empress, displeased by their freedom, had written full accounts to her husband of this movement of sympathy, begging him never to let it be known that she had mentioned the matter to him. That she had done so she confided to M. de Rémusat, who expressed his disapproval, but kept her secret. When M. de Talleyrand joined the Emperor, he too related what had been taking place at Mayence, but more with the intention of amusing Napoleon than from any hostility toward the Lady of Honor, whom he neither liked nor disliked. Bonaparte was, however, greatly displeased with her, and the first time they met he reproached her with his usual violence for her opinions and her utterances. Mme. de la Rochefoucauld was taken by surprise, and, for want of a better excuse, denied everything. The Emperor rejoined by a positive reiteration, and, when she inquired who had made this fine report about her, he instantly named M. de Rémusat. On hearing this, Mme. de la Rochefoucauld was astounded. She was friendly to my husband and to me; and, believing rightly that she might rely on our discretion, she had often confided her most secret thoughts to us. She felt, therefore, extreme surprise and anger, the more so that she herself was a sincere person, and incapable of such baseness as that attributed to my husband.

Being thus prejudiced against him, she avoided any opportunity of explanation, but was cold and constrained in her demeanor. For a long time he could not understand the reason of the estrangement; but, a few months afterward, some circumstances connected with the divorce rendered certain interviews and conversations between Mme. de la Rochefoucauld and ourselves necessary, and she questioned my husband on the matter which I have just related, and then learned the whole truth. She had made an opportunity of speaking freely to the Empress, who did not undeceive her, but allowed suspicion still to rest on M. de Rémusat, adding only that M. de Talleyrand had probably said more than he. Mme. de la Rochefoucauld was an intimate friend of M. de Ségur, Grand Master of Ceremonies, and she confided her feelings to him. For a time this caused a coolness between him and us; it also set him against M. de Talleyrand, the sharpness and occasional bitterness of whose satire leagued all commonplace people together against him, and he amused himself mercilessly at their expense. They took their revenge when and how they could. The Emperor did not confine his reproaches to persons of the Court; he complained likewise of high society in Paris. He rebuked M. Fouché for the imperfection of his supervision; he sent certain ladies into exile, threatened some persons of distinction, and implied that, to avoid the effects of his displeasure, former acts of indiscretion must be repaired by steps which would show that his authority was recognized. Many persons felt themselves in consequence obliged to be presented at Court; some few made their own safety a pretext for this, and the splendor of his Court was increased.

As he always took care to make his presence felt by disturbing everybody, he did not spare his own family. He severely, though very ineffectually, scolded his sister Pauline for her lightness of conduct, which Prince Borghese beheld with real or affected indifference. Nor did he hide from his sister Caroline that he was aware of her secret and ambitious projects. She bent before the inevitable storm with her usual suppleness, and brought him by degrees to own that, with such blood running in her veins, she was not very guilty in desiring a superior rank, while she took care to make her defense with all her usual charm. When he had thus, to use his own expression, roused up everybody all round, he felt satisfied with the terror he had excited, and, appearing to forget what had passed, resumed his customary way of life.

M. de Talleyrand, whose return occurred a little later, expressed great pleasure at meeting M. de Rémusat. He now took up a habit of frequently coming to see me, and our intimacy became closer. I recollect that, at first, notwithstanding the gratitude with which his kindness inspired me, and the great pleasure I felt in his conversation, I was for a long time ill at ease in his company. M. de Talleyrand was justly reckoned as a very clever man; he was a very important personage; but he was said to be hard to please and of a sarcastic disposition. His manners, although highly polished, seem to place the person whom he is addressing in a relatively inferior position. Nevertheless, as the customs of society in France always accord to women a certain importance and liberty, they could, if they chose, hold their own with M. de Talleyrand, who likes women and is not afraid of them. Yet few of them chose to do so; the desire of pleasing restrained them. They hold themselves in a sort of bondage to him, and, in fact, to use a common expression, they have *spoiled him*. Lastly, as he is reserved, *blasé* on a multitude of subjects, indifferent on many others, and with feelings difficult to touch, a woman who designs to conquer or retain him, or even only to amuse him, undertakes a hard task.

All that I knew about him, all that I discovered in becoming more intimate with him, made me constrained in his presence. I was gratified by his friendliness, but I did not venture to tell him so; I was afraid of disclosing my habitual thoughts and anxieties, because I imagined they would excite his sarcasm. I asked him no questions either about himself or on public affairs, for fear he might think me curious. My mind was strained in his presence, so that I sometimes experienced actual fatigue. I listened to him with the greatest attention, in order that, even if I could not always reply fittingly, at least I should have procured him the pleasure of an attentive auditor; for I own that pride was flattered by his preference for me. When I think it all over now, I am amused at the mingled distress and pleasure which I experienced when my folding-doors were opened (on both sides) and the Prince of Benevento was announced. Large drops sometimes stood on my forehead from the efforts I made to express myself wittily, and there is no doubt that I was in consequence less agreeable than had I behaved more naturally, when, at any rate, I should have had the advantage of sincerity and of harmony in my whole deportment. Although naturally grave and inclined to deep feeling, I tried to emulate the lightness with which he could pass from one subject to another. I was kind-hearted by nature, and averse to malicious talk, and yet I was always ready to smile at his jests. At the beginning, then, he exerted over me the influence which was customary to him; and, had our intimacy continued on the same footing, I should have seemed to him but one woman the more to swell the ranks of those worshippers who rivalled each other in applauding his defects and encouraging the worst points of his character. He would probably have ended by breaking with me, for I should have ill sustained a rôle for which I was so little suited. I will presently relate the painful circumstances which made me resume my natural character, and which caused me to conceive a sincere affection for him, which has never wavered.

Our new-formed intimacy was soon remarked at Court, and the Emperor did not at first seem displeased. M. de Talleyrand was not without influence over him; the opinions he pronounced in speaking of M. de Rémusat were of service to us; a few words let us perceive that we were held in increased esteem. The Empress, who found in most things a subject for fear, showed me great kindness, thinking I might serve her cause with M. de Talleyrand. His enemies at Court watched us, but, as he was powerful, we were treated with great consideration. His numerous circle of acquaintance began to look with curious eyes on a quiet, straightforward, and taciturn man, who never flattered and was incapable of intrigue, yet whose abilities were praised, and whose society was courted by M. de Talleyrand. I myself, a little person of twenty-seven years of age, ordinary-looking, cold and reserved, in nowise remarkable, devoted to the duties of a pure and virtuous life, thus distinguished by the notice of so eminent a personage, also became an object of attention! It was probable that M. de Talleyrand, being just then in want of amusement, found something novel and attractive in gaining the affection of two persons completely outside his own sphere of ideas, so that, when wearied by the constraint of his existence, he turned sometimes with relief to a companionship which he knew he could trust; while our attachment to him, openly professed at a time when his disgrace shook our own position, caused a solid friendship to succeed to mutual liking.

It was then that, visiting oftener at his house, which we had not before this been in the habit of frequenting, I became acquainted with a section of society hitherto almost unknown to me. There were always a number of people at M. de Talleyrand's—foreigners who paid him obsequious attention, great nobles of the former order of things, and men of the new, all wondering at finding themselves under the same roof —all remarkable for some reason or other, but whose character was not always equal to their celebrity. Well-known women were there also, of whom it must be said he had in general been rather the lover than the friend, and who were on the kind of terms with him that he preferred.

His wife must be named first among the persons to whom I allude. Her beauty was daily waning on account of her increasing size. She was always handsomely dressed, and occupied by right the place of honor, but was unacquainted with most of the com-

pany. M. de Talleyrand never seemed to perceive
that she was present; he never spoke to her, still less
did he listen to what she said, and I believe he suffered acutely, but with resignation, for the error
which had forced him into this extraordinary marriage. His wife seldom went to Court: the Emperor
treated her coldly, and she received no consideration
there. It never occurred to M. de Talleyrand to complain of this, nor yet of the compensation she was
said to seek in the attentions of certain strangers.
Bonaparte would sometimes jest on this subject with
M. de Talleyrand, who would answer with indifference and let the matter drop. Mme. de Talleyrand
habitually disliked all her husband's friends, whether
men or women. It is probable that she made no exception in my favor, but I always behaved to her with
such ceremonious civility, I held myself so totally
aloof from her private affairs, that we scarcely came
into contact.

In these reception-rooms I also met some old
friends of M. de Talleyrand, who began to regard
me with curiosity, much to my amusement. Among
these were the Duchesse de Luynes and the Princesse
de Vaudemont, both of them excellent women. They
were sincerely attached and true to him, and very
kind to me because they saw that my regard for him
was sincere, straightforward, and without any ulterior
design. The Vicomtesse de Laval was less well
pleased, and, being rather ill-natured, she judged me
with some severity. The Princesse de Lieskiewitz,
sister of Prince Poniatowski, had lately made the acquaintance of M. de Talleyrand at Warsaw, and had
followed him to Paris. This poor lady, notwithstanding her forty-five years and her glass eye, was
unfortunately passionately in love with him; and her
attachment, of which he was manifestly weary, made

her alive to the least preference shown by him. It is possible she may have honored me with a little jealousy. The Princesse de X—— yielded to the same infirmity, for it was truly an infirmity to " love " M. de Talleyrand. I also met the Duchesse de Fleury, a very clever woman, who had obtained a divorce from her husband, M. de Montrond; Mesdames de Bellegarde, whose only claim to importance in society was their extreme license of speech; Mme. de K——, to whom M. de Talleyrand paid attention, in order to keep on good terms with the Grand Equerry; Mme. de Brignoli, one of the Ladies-in-waiting—a very agreeable and elegant Genoese; and Mme. de Souza, formerly Mme. de Flahaut—a talented woman, who had been in her early youth a friend of M. de Talleyrand, and for whom he still retained much regard. She had written several pretty tales, and was, at the time of which I speak, the wife of M. de Souza, who had been ambassador to Portugal. Lastly, I met the ambassadresses, the foreign princesses then in Paris, and a great number of all the distinguished people in Europe.

I was entertained by this social magic lantern; but, warned by an instinctive feeling to make no friendships among the crowd, I always stood on the strictest ceremony, and much preferred receiving M. de Talleyrand at my own fireside. My own circle felt some surprise at his so frequently joining us—some of my friends were even alarmed; for he inspired a general apprehension lest, immersed in important affairs as he was, he might find himself in a dangerous position and drag us down in his fall. We did not share the alarm of these friends, as perhaps we ought to have done. M. de Rémusat's office as First Chamberlain brought us into contact with M. de Talleyrand, and it was pleasanter that our intercourse should be friendly; we held aloof from all serious affairs, and had no thought of benefiting by his influence. Disinterested persons are apt to deceive themselves on this head; they imagine that others must know, or at any rate must perceive, what their real motives are, and as they act with simple sincerity they do not apprehend that they will be suspected of double-dealing. It was a great blunder, at that time, to expect to be estimated at one's real worth.

The Emperor saw Louis's second son when he went to Saint Cloud, and treated him affectionately, so that the Empress began to hope he would think of this child as his heir, as he had formerly thought of the elder boy. Bonaparte had been impressed by the extreme rapidity of the progress of the disease that had so suddenly carried off the elder brother, and he offered a competitive prize of twelve thousand francs for essays upon the malady called croup. Some valuable works were published in consequence.

The pacification of Europe did not at once bring back the whole army to France. In the first place, the King of Sweden, prevailed on by the English Government, and in spite of the opposition of his people, announced the rupture of his armistice with us. Thirteen days after the signature of peace at Tilsit, a partial war broke out in Pomerania. Marshal Martier was at the head of this expedition; he entered Stralsund, and obliged the King of Sweden to take ship and escape. On this the English sent a considerable fleet to the Baltic, and, having attacked Denmark, laid siege to Copenhagen, of which they soon obtained possession. These various events were chronicled in the " Moniteur," accompanied with notes attacking the English as usual, while the aberration of mind of the King of Sweden was proclaimed to Europe.

Speaking of the subsidy which the English Government allowed the Swedes for carrying on the war, the Emperor expressed himself as follows in the " Moniteur ": " Gallant and unfortunate Swedes, this subsidy costs you dear! If England could only repair the harm she does to your trade and to your honor, or could replace the blood she has already cost and still costs you! But you must feel that you are to be pitied for having lost all your privileges and all consideration, and for being, thus defenseless and disorganized, subject to the caprices of an invalid King."

General Rapp remained at Dantzic as governor, with a garrison. He was a brave and honest man—rather rough in his ways, faithful, frank, careless of what went on about him, and of everything except the orders he received. He served his master with great fidelity, more than once nearly losing his life for him, without having ever made the least inquiry into the qualities or the vices of his character.

The Emperor also considered himself bound to support the new constitution established in Poland by the King of Saxony, and sent a considerable garrison thither to be added to the Polish garrison. Marshal Davoust had the command of this cantonment. By thus dispersing his troops through Europe, Bonaparte secured his influence over his allies, kept his soldiers in practice, and relieved France from the burden of supporting so many armed men. His aggressive policy obliged him to be always in readiness; and, moreover, to insure the entire devotion of his army, it was necessary to keep the men far from their homes. He succeeded in so completely altering the nature of his troops that they became unreservedly devoted to his service; they lost all national sentiment, and cared only for their chief, for victory, and for plunder, which in the eyes of a soldier is a great embellishment of danger. They drew down by degrees on the fatherland which they had forgotten those feelings of hatred and revenge which resulted in the European crusade against us in 1813 and 1814.

Fresh adulation awaited the Emperor on his return. Language was exhausted for formulas of praise, to which he listened with disdainful composure. There is little doubt, however, that his indifference was feigned; for he loved praise from no matter what lips, and more than once he was duped by it. There were men who had influence over him only because their compliments were inexhaustible. Unfailing admiration, even though somewhat foolishly expressed, never failed to please him.

On the 10th of August he sent a message to the Senate, announcing the elevation of M. de Talleyrand to the dignity of Vice-Grand Elector, and that of Marshal Berthier to the rank of Vice-Grand Constable. General Clarke succeeded to the latter as Minister of War, and found opportunities for displaying the devoted admiration to which I have alluded, even more fully than before. The Emperor's habitual attention to all war matters, the high intelligence of Berthier, Major-General of the army, and the careful administration of General Dejean, the chief of the Commissariat, made any great abilities in General Clarke unnecessary. Punctual, upright, and submissive, he fulfilled all the requirements of his position. MM. Champagny and Cretet obtained the two ministerial posts of which I have spoken, and State Councilor Regnault was made State Secretary to the Imperial Family.

Meanwhile we read every day of fresh military promotions, of the distribution of rewards, of the creation of official posts—in fact, of everything that tends to keep ambition, covetousness, and vanity on the alert. Then the Corps Législatif opened its session. M. de Fontanes, who, as usual, was named President, made, as usual, a fine speech on the truly brilliant position of France. A very great number of laws appertaining to rule and order were brought before the Assembly for its sanction, as was likewise a budget which proclaimed our finances to be in a flourishing condition; and, lastly, an account of the public works of all kinds in contemplation, or begun, or already terminated, in all parts of the Empire. The cost of all these was defrayed by the contributions exacted throughout Europe, and all France might witness improvements which nevertheless did not augment a single tax. The Emperor, in addressing the legislative bodies, spoke to the whole French nation; gave them an account of his victories; mentioned the 5,179 officers and the 123,000 subalterns and privates taken prisoners in this war; spoke of the complete conquest of Prussia, of his soldiers encamped on the banks of the Vistula, of the fall of the power of England, which, he said, must be the result of so many victories; and ended by an expression of satisfaction with the nation, which had so faithfully served him in gaining for him such triumphant success. " Frenchmen," he said, " I am well pleased with you; you are a good and a great people."

The opening of the Corps Législatif was an imposing ceremony. The hall had been lavishly decorated; the dress of the deputies was handsome, that of the courtiers surrounding the Emperor was magnificent, and he himself was resplendent in gold and diamonds on that day. Although in every ceremonial he was too precipitate, the great pomp he insisted upon took the place of that dignity which was wanting. When Bonaparte, in the course of any ceremony, had to walk toward the throne prepared for him, he always seemed to rush at it. One could not but feel, on observing him, that this was no legitimate sovereign taking peaceful possession of the royal seat bequeathed to him by his ancestors; but an all-powerful master, who, each time that he wore the crown, seemed to reiterate the words he had once uttered at Milan, " Guai à chi la toccherà."

On these state occasions Bonaparte's incorrect pronunciation was a great drawback. In general he had his speech drawn up for him. M. Maret, I believe, most frequently undertook that task, but sometimes it fell to M. Vignaud, or even to M. de Fontanes; and he would try to learn it by heart, but with little success; for the least constraint was insupportable to him. He always ended by resolving to read his speech, and it was copied out for him in a large hand; for he was little accustomed to read writing, and could have made nothing out of his own. Then he would be instructed in the proper pronunciation of the words; but when he came to speak he forgot his lesson, and in a muffled voice, with lips scarcely parted, would read the speech in an accent more strange even than it was foreign, most unpleasant, and indeed vulgar. I have heard numbers of persons say that they always felt a painful sensation on hearing him speak in public. The indisputable testimony of his accent to the fact that he was a foreigner struck painfully on the ear and the mind alike. I have myself sometimes experienced this involuntary sensation.

The fêtes of the 15th of August were splendid. The whole Court, glittering with precious stones, was present at a concert in the palace, and at the ballet which followed it. The reception-rooms of the Tuileries were thronged with a brilliant and gorgeous company; there were ambassadors, the greatest nobles of all Europe, princes, and many kings who, although new-made, appeared in becoming state. There, too, were lovely women, magnificently attired, who, together with the first musicians in the world, and all that the opera-ballets could lend of grace and elegance, combined to form a scene of Oriental splendor.

Public games and rejoicings were given to the city of Paris. The Parisians, who are naturally gay when gathered together, and eager to join any crowd, hurried into the streets to see the illuminations and the fireworks, and showed the delight they felt in scenes of pleasure and in the beauty of the season. But there were no acclamations in honor of the Emperor. There seemed to be no thought of him, as the people enjoyed the amusements he had provided for them; but every one diverted himself according to his own character and taste, and these, perhaps, make the French the least serious people in the world, but the most pleasant.

English people who were present at these rejoicings were quite astonished at the good order, the frank gayety, and the harmony which reign on such occasions throughout all classes of society. Every one enjoys himself, and does not think of interfering with his neighbor's enjoyment; there is no quarreling nor ill humor, no revolting and dangerous drunkenness. Women and children may mix with impunity in the crowd, and are protected. People who are strangers to each other take their pleasure together; they sing and laugh in chorus, though they have never met before. On such occasions an unobservant sovereign might easily be misled. This constitutional hilarity, temporarily called forth by extraneous circumstances, may be mistaken for the expression of the feelings of a contented and loyal people. But, if the sovereigns who are destined to reign over Frenchmen do not want to be deceived, they will interrogate their own conscience rather than the popular cry, if they would learn whether they inspire affection and give happiness to their people.

In this respect the flattery of a Court is really astonishing; numbers of courtiers, in describing the behavior of the Parisian public, endeavored to represent it to the Emperor as a proof of the people's gratitude toward him! I will not affirm that he was never deceived by this, but for the most part he remained stolidly unmoved. Bonaparte seldom listened to others, and joyousness was foreign to his nature.

During the month of August several of the German princes arrived in Paris—some in order to visit the Emperor, others to solicit some favor, or some liberty in behalf of their petty states.

The Prince Primate of the Confederation of the Rhine came at about this time, to celebrate the marriage of Princess Catherine of Würtemberg, who herself arrived on the 21st of August, She was, I think, about twenty years of age, and was a nice-looking girl; her figure was already rather stout, and seemed to indicate that she would take after her father, whose size was so enormous that he could only sit on chairs specially constructed for him, and had to dine at a table which had been hollowed out in a semicircle to make room for his unwieldy figure.

This King of Würtemberg was a very able man, but had the reputation of being the most worthless prince in Europe. He was hated by his subjects, who, it is said, more than once tried to rid themselves of him. He is now dead.

The marriage of Princess Catherine and the King of Westphalia took place at the Tuileries with great splendor. The civil ceremony was performed in the Gallery of Diana, as in the case of the Princess of

Baden's wedding; and on Sunday, the 23d, at eight in the morning, the religious marriage was solemnized at the Tuileries, in presence of the whole Court.

The Prince and Princess of Baden had also come to Paris. She was prettier than ever. The Emperor did not appear to notice her particularly. I will speak of her again presently.

The King and Queen of Holland arrived at the end of August. They seemed to be on good terms, but still depressed on account of their loss. The Queen was thin, and suffering all the *malaise* of an early stage of pregnancy. She had been a very short time in Paris when seeds of the old distrust and disquiet were once more sown in the mind of her husband. Evil tongues insinuated falsehoods respecting the life that the unhappy woman had led at the Pyrenean watering-place. Her grief, the tears that were still flowing, her downcast air, her too evident ill health, failed to disarm her enemies. She talked of the excursions she had made among the mountains, and of the soothing effects of the mountain scenery. She told how she had met M. Decazes, and pitied the profound grief into which his wife's death had plunged him. All this she related in the most frank and simple manner, but calumny laid hold of it, and the suspicions of Louis were reawakened. He wished, naturally but selfishly, to take his wife and son back to Holland. Mme. Louis was as submissive as he could require her to be; but the Empress, alarmed by the declining state of her daughter, insisted on a consultation of physicians being held. The doctors were unanimous in pronouncing the climate of Holland unfit for a woman in the Queen's situation, whose chest was already delicate; and the Emperor settled the question by announcing that he intended to keep his step-daughter and her child with himself for the present. The King submitted sullenly, and bitterly resented to his wife a decision which she had not solicited, but which, I believe, was in accordance with her wishes. Discord once more reigned in that wretched household; and Queen Hortense, profoundly offended this time by the jealous suspicions of her husband, lost for ever the interest which she had recently felt in him, and conceived a positive aversion toward him. " From that time forth," she has often said to me, " I was fully aware that my unhappiness must always be irremediable. I regarded my hopes as entirely and irrevocably ruined. All grandeur inspired me with horror. As for the throne, and what so many people called my ' luck,' I cursed them many a time. I was a stranger to every enjoyment of life. All my dreams had vanished; I was wellnigh dead to all that was passing around me."

About this time the Academy lost two of its most distinguished members: Le Brun the poet, who has left some beautiful odes and the reputation of great poetical talent, and M. Dureau de la Malle, the esteemed translator of Tacitus and the intimate friend of Delille.

M. Delille lived peaceably in the enjoyment of a moderate fortune, surrounded by friends, popular in society, left to his repose and his freedom by the Emperor, who had given up the idea of conquering him. He published certain works from time to time, and reaped the reward of his natural amiability in the favor with which they were received. His life was indeed a peaceful one, untroubled by any bitter thoughts or hostile opinions. M. Delille was a professor at the College of France, and received the salary of a chair of literature, but Le Gouvé did its work for him. This was the only boon which he consented to accept from Bonaparte. He prided himself on preserving a faithful remembrance of Queen Marie Antoinette, whom he called his benefactress. It was known that he was composing a poem in honor of her, the King, and the *émigrés,* but no one resented this to him. A Government which was always anxious to efface such memoirs respected them in Delille, and would not have ventured to incur the odium of persecuting the amiable, grateful, and generally beloved old man.

The two vacant seats in the Academy were much discussed in the salons of Paris. M. de Chateaubriand was mentioned for one of them. The Emperor was angry with him, and the young writer— who was pursuing a course which gained him celebrity, procured him the support of a party, and nevertheless did not expose him to any real danger—kept up an opposition which gained strength from the fact that it excited the Emperor's anger. The French Academy, imbued at that time with the revolutionary and would-be philosophical incredulity that had come into fashion in the last century, opposed the choice of a man who had hoisted religious colors as the banner of his genius. It was said by those who most frequented M. de Chateaubriand's society, that the habits of his life were by no means in harmony with the precepts that adorned his compositions. Excessive pride was imputed to him. Women, captivated by his talents, his peculiar manner, his handsome face, and his reputation, vied with each other in admiring and petting him, and he showed himself by no means insensible to their advances. His extreme vanity, the exalted opinion of himself which he entertained, made us all believe that, if the Emperor had only coaxed him a little, he would have succeeded in gaining him over to his side, although, of course, he would have to pay the high price at which M. de Chateaubriand himself would have rated his partisanship.

The silent labors of the Corps Législatif were continued. It ratified all the laws that emanated from the Council of State, and the administrative organization of the power of the Emperor was completed without opposition. It was now certain that he could rule France, by the strength of his own genius and by the proved ability of the members of this Council of State, with an appearance of legality which reduced the country to silence and pleased his orderly mind; and, regarding the remains of the Tribunate as merely a center of opposition, which, however feeble, might be troublesome to him, he resolved to make an end of it. The Tribunate had been considerably lessened in number under the Consulate. By a *senatus consultum* the tribunes were transferred to the Corps Législatif, and the session was immediately closed. The speeches delivered at the last sitting of the Tribunate are remarkable. It is surprising that men should mutually consent to act such a farce, and yet we had become so much accustomed to that sort of thing, that nobody noticed it particularly at the time.

First, M. Béranger, Councilor of State, appeared with certain of his colleagues, and, after having recapitulated the services which the Tribunate had rendered to France, he went on to say that the new decree was about to confer on the Corps Législatif a plenitude of importance which guaranteed national rights. The President replied, on behalf of the entire Tribunate, that this resolution was received with respect and confidence by them all, and that they appreciated its positive advantages. Then a tribune (M. Carrion-Nisas) moved that an address should be presented to the Emperor thanking him for the evidence of esteem and regard which he had deigned to offer to the Tribunate; and the speaker added that he believed himself to be the interpreter of the feelings of each of his colleagues, in proposing to lay at the foot of the throne, as the last act of an honorable existence, an address which should impress the people with the idea that the tribunes, whose attachment to the monarchy was unalterable, had received the act of the Senate without regret, and without solicitude for the country. This proposition was adopted with unanimity. The President of the Tribunate, Fabre de l'Aude, was named Senator.

At this time the Emperor organized the Cour des Comptes, and, his displeasure with M. Barbé-Marbois having passed away, he recalled him and made him President of that Court.

In September the Emperor of Austria married for the second time. His bride was his first cousin, the daughter of the old Archduke Ferdinand of Milan. Shortly afterward his brother, the Grand Duke of Würzburg, who is now Grand Duke of Tuscany, came to Paris.

The Court was increased from time to time by the arrival of a number of great personages. Toward the end of September a sojourn at Fontainebleau was announced. On this occasion the greatest magnificence was to be displayed; fêtes were to take place in honor of the Queen of Westphalia; the *élite* of the actors and musicians of Paris were to be brought down to the palace, and the Court received orders to appear in the utmost splendor. The Princes and Princesses of the Imperial family brought a portion of their households, and they, as well as the great dignitaries and the Ministers who were to accompany the Emperor, were to have separate tables.

On the 21st of September Bonaparte left Paris with the Empress, and during the following days the

Queen of Holland, the Queen of Naples, the King and Queen of Westphalia, the Grand Duke and Grand Duchess of Berg, the Princess Pauline, Madame Mère, the Grand Duke and Grand Duchess of Baden, the Prince Primate, the Grand Duke of Würzburg, the Princes of Mecklenburg and Saxe-Gotha, M. de Talleyrand, the Prince de Neufchâtel, Maret (Secretary of State), the great officers of the Imperial houses, several Ministers of the kingdom of Italy, and a number of Marshals, arrived at Fontainebleau. M. de Rémusat, several Chamberlains, the Ladies of Honor, the Ladies-in-Waiting, and the Women of the Bedchamber were included in the traveling party. We were all summoned by a letter from the Grand Marshal Duroc, which announced to each that she had been selected by the Emperor. I had just come from Aix-la-Chapelle, and, being comprised in the list, I rejoined the Court and my husband at Fontainebleau, after the delay of a few days in Paris with my mother and my children.

Marshal Lannes had been nominated Colonel-General of the Swiss Guard on the 20th of September.

CHAPTER XXVI

(1807.)

LET us suppose an individual, ignorant of all antecedent events, and suddenly introduced to the life of the palace at Fontainebleau at the time of which I am speaking. That individual, dazzled by the magnificence of this royal dwelling, and struck by the authoritative air of the master and the obsequious reverence of the great personages who surrounded him, would undoubtedly have believed that he beheld a sovereign peacefully seated upon the greatest throne in the world, in virtue of the joint rights of power and legitimacy.

Bonaparte was then king in the eyes of all and in his own eyes; he forgot the past, he did not fear the future. He walked with a firm step, foreseeing no obstacles, or at least certain that he could easily overthrow any which might arise. It appeared to him, it appeared to us, that he could not fall except by an event so unforeseen, so strange, and which would produce so universal a catastrophe, that all the interests of order and tranquillity were solemnly pledged to his support. He was either the master or the friend of all the continental kings. He was allied to several of them either by foreign treaties or by foreign marriages. He had made sure of Europe by the partitions which he had effected. He had strong garrisons upon his most distant frontiers to insure the execution of his will, and all the resources of France were placed absolutely in his hands. He possessed an immense treasury; he was in the prime of life, admired, feared, and scrupulously obeyed. Had he not then surmounted every obstacle?

For all this, a worm was gnawing at the vitals of his glory. The French Revolution was not a process by which the public mind was to be led to submit to arbitrary power; the illumination of the age, the progress of sound principles, the spread of liberty, were all against him, and they were destined to overthrow this brilliant edifice of authority, founded in opposition to the march of the human intellect. The sacred flame of liberty was burning in England. Happily for the welfare of nations, that sanctuary was defended by a barrier which the armies of Bonaparte could not break down. A few leagues of sea protected the civilization of the world, and saved it from being forced to abandon the field of battle to one who might not perhaps have utterly beaten it, but who would have stifled it for the space of a whole generation.

The English Government, jealous of so colossal a power, and, notwithstanding the ill success of so many enterprises, though always conquered, never discouraged, found an unfailing resource against the Emperor in the national sentiments. The pride and industry of England, attacked both in its position and its interests, were equally irritated, and the people consented eagerly to every sacrifice which was demanded of them. Large sums were voted for the augmentation of a naval service which should secure the blockade of the entire continent of Europe.

The kings who were afraid of our artillery submitted to the prohibitive system which we exacted of them, but their people suffered. The luxuries of life, the necessities created by prosperity, the innumerable wants which are the result of high civilization, all fought the battle of the English. Murmurs arose at

St. Petersburg, on the Baltic, in Holland, in all the French ports; and the discontent which dared not express itself took all the deeper root in the public mind that it might be long before it could find a voice.

The threats or reproaches which we were suddenly made aware our Government was addressing to its allies were, however, indications of the true state of things. We in France were in complete ignorance of all that was passing outside of us, without communications (at least of an intellectual kind) with other nations, incredulous of the truth of the articles written to order in our dull journals; but, nevertheless, we were led by the line taken in the "Moniteur" to the conclusion that the Imperial will was balked by the necessities of the nation. The Emperor had bitterly reproached his brother Louis with a too feeble execution of his orders in Holland. He now sent him back to his kingdom with a positive injunction that his will was to be scrupulously obeyed.

"Holland," said the "Moniteur," "since the new measures taken there, will no longer correspond with England. English commerce must find the whole continent closed to it, and these enemies of the nations must be outlawed. There are peoples who know not how to do anything but complain; they must learn to suffer with fortitude, to take every means of injuring the common enemy and obliging him to recognize the principles which actuate all the continental nations. If Holland had taken her measures from the commencement of the blockade, perhaps England would have already made peace."

At another time every effort was made to stigmatize what was called the invasion of continental liberties. The English Government was compared, in its policy, to Marat. "What did he ever do that was more atrocious?" was asked. "The spectacle of a perpetual war is presented to the world. The oligarchical ring-leaders who direct English policy will end, as all exaggerated and infuriated men do end, by earning the opprobrium of their own country and the hatred of other nations."

The Emperor, when dictating this and similar tirades against oligarchical governments, was using for his own purposes the democratic idea which he well knew existed in the nation. When he employed some of the revolutionary phrases, he believed that he was carrying out the principles of the Revolution. " Equality "—nothing but "Equality "—was the rallying-cry between the Revolution and him. He did not fear its consequences for himself; he knew that he had excited those desires which pervert the most generous dispositions; he turned liberty aside, as I have often said, he bewildered all parties, he falsified all meanings, he outraged reason. The power which his sword conferred upon him he sustained by sophistry, and proved that it was from motives of sound wisdom that he deviated from the path of progress and set aside the spirit of the time. He called the power of speech to his aid, and perverted language to lead us astray.

That which makes Bonaparte one of the most remarkable of human beings, which places him apart, and at the head of all those powerful men who have been called to rule over their fellows, is that he perfectly knew and always contended with his epoch. Of his own free will he chose a course which was at once difficult and contrary to the spirit of his time. He did not disguise this from himself; he frequently said that he alone had checked the Revolution, and that after him it would resume its course. He allied himself with the Revolution to oppress it; but he presumed too far upon his strength, and in the end the Revolution recovered its advantage, conquered and repulsed him.

The English Government, alarmed by the fervor with which the Czar, who was rather fascinated than convinced, had embraced the policy of the Emperor, closely attentive to the troubles which were beginning to manifest themselves in Sweden, uneasy at the sentiments which Denmark manifested toward us, and which must lead to the closing of the Sound against themselves, increased their armament, and assembled their forces for the blockade of Copenhagen. They succeeded in taking that city; but the Prince Royal, fortified by the love of his people, defended himself bravely, and fought even after he had lost his capital, so that the English found themselves obliged to evacuate Copenhagen, and to content themselves, there as elsewhere, with the general blockade.

The Opposition declared against the expedition, and the Emperor, in his ignorance of the British Constitution, flattered himself that the Parliamentary debates on this point would be useful to him. Little accustomed to opposition, he estimated that of a political party in England by the effect which would have been produced in France had the same violence of opinion which he remarked in the London journals been manifested here, and he believed the English Government was lost on the evidence of the diatribes of the " Morning Chronicle." These articles were a welcome aliment to his own impatience, but his hopes always proved vain. The Opposition declaimed, but its remonstrances came to nothing, and the Government always found means to carry on the necessary struggle.

Nothing could exceed the Emperor's anger when he read the debates in the English Parliament, and the violent attacks upon himself in which the free English press indulged. He took advantage, on his own part, of the liberty of the press in England to hire writers in London, who might print what he wanted with impunity. These duels of the pen served no purpose. The abuse which he dictated was answered by abuse of him which reached Paris. All these articles had to be translated and shown to him. Those whose duty it was to bring them under his notice trembled as they did so, so terrible was his anger, whether silent or displayed in violent passion; and ill indeed was the fortune of any one whose position in the household brought him in contact with the Emperor immediately after he had read the English newspapers. We were always made aware of the state of his temper on those occasions. The officials whose business it was to provide for his amusements were much to be pitied. At this time what I must really call the " torture " of M. de Rémusat commenced. I shall have more to say of this subject when I have to describe our Court life at Fontainebleau.

All those persons who were to accompany their Majesties were assembled, and informed of the rules which they would have to observe. The different evenings of the week were to be passed in the respective apartments of the great personages. On one evening the Emperor would receive; there would be music, and afterward cards. On two other evenings there would be a play—on one, followed by a ball in the apartment of the Grand Duchess of Berg, and, on the other, by a ball in the apartment of the Princess Borghese. On the fifth, there would be a reception and cards in the apartment of the Empress. The Princes and Ministers were to give dinners, and to invite all the members of the Court in turn. The Grand Marshal was to do the same; twenty-five covers were to be laid at his table every day. The Lady of Honor was likewise to entertain. And, lastly, there was to be a table for all those who had not received a special invitation elsewhere. Princes and Kings were to dine with the Emperor only when invited. He reserved to himself the liberty of his *tête-à-tête* dinner with his wife, and chose whom he pleased when he thought fit to depart from that rule.

Hunting took place on fixed days, and the guests were invited to accompany the hunt, either on horseback or in elegant *calèches*.

The Emperor took it into his head that the ladies should have a hunting costume, and to that the Empress agreed very willingly. The famous costumer Leroy was consulted, and a very brilliant uniform was arranged. Each Princess selected a different color for herself and her household. The costume of the Empress was amaranth velvet, embroidered in gold, with a *toque* also embroidered in gold, and a plume of white feathers. All the Ladies-in-Waiting wore amaranth. Queen Hortense chose blue and silver; Mme. Murat, pink and silver; Princess Borghese, lilac and silver. The dress was a sort of tunic, or short *redingote* in velvet, worn over a gown of embroidered white satin; velvet boots to match the dress, and a *toque* with a white plume. The Emperor and all the gentlemen wore green coats, with gold or silver lace. These brilliant costumes, worn either on horseback or in carriages, and by a numerous assemblage, had a charming effect in the beautiful forest of Fontainebleau.

The Emperor liked hunting rather for the exercise which it forced him to take than for the pleasure of the chase itself. He did not follow the deer very carefully, but, setting off at a gallop, would take the first road that lay before him. Sometimes he forgot the object of the hunt altogether, and followed the winding paths of the forest, or seemed to abandon himself to the fancy of his horse, being plunged the while in deep reverie. He rode well, but ungracefully. He preferred Arab horses, because they are so trained that they stop on the instant. Horses of this kind were very carefully broken for him, as, from his habit of starting at full gallop with a loose rein, he would have been in danger of falling had not great precaution been taken. He would go down steep hills at full speed, to the great risk of those who had to follow him at the same pace. He had a few severe falls, but they were never alluded to. He would not have liked any mention of them.

He took up for a while a fancy for driving a *calèche* or a buggy, and he was a very unsafe coachman, for he took no precaution in turning corners or to avoid difficult roads. He was determined always to conquer every obstacle, and would retreat before none. One day, at Saint Cloud, he undertook to drive four-in-hand, and turned the horses, which he could not manage, so awkwardly through a gateway, that the carriage was upset. The Empress and some other persons were in the vehicle and were all thrown out; but, fortunately, no serious accident occurred, and he himself escaped with a sprained wrist. After that he gave up driving, remarking, with a laugh, that " in even the smallest things every man should stick to his own business."

Although he took no great interest in the success of a hunt, he would scold violently if the deer were not taken, and be very angry if it were represented to him that he had, by changing the course, misled the dogs. He was surprised and impatient at the slightest non-success.

He worked very hard at Fontainebleau, as, indeed, he did everywhere. He rose at seven, held his *levée,* breakfasted alone, and, on the days when there was no hunt, remained in his cabinet or held councils until five or six o'clock. The Ministers and Councilors of State came from Paris as if we had been at Saint Cloud. He never considered distances, and carried this to such an extent that, having expressed an intention to " receive " on Sunday, after Mass, as he did at Saint Cloud, people had to leave Paris in the night in order to reach Fontainebleau at the prescribed hour. The persons who had made this journey would be placed in one of the galleries of the château, through which he would walk, sometimes without taking the trouble of rewarding them by a word or a look for the fatigue and inconvenience they had undergone.

While he remained all the morning in his cabinet, the Empress, elegantly dressed, breakfasted with her daughter and her ladies, and afterward went into her drawing-room and received visits from persons living in the château. Such of us as cared to do so might occupy ourselves with needlework, and this was a great relief to the fatigue of idle and trifling conversation. Mme. Bonaparte did not like to be alone, but she had no taste for any kind of occupation. At four o'clock we left her; she then gave herself up to the business of her toilet, we to the business of ours, and this was a momentous affair. A number of Parisian shopkeepers had brought their very best merchandise to Fontainebleau, and they easily disposed of it by presenting themselves at our rooms.

Between five and six o'clock the Emperor would go down to his wife's apartment, and then go out in a carriage alone with her for a drive before dinner. At six o'clock we dined, and afterward we met in the theatre or at the apartment of the person who was charged with providing the especial amusement of the particular evening.

The princes, marshals, great officers, or chamberlains who had the *entrée,* might present themselves at the Empress's apartment. They knocked at the door, the chamberlain on duty announced them, and the Emperor said, " Let them come in." Ladies would sit down in silence; gentlemen would remain standing against the wall in the order in which they entered the room. The Emperor would generally be walking backward and forward, sometimes silently and deep in thought, without taking any notice of those around; at others, he would make an opportunity of talking, but almost without interruption, for it was always difficult to reply to him, and had become more so than ever. He neither knew how to put people at their ease nor cared to do so; for he dreaded the slightest appearance of familiarity, and he inspired all who were in his presence with the apprehension that some disparaging or unkind word would be said to him or her before witnesses.

The receptions did not differ much from these more private and privileged occasions. All about him suffered from *ennui;* he did so himself, and frequently complained of the fact, resenting to others the dull and constrained silence which was in reality imposed by him. I have heard him say: " It is a singular thing: I have brought together a lot of people at Fontaine-bleau; I wanted them to amuse themselves; I arranged every sort of pleasure for them; and here they are with long faces, all looking dull and tired."

" That," replied M. de Talleyrand, " is because pleasure can not be summoned by beat of drum, and here, just as when you are with the army, you always seem to say to us all, ' Come, ladies and gentlemen, forward! march!' " The Emperor was not annoyed by this speech; he was in a very good humor at this time. M. de Talleyrand passed long hours alone with him, and was then free to say anything he chose; but, in a great room and among forty other persons, M. de Talleyrand was just as silent as the rest.

Of the whole Court, the person who was most oppressed by the care of the Emperor's pleasures was, beyond all comparison, M. de Rémusat. The fêtes and the plays were in the department of the Grand Chamberlain, and M. de Rémusat, in his capacity as First Chamberlain, had all the responsibility and labor. That word is perfectly appropriate, for the imperious and harassing will of Bonaparte rendered this sort of business exceedingly troublesome. It always was, as M. de Talleyrand said, a case of "amusing the unamusable."

The Emperor chose to have two plays in the week, and that they should always be different. Only the actors of the Comédie Française performed in these plays, which alternated with representations of Italian operas. Nothing but tragedy was played—Corneille frequently, a few of Racine's pieces, and Voltaire, whose dramatic works Bonaparte did not like, very rarely.

The Emperor approved the entire repertory for Fontainebleau, positively insisted that the best actors of the company must perform there, and commanded that the representations in Paris should undergo no interruption; all the arrangements were made accordingly. Then, all of a sudden, he would upset the whole arrangement, demand another play or another actor, and that on the morning of the day on which the piece, as previously set down, was to be acted. He would not listen to any observation on the subject, and sometimes would be quite angry about it; and the best that was to be hoped for was that he would say, with a smile: "Bah! take a little trouble, and you will succeed. I wish it to be so; it is your business to find the means."

When the Emperor uttered that irrevocable *Je le veux,* the words echoed through the whole palace. Duroc, and especially Savary, pronounced them in the same tone as himself, and M. de Rémusat was obliged to repeat them to the unfortunate actors, who were bewildered and overtaxed by the sudden efforts of memory, or the entire disarrangement of their studies, to which they were subjected. Then messengers would be dispatched at full speed to seek the necessary persons and " properties." The day passed in a whirl of petty agitation—in the fear that an accident, or an illness, or some unforeseen circumstance might prevent the execution of the order; and my husband, who occasionally came to my room for a moment's rest, would sigh at the thought that a reasonable man should be forced to exhaust his patience and all the efforts of his intellect in such trifles, which, however, were of real importance because of the consequences to which they might lead.

One would need to have lived in courts to realize how small things can become grave matters, and how hard to bear is the displeasure of the master, even when its cause is utterly insignificant. Kings are in the habit of displaying their displeasure before everybody, and it is unbearable to receive a complaint or a rebuff in the presence of a number of people who look on it as if they were at a play. Bonaparte, the most arbitrary of sovereigns, never hesitated to " scold " in the harshest way, frequently without the slightest reason, and would humiliate or threaten anybody at the prompting of a whim. The fear which he excited was infectious, and his harsh words resounded long and far.

When with very great trouble one had succeeded in satisfying him, it is not to be supposed that he would testify that satisfaction. Silence was the best one had to expect. He would go to the play preoccupied, irritated by reading some English journal, or, perhaps, only fatigued with the day's hunting, and he would either fall into reverie or go to sleep. No applause was permitted in his presence, and the silent representation was exceedingly dull and cold. The Court grew intolerably weary of these eternal tragedies. The younger ladies simply slept through them; every one went away depressed and dissatisfied. The Emperor perceived this, was angry at it, attacked his First Chamberlain, blamed the actors, insisted on others being found, although he had the best, and would command different pieces for the ensuing days, which were received in precisely the same manner. It rarely happened otherwise, and our theatrical experiences were, it must be confessed, eminently unpleasant. Those days at Fontainebleau were a constantly recurring source of misery to me; the frivolity of the thing itself, and the importance of its consequences, rendered it a great trial.

The Emperor admired Talma's acting; he persuaded himself that he liked it very much, but I think he rather knew than felt that Talma was a great actor. He had not in himself that which enables one to take pleasure in the representation of a fiction on the stage; he was deficient in education, and his mind was too rarely disengaged, he was too entirely occupied by his own actual circumstances, to be able to give his attention to the development of a feigned passion. He occasionally appeared moved by a scene, or even by a word pronounced with great effect; but that emotion detracted from his pleasure as a whole, because he wanted it to be prolonged in all its strength, and he never took those secondary impressions into account, which are produced by the beauty of the verse or the harmony which a great actor lends to his entire *rôle*.

In general, he thought our French drama cold, our actors too measured, and he resented to others that he found it impossible to be pleased with what the multitude accepted as a diversion.

It was the same with regard to music. He had little feeling for the arts, but he had an intellectual appreciation of them, and, demanding from them more than they could give him, he complained of not having felt what his nature did not permit him to experience.

The first singers in Italy had been attracted to the Emperor's Court. He paid them largely; his vanity was gratified by the power of taking them away from other sovereigns; but he listened to their strains moodily, and seldom with any interest. M. de Rémusat bethought himself of enlivening the concerts by a sort of representation of the pieces of music that were executed in the Emperor's presence. These concerts were sometimes given on the stage, and they included the finest scenes from the Italian operas. The singers wore the appropriate costumes, and really acted; the decorations represented the scene in which the action of the song was supposed to pass. All this was arranged and mounted with the greatest care, but, like everything else, failed in its effect. And yet not completely; for it must be said that, if so much attention and pains were labor lost so far as his pleasure was concerned, the pomp of all these various spectacles and entertainments pleased Bonaparte, for it consorted with his policy, and he liked to display a superiority which extended to everything before the crowd of foreigners who surrounded him.

The same moody and discontented temper, which was inseparable from him, cast a cloud over the balls and receptions at Fontainebleau. At eight o'clock in the evening, the Court, all in splendid attire, would assemble in the apartment of the Princess whose turn it was to receive company. We placed ourselves in a circle, and looked at each other without speaking. Thus we awaited the arrival of their Majesties. The Empress came in first, made the tour of the reception-room with her unfailing grace, and then took her place and kept silence like the rest, until the Emperor at length appeared. He would seat himself by her side, and look on at the dancing with a countenance so little encouraging to gayety, that enjoyment was out of the question on these occasions. Sometimes, during a pause in the dancing, he would walk about the room, addressing some trifling remarks to the ladies. These observations were, for the most part, jests about their attire, of anything but a delicate kind. He withdrew very soon, and shortly afterward the party would break up.

During the sojourn of the Court at Fontainebleau, a very pretty woman made her appearance, and attracted the attention of the Emperor. She was an Italian. . . . M. de Talleyrand had seen her in Italy, and persuaded the Emperor to appoint her " Reader " to the Empress. Her husband was made Receiver-General. The Empress was at first indignant at the appearance of this fair lady on the scenes; but she promptly made up her mind to lend herself with complacency to what she was powerless to oppose, and this time she shut her eyes to the state of affairs. The lady was a quiet person, acquiescent rather than elated; she yielded to her master from a sort of conviction that she ought not to resist him. But she made no display, she gave herself no airs in consequence of her success, and she contrived to combine a real attachment to Mme. Bonaparte with submission to Bonaparte's fancy for her. The result was that the affair was conducted without any scandal or disturbance. This lady was certainly the handsomest woman in the

Court, which boasted a number of beauties. I have never seen more beautiful eyes, finer features, or a more exquisitely harmonious face. She was tall, and had an elegant figure, but she was a little too slight. The Emperor never cared very much for her; he told his wife all about the affair at once, and made her mind quite easy by his unreserved confidence respecting this brief and unsentimental *liaison*. The lady was lodged in the palace of Fontainebleau in such a manner as to be within call whenever he desired her presence. It was whispered about that she came down in the evening to his apartment, or he went to hers; but in the ordinary circle he did not talk to her more than to any other lady, and the Court paid no great attention to this affair, because it was plainly unlikely to lead to any change. M. de Talleyrand, who had in the first instance persuaded Bonaparte to select this Italian as a mistress, received his confidences concerning her, and that was all.

If I were asked whether the idleness of our Court life at Fontainebleau led to the formation of *liaisons* of a similar kind on the part of the courtiers, I should hardly know how to answer that question. The Emperor's service demanded such entire subjection, and involved such close though trifling occupation, that the men had not time for gallantry, and the women were too much afraid of what Bonaparte might say of them to yield without very great precaution. In so cold, constrained, and conventional a society, in which no one would venture on a word or a movement more than the others, no coquetry was ever displayed, and every arrangement was made in silence, and with a promptitude which eluded observation. Another peculiarity of the time which acted as a safeguard to women was that men took no pains to please: they merely asserted the pretensions of victory without wasting time in the preliminaries of love. Thus, among the Emperor's surroundings, only passing intrigues, whose *dénoûment* both parties seemed anxious to hasten as much as possible, took place. Besides, Bonaparte desired that his Court should be grave, and he would not have permitted women to assume the slightest ascendency in it. To himself alone he reserved the right to every kind of liberty. He tolerated the misconduct of certain members of his own family, because he knew that he was powerless to restrain them, and that the attempt to do so only gave the facts additional publicity. For the same reason, he would have dissembled the anger he might have felt had his wife allowed herself any " distractions "; but at this period she no longer seemed disposed to do so. I am absolutely unacquainted with the secrets of her private life, and I always saw her exclusively occupied with the difficulties of her own position, and tremblingly apprehensive of displeasing her husband. She was entirely devoid of coquetry; her manner was perfectly modest and reserved; she never spoke to men, except to find out what was going on; and her grand subject of care and dread was the divorce which was always hanging over her head. Lastly, the women of that Court had great need to be on their guard and to take care what they did; for, whenever the Emperor was informed of anything— and he always was informed—he would invariably make the husband acquainted with the facts of the case. It is true that he interdicted any complaint or action in consequence. Thus, we all know that he has made S—— aware of certain adventures of his wife's, and so imperiously ordered him to display no anger that S——, who was always entirely submissive to him, consented to allow himself to be deceived, and ended, partly through this weak compliance, and partly through his desire to think his wife innocent, by not believing facts which were of public notoriety.

Mme. de X—— was at Fontainebleau, but the Emperor never paid her any attention; and, if the rumor that the former *liaison* between them was temporarily renewed had any truth at all in it, the revived intimacy must have been very transitory, and it did not restore any of her vanished importance to the lady.

We had, however, during our stay at Fontainebleau, the spectacle of one really ardent love-affair. Jérôme, as I have already said, had recently married the Princess Catherine, and his young wife became deeply attached to him, but very shortly after their marriage he gave her cause for jealousy. The young Princess of Baden was at this time a very fascinating person, and on very bad terms with her husband. She was coquettish, frivolous, gay, and clever, and she had a great success in society. Jérôme fell in love with her, and his passion seemed to afford her considerable amusement. She danced with him at all the balls. The Princess Catherine, who was even then too fat, did not dance, and she would remain seated, sadly contemplating the gayety of the two young people, who passed and repassed before her, quite indifferent to the pain they were inflicting on her. At length, one evening, in the midst of a fête, the good understanding between them being too plain to be mistaken, the young Queen of Westphalia was observed to turn deadly pale, and burst into tears; in another minute she had slid from her chair and swooned completely away. The ball was interrupted; she was carried into another room, the Empress and some of the ladies hastened to her aid, and we heard the Emperor address a severe rebuke to his brother, after which he retired. Jérôme, greatly frightened, went at once to his wife, took her upon his knee, and endeavored to restore her to consciousness by his caresses. The Princess, on coming to herself, wept bitterly, and seemed to be unaware that a number of persons surrounded her. I looked on at this scene in silence, deeply impressed by its strangeness, by the sight of this Jérôme—whom a succession of circumstances, all entirely independent of any merit of his own, had raised to a throne—figuring as the object of the passionate love of a real Princess, with the right to her love, and also a right to neglect her. I can not describe what I felt at seeing her sitting upon his knees, her head upon his shoulder, and receiving his kisses, while he called her by her name, " Catherine," over and over again, entreating her to calm herself, and using the familiar *tutoiement*. A few minutes later the young couple retired to their own apartment.

On the following day Bonaparte ordered his wife to speak strongly to her young niece, and I also was instructed to make her listen to reason. She received me very well, and listened to me with attention. I represented to her that she was compromising her future, and urged upon her that her duty and her interest alike bound her to live on proper terms with the Prince of Baden; that she was destined to live in other countries than France; that levity which might be tolerated in Paris would probably be resented in Germany; and that she ought most carefully to avoid giving any excuse for the spread of calumny against her. She acknowledged that she had more than once reproached herself for the imprudence of her behavior, but that there really was nothing in it except the desire to amuse herself; and she added that she was quite aware that all her present importance was due to her being Princess of Baden, for she was no longer treated at the French Court as she had been in times past. This was, in fact, quite true; for the Emperor, who had outlived his fancy for her, had changed the whole ceremonial with respect to her, and, paying no attention to the rules which he had himself laid down at the time of her marriage, no longer treated her as his adopted daughter, but accorded her merely the precedence of a Princess of the Confederation of the Rhine, which came very far after that of the Queens and Princesses of the Imperial family. Lastly, she knew that she was a cause of disturbance, and the young Prince, who did not venture to express his displeasure, manifested it only by his extreme dejection. Our conversation lasted for a long time, and she was much impressed by it and by her own reflections. When she dismissed me, it was with an embrace, and saying, " You shall see that you will be pleased with me."

That same evening there was a ball, and the Princess approached her husband, and spoke to him in an affectionate manner, while toward all others she adopted a reserved demeanor, which everybody observed. During the evening she came to me, and asked me, in the sweetest and most graceful way, whether I was pleased with her; and from that moment, until the end of the sojourn of the Court at Fontainebleau, not a single disparaging observation could possibly be made respecting her. She showed no reluctance to return to Baden; when there, she conducted herself well. She has since had children by the Prince, and lived happily with him; she also won the affection of his subjects. She is now a widow, and has only two daughters left; but she is held in high consideration by her brother-in-law, the Emperor of Russia, who has on several occasions evinced a great interest in her.

As for Jérôme, he went shortly afterward to take possession of his kingdom of Westphalia, where his conduct must have given the Princess Catherine cause more than once to shed tears: this, however, did not cure her of her love for him, for since the Revolution of 1814 she has never ceased to share his exile.

While pleasure, and especially etiquette, reigned at Fontainebleau, the poor Queen of Holland lived in the château, as much apart as she could from all; suffering much from her condition, grieving incessantly for her son, spitting blood at the least exertion, quite disconsolate, and unable even to wish for anything except rest. At this time she often said to me, with tears in her eyes: " I hold by life for my brother's sake only. When I think of him, I take pleasure in our greatness; but to myself it is a torment." The Emperor displayed invariable esteem and affection for his step-daughter; it was always to her that he intrusted the task of conveying to her mother such hints as he thought necessary. Mme. Bonaparte and her daughter were good friends, but they were too dissimilar to understand each other, and the former was conscious of a certain inferiority which affected her to some extent. And, then, Hortense had experienced such great trials that she could not deeply compassionate cares which seemed to her so light in comparison with the burden that she herself had to carry. When the Empress would tell her of a quarrel with Bonaparte about some foolish expense or some passing fit of jealousy, or would talk of her fear of divorce, her daughter would say, with a melancholy smile, " Are these things misfortunes? " The two undoubtedly loved, but I do not think they ever understood, each other.

The Emperor, who had, I believe, a much greater regard for Mme. Louis than for his brother, but who was, nevertheless, swayed to a certain extent by the spirit of the family, interfered in their domestic affairs with reluctance and caution. He had consented to keep his step-daughter with him until after her con-

finement, but he always spoke in the sense of wishing
that she should ultimately return to Holland. She
told him repeatedly that she would not go back to a
country in which her child had died, and where misery
awaited her. "My reputation is blasted," said she;
"my health is destroyed; I expect no more happiness
in this life. Banish me from your Court, if you will;
place me in a convent: I want neither throne nor
fortune. Give my mother peace, and Eugène the *éclat*
which he deserves, but let me live quietly and in
solitude." When she spoke thus, she succeeded in
touching the Emperor's feelings; he consoled and
encouraged her, promising her his aid and support,
and advising her to trust to time, but he utterly
scouted the idea of a divorce between her and Louis.
He was, no doubt, thinking of his own, and felt that
a repetition of the same incident in the family would
bring them into ridicule. Mme. Louis submitted, and
let time pass by; but she was privately quite resolved
that nothing should induce her to renew a union, at
the thought of which she shuddered. It did not seem
that the King wished for her return; on the contrary,
he was embittered against his wife, loved her no better
than she loved him, and in Holland, where he wanted
to pass for a victim, openly accused her. Many people
believed his story: kings easily find credulous ears.
One thing is certain: the husband and wife were most
unhappy, but my belief is that, with his disposition,
Louis would have made troubles for himself anywhere,
under any circumstances; whereas Hortense was eminently calculated for a calm and happy domestic life.
She did not seem to know the meaning of passion;
her mind and feelings were disposed toward profound
quiet.

The Grand Duchess of Berg applied herself to being
extremely agreeable to us all at Fontainebleau. She

could be very gay and pleasant when she was in the humor, and she could even assume an air of *bonhomie*. She lived in the château at her own expense, very luxuriously, and kept a sumptuous table. She always used gilt plate, in this outdoing the Emperor, whose silver-gilt services were used on state occasions only. She invited all the dwellers in the palace by turns, receiving them most graciously, even those whom she did not like, and appeared to be thinking of nothing but pleasure; but, nevertheless, she was not wasting her time. She frequently saw Count Metternich, the Austrian Ambassador. He was young and handsome, and he appeared to admire the sister of the Emperor. From that time forth, whether from a spirit of coquetry or from a far-sighted ambition which prompted such a measure of precaution, she began to accept the homage of the Minister with readiness. He was said to be held in high consideration and to have great influence at his Court, and he might be placed, by the course of events, in a position to serve her. Whether she had this idea beforehand or not, events justified it, and Metternich never failed her.

In addition to this, she took the influence of M. de Talleyrand into consideration, and did her best to cultivate him while keeping up as secretly as possible her relations with Fouché, who visited her with extreme precaution, in consequence of the displeasure with which the Emperor regarded any intimacy of the kind. We observed her making up to M. de Talleyrand in the drawing-room at Fontainebleau, talking to him, laughing at his *bons mots,* looking at him when she said anything remarkable, and even addressing such observations to him. M. de Talleyrand showed no reluctance, but met her advances, and then their interviews became more serious. Mme. Murat did not conceal from him that the spectacle of her brothers seated on thrones inspired her with envy, as she felt herself quite capable of wielding a scepter, and she reproached him with opposing this. M. de Talleyrand objected that Murat's abilities were not brilliant, and made some jokes at his expense, which were not resented very strongly. The Princess delivered up her husband to M. de Talleyrand's sarcasms readily enough, but she urged that she would not leave the whole charge of ruling in Murat's hands; and she gradually, by certain seductive methods, led M. de Talleyrand to be less opposed to her wishes. At the same time she also flattered and cultivated M. Maret, who, in his heavy way, repeatedly praised the intelligence and ability of the Emperor's sister to her all-powerful brother.

Bonaparte himself had a great opinion of her, and he found it supported by a variety of testimony which he knew was not concerted. He began to treat his sister with greater consideration, whereat Murat, who lost something by what she gained, thought proper to take offense and complain. Thence ensued conjugal "scenes," in which the husband insisted on resuming his right and his rank. He bullied the Princess, and she was a good deal frightened; but, partly by adroitness, partly by threats—by being now caressing, and again haughty and distant, by acting on some occasions the submissive wife, and on others the sister of the master of all—she bewildered her husband, resumed her ascendency, and proved to him that she was serving his interests in all she was doing. It seems that quarrels of the same kind occurred when she was at Naples, that Murat's vanity took umbrage, and that he was deeply hurt; but every one agrees that, if he made mistakes, it was always when he ceased to follow her advice.

I have said that the sojourn of the Court at Fontainebleau was marked by a brilliant succession of foreign visitors. With the Prince Primate we had very agreeable conversations; he was witty, had fine manners, delighted in recalling the days of his youth, when he had been acquainted in Paris with all the men of letters of the epoch. The Grand Duke of Würzburg, who remained all the time at Fontainebleau, was very good-natured, and put every one at ease with him. He was passionately fond of music, and had a voice like that of a precentor; but he enjoyed himself so much when he was allowed to take a part in a piece of concerted music that no one had the heart to spoil his harmless pleasure by smiling at his performance.

Next to the two whom I have just mentioned, the Princes of Mecklenburg were objects of special attention. They were both young, and very polite—indeed, even obliging—to everybody. They were in some awe of the Emperor; the magnificence of his Court dazzled them, and so impressed were they by his power and the splendor amid which it was displayed that they were in a state of perpetual admiration, and paid court even to the chamberlains.

The Prince of Mecklenburg-Strelitz, brother to the Queen of Prussia, was rather deaf, and found it difficult to communicate his ideas; but the Prince of Mecklenburg-Schwerin, who was also young and very good-looking, was extremely affable. His object in coming was to endeavor to obtain the removal of the French garrisons from his states. The Emperor kept him amused by fair promises; he explained his wishes to the Empress, and she listened to him with gracious patience. The unfailing kindness that distinguished Josephine, her sweet face, her lovely figure, the suave elegance of her person, were not without their effect on the Prince. We saw, or believed we saw, that he was captivated; she laughed, and was amused. Bonaparte also laughed, but he afterward took the matter ill. This change of his humor occurred on his return from a journey to Italy, which he made at the end of the autumn. The two Princes were treated with less cordiality toward the close of their stay in Paris.

I do not think Bonaparte felt any real annoyance, but he did not choose to be the subject of any kind of jest. The Prince, no doubt, retained some sort of feeling for the Empress; for she told me that, on the occasion of the divorce, the Emperor suggested to her that, if she wished to marry again, she should select the Prince of Mecklenburg as her husband, and she declined. I am not quite sure whether she did not tell me that the Prince had written to ask for her hand.

Such of the Princes as were not invited to the Emperor's table dined with the Queens, the Ministers, the Grand Marshal, or the Lady of Honor. Mme. de la Rochefoucauld had a fine suite of rooms, where the foreigners were accustomed to assemble. She received them with much grace and cordiality, and time passed there pleasantly.

How curious a spectacle is a Court! There we see the most illustrious personages of the time, men of the highest social rank; each of them is supposed to be occupied with important interests; but the silence enforced by prudence and custom reduces all conversation to complete insignificance, and it frequently happens that princes and other great men, not daring to act like men under such circumstances, assume the behavior of mere children. This reflection was forced upon my mind even more strongly at Fontainebleau than elsewhere. All these foreigners were aware that they were drawn thither by force. All were more or less vanquished or dispossessed; they had come to

entreat either favor or justice; they knew that in a
corner of the château their fate was being decided;
and all of them, assuming a similar appearance of good
spirits and entire freedom of mind, followed the chase,
and acquiesced in everything required of them. These
requirements included dancing, playing at blind-man's-
buff, and other games, so that, being thus employed,
no one need either listen or reply to them. How often
have I sat at Mme. de la Rochefoucauld's piano, playing, at her request, those Italian dances which our
lovely Italian inmate had brought into fashion!
Princes, Electors, Marshals, and chamberlains, conquerors and conquered, nobles and plebeians, passed
before me, dancing indiscriminately together; all the
quarterings of Germany contrasting with the Revolutionary swords or the decorated uniforms of our
" illustration "—an " illustration " much more real
and weighty, at that period, than that of the ancient
title-deeds and patents which the smoke of our guns
had nearly obliterated. I often reflected very seriously
on the events then taking place before my eyes, but I
took good care not to confide these thoughts to any of
my companions, and would not have ventured for the
world to smile at either them or myself. " Herein is
the wisdom of courtiers," says Sully. " It is agreed
that, though they all wear grotesque masks, none shall
ever be held to be ridiculous by the others! "

In another place he says: " A truly great man
knows how to be everything by turns and according to
circumstances—a master or an equal, a king or a
citizen. He loses nothing by thus accommodating himself in private, provided that on other occasions he
shows himself equally able to political and military
affairs; the courtier will never forget that he is in the
presence of his master."

But the Emperor was by no means disposed to adopt

these axioms, and, from design as well as from inclination, he never relaxed his kingly state. And, indeed, a usurper could, perhaps, hardly do so with impunity.

When the hour struck for us to leave our childish games in order to present ourselves before him, the expression of every face became constrained. Each of us wore a serious countenance, as we proceeded slowly and ceremoniously to the great apartments. Hand in hand, we entered the Empress's anteroom. A chamberlain announced the names. Then, sooner or later, we were received—sometimes only those who had the *entrée,* at other times everybody. We silently fell into our places, as I have said before, and listened to the few and vague phrases the Emperor addressed to each. Wearied like us, he soon called for the card-tables, to which we would sit down for appearance' sake, and shortly after the Emperor would retire. Nearly every evening he sent for M. de Talleyrand, with whom he sat up far into the night.

The state of Europe at this time was, doubtless, the ordinary subject of their conversations. The expedition of the English into Denmark had greatly angered the Emperor. He found himself totally unable to assist his ally, and this, added to the destruction of the Danish fleet and the blockade established everywhere by English ships, made him eagerly seek every opportunity of harming them. He exacted with greater urgency than ever that his allies should devote themselves to carrying out his vengeance. The Emperor of Russia, who had taken steps toward a general peace, having been repulsed by the English Government, threw himself thoroughly into the alliance with Bonaparte. On the 26th of October he made a declaration, by which he announced that he had broken off all communication with England up to the time when she should enter into a treaty of peace with us. His ambassador, Count Tolstoi, arrived at Fontainebleau shortly afterward; he was received with great honor, and included among the "members of the Journey," as it was called.

At the beginning of the month a rupture took place between ourselves and Portugal. The Prince Regent of that kingdom gave no support to those continental prohibitions which so harassed the people. Bonaparte grew angry; violent paragraphs against the house of Braganza appeared in the newspapers, the ambassadors were recalled, and our army entered Spain in order to march on Lisbon. Junot was in command. In November the Prince Regent, seeing he could offer no resistance to such an invasion, resolved to emigrate from Europe, and to go and reign in Brazil. He embarked on the 29th of November.

The Spanish Government had taken good care not to oppose the passage of the French troops through its territories. A great deal of scheming was going on at that time between the Court of Madrid and that of France. For a long time past there had been a close correspondence between the Prince of the Peace and Murat. The Prince, absolutely master of his King's mind, and the implacable enemy of the Infante Don Ferdinand, heir to the throne, had devoted himself to Bonaparte and served him zealously. He repeatedly promised Murat to satisfy him on every point, and the latter, in return, was instructed to promise him a crown (the "kingdom of the Algarves"), and efficient support from us. A crowd of schemers, both French and Spanish, were mixed up in all this. They deceived Bonaparte and Murat as to the true spirit of Spain, and they most carefully concealed that the Prince of the Peace was hated throughout the kingdom. Having gained over this Minister, we fancied ourselves masters of the country, and we fell willfully into many errors for which we have since had to pay very dearly.

M. de Talleyrand was not always consulted or believed on these points. Better informed than Murat, he often spoke to the Emperor of the true state of the case, but he was suspected of being jealous of Murat. The latter asserted that it was to injure him that Talleyrand threw a doubt upon the success for which the Prince of the Peace made himself answerable, and Bonaparte allowed himself to be deceived. It has been said that the Prince of the Peace made enormous presents to Murat; the latter flattered himself that, after betraying the Spanish Minister, and by his means causing a rupture between the King of Spain and his son, and finally bringing about the wished-for revolution, he would have the throne of Spain as his reward; and, dazzled by this prospect, he would not permit himself to doubt the truth of all the flattery that was lavished upon him.

It happened that a conspiracy was suddenly formed at Madrid against the King; Prince Ferdinand was accused in the reports that were made to King Charles, and whether there was truth in the matter, or it was only a wretched intrigue against the life of the young Prince, the charge was published widely. The King of Spain, having caused his son to be put on his trial before a tribunal, suffered himself to be disarmed by the letters which fear dictated to the Infante—letters in which he acknowledged his crime, real or pretended —and the Court was in a deplorable state of turmoil. The King's weakness was extreme; he was infatuated with his Minister, who ruled over the Queen with all the authority of a master and former lover. The Queen detested her son, to whom the Spanish nation was attached in consequence of the hatred inspired by the Prince of the Peace. There was in this situation sufficient to flatter the Emperor's hopes. If we add the state of Spain itself, the political incapacity of the effete nobility, the ignorance of the people, the influence of the clergy, the prevalence of superstition, the miserable state of the finances, the influence which the English Government was trying to gain, and the occupation of Portugal by the French, it is plain that such a condition of things threatened revolution.

I had often heard M. de Talleyrand talking to M. de Rémusat of the situation of Spain. Once, when he was conversing with us about the establishment of Bonaparte's dynasty, he said, "A Prince of the house of Bourbon is but a bad neighbor for him, and I do not think he will be able to retain him." But at this date, in 1807, M. de Talleyrand, thoroughly well informed as to the real disposition of Spain, was of opinion that, far from intriguing by means of a man of so little capacity and so ill esteemed as the Prince of the Peace, the way to propitiate the nation was by procuring his dismissal, and, if the King refused this, by declaring war, taking part with the people against him, and, according to events, either dethroning all the Bourbon family or making a compromise in Bonaparte's interest by marrying Prince Ferdinand to a lady of the Imperial house. It was toward this latter plan that M. de Talleyrand was most inclined, and he predicted even then to the Emperor that any other line of conduct would involve him in difficulties.

One of the greatest defects of Bonaparte—I do not know if I have already mentioned it—was to jumble all men together on the level of his own views, ignoring the differences in character which manners and customs produce. He looked upon the Spaniards as he looked upon any other nation. He knew that in France the progress of skepticism had led to indifference toward the priests, and he persuaded himself that, by holding forth on the other side of the Pyrenees in the philosophic language which had preceded the French Revolution, he would induce the inhabitants of Spain to join the movement which had carried away the French. "When I come," said he, "with the words *liberty, deliverance from superstition, destruction of the nobility,* inscribed upon my banner, I shall be received as I was in Italy, and all truly national classes will be with me. I shall rouse a once generous people from their interest; I shall develop them in industry which will increase their wealth, and you will see that I shall be looked upon as the liberator of Spain."

Murat carried some of this talk to the Prince of the Peace, who did not fail to assure him that such results were, in fact, highly probable. M. de Talleyrand's warnings were vain; they would not listen to him. This was the first check to his influence, and it shook it at first imperceptibly, but his enemies took advantage of it. M. Maret adopted the tone of Murat, finding that it pleased the Emperor. The Minister of Foreign Affairs, humiliated at being reduced to functions of which M. de Talleyrand took the best part from him, thought proper to adopt and hold a different opinion from his. The Emperor, thus circumvented, allowed himself to be deceived, and a few months later embarked in this perfidious and deplorable enterprise.

While we were at Fontainebleau, I saw a great deal of M. de Talleyrand. He often came to my apartment, and seemed to be amused by my observations about our Court; he also gave me his own opinions, which were entertaining. Sometimes, indeed, our conversations took a serious turn. He would come in wearied or even displeased with the Emperor, and would then dwell upon the more or less hidden vices of his character; and, thus enlightening me with truly funereal gleams, he fixed my as yet unsettled opinions, and caused me much sincere concern.

One evening, when more communicative than usual, he told me some of the anecdotes which I have related in these pages; and, as he was insisting strongly on what he called the *knavery* of our master, representing him as incapable of a single generous sentiment, he was astonished to observe that, as I listened, I was weeping silently. " What is it?" he exclaimed. " What is the matter with you?" " The matter is," I replied, " that you make me really wretched. You politicians do not want to feel any affection for those you serve. As for me, a poor woman, how do you suppose I can endure the disgust your stories inspire, and what will become of me if I must remain where I am without being able to retain a single illusion?"

" Child that you are," replied M. de Talleyrand, " must you always want to put your heart into all you do? Take my advice: do not try to feel any affection for this man, but rest assured that, with all his faults, he is at present necessary to France. He knows how to uphold the country, and each of us ought to do his best to aid him. However," added he, " if he listens to the sage advice he is receiving at present, I will not answer for anything. He is now embarked in a pitiable intrigue. Murat wants to be King of Spain; they are cajoling the Prince of the Peace, and want to gain him over, as if he had any importance in Spain! It is fine policy for the Emperor to arrive in a country with the reputation of a close alliance with a detested minister. I know well enough that he deceives that minister, and will throw him over when he perceives that he counts for nothing; but he might have spared himself this despicable perfidy.

" The Emperor will not see that he was called by his destiny to be everywhere and always *the man of the nations,* the founder of useful and possible inno-vations. To restore religion, morality, and order to France; to applaud the civilization of England while restraining her policy; to strengthen his frontiers by the Confederation of the Rhine; to make Italy a king-dom independent both of Austria and himself; to keep the Czar shut up at home, by creating the natural barrier which Poland offers—these are what ought to have been the Emperor's designs, and it was to these that each of my treaties was leading him. But ambi-tion, anger, pride, and the fools to whom he listens, often mislead him. He suspects me whenever I speak to him of ' moderation '; and, if ever he ceases to trust me, you will see he will compromise both himself and us by imprudence and folly. Nevertheless, I shall watch over him to the end. I have associated myself with the creation of his Empire; I should like it to hold together as my last work; and, so long as I can see my way to the success of my plan, I will not renounce it."

The confidence which M. de Talleyrand reposed in me pleased me very much. He soon saw how well founded it was, and that, both by taste and by habit, I brought perfect trustworthiness to our friendly inter-course. With me he enjoyed the rare pleasure of being able to speak freely, to give vent to his feelings without any misgivings, and this just when he felt inclined; for I never sought his confidences, and I always stopped where he pleased. As he was endowed with great tact, he quickly discerned my reserve and discretion, and they formed a new link between us. When this business or our duties gave us a little leisure, he would come to my rooms, where we three passed a good deal of time together. In proportion as M. de Talleyrand grew more friendly toward me, I felt more at my ease with him. I resumed the manners natural to my disposition, the little prejudice of which I have spoken melted away, and I gave myself up to a pleasure all the greater to me that it was to be found within the walls of a palace where solicitude, fear, and mediocrity hindered all real companionship between its inmates.

This intimacy, moreover, became very useful to us. M. de Talleyrand, as I have said, talked to the Emperor about us, and convinced him that we were well qualified to keep a great house, and to entertain the foreigners who would undoubtedly frequent Paris in great numbers thenceforth. Upon this the Emperor determined to give us the means of establishing ourselves in Paris in handsome style. He increased M. de Rémusat's salary on the condition that, on his return to Paris, he should set up a house; he appointed him superintendent of the Imperial theatres. M. de Talleyrand was commissioned to announce these favors to us, and I was very happy to owe them to him. This moment was the culminating point of our position, for it opened to us an agreeable prospect of ease and many opportunities of amusement. We received several congratulations, and we experienced the greatest, the only pleasure of a life passed at Court —I mean that of becoming important.

In the midst of all these things the Emperor worked incessantly, and issued decrees almost daily. Some of these were of great utility. For example, he improved the public offices in the departments, increased the salaries of the curés, and reëstablished the Sisters of Charity. He caused a *senatus consultum* to declare the judges irremovable at the end of five years. He also took care to encourage talent, especially when his own glory was the aim of its efforts. The " Triomphe de Trajan " was given at the Paris Opéra. The poem was by Esménard, and both he and the composer received presents. The work admitted of significant applications. Trajan was represented burning papers that contained the secret of a conspiracy with his own hand. This recalled what Bonaparte had done at Berlin. The triumph of Trajan was represented with magnificent pomp. The decorations were superb; the conqueror appeared in a chariot drawn by four white horses. All Paris flocked to the spectacle; the applause was unstinted, and charmed the Emperor. Soon afterward " La Vestale," the libretto by Mme. Jouy, the music by Spontini, was performed. This work, which is good as a poem, and remarkable as a musical composition, also included a " triumph," which was much applauded, and the authors received a liberal recompense.

About this time the Emperor appointed M. de Caulaincourt ambassador to St. Petersburg. He had great trouble in inducing him to accept this mission; M. de Caulaincourt was very reluctant to part from a person whom he loved, and he refused. Bonaparte at length, by dint of flattering and affectionate persuasions, brought him to consent, promising that his brilliant exile should not be prolonged beyond two years. An immense sum was granted to the ambassador for the expenses of his establishment, and his salary was fixed at from seven to eight hundred thousand francs. The Emperor charged him to eclipse all the other ambassadors in splendor. On his arrival at St. Petersburg, M. de Caulaincourt found himself at first in an embarrassing position. The crime of the death of the Duc d'Enghien had left a stain upon him. The Empress-Mother would not see him; a great number of ladies refused to receive him. The Czar received him graciously, and soon conceived a liking for him, which grew into friendship; and then the great world, following his example, treated the am-

bassador with less severity. When the Emperor
learned that a mere memory of this kind had affected
the position of his ambassador, he was astonished.
"What!" said he, "do they remember that old
story?" He made use of the same expression every
time he found that the circumstance was not forgotten,
which indeed was frequently; and he would add:
"What childishness! Nevertheless, what is done, is
done."

Prince Eugène was Arch-Chancellor of State. M.
de Talleyrand had to replace the Prince in the discharge of the functions attached to that post; so that
the former united a number of dignities in his own
person. The Emperor also began to settle great revenues on his marshals and generals, and to found those
fortunes which seemed immense, and which were
destined to disappear with himself. A man would
find himself endowed with a considerable revenue,
perhaps declared proprietor of a vast number of
leagues of territory in Poland, Hanover, or Westphalia. But there were great difficulties about realiz-
ing the revenues. The conquered countries gave them
up reluctantly, and the agents sent to collect them
found themselves in an embarrassing position. Transactions and concessions became inevitable; a portion
of the promised sums only could be had. Nevertheless, the desire of pleasing the Emperor, the taste for
luxury, an imprudent confidence in the future, induced
these men to place their expenditure on the footing of
the presumed income which they expected to receive.
Debts accumulated, embarrassments cropped up, in the
midst of this seeming opulence; the public, beholding
extreme luxury, took immense fortunes for granted;
and yet nothing real, nothing secure, was at the bottom
of all this.

We have seen most of the Marshals coming to the

Emperor, when pressed by their creditors, to solicit aid, which he granted according to his fancy, or the interests to be served by binding certain persons to himself. These demands became excessive, and perhaps the necessity for satisfying them counted for much among the motives of the subsequent wars. Marshal Ney bought a house; its purchase and the sums expended upon it cost him more than a million, and he has since complained bitterly of the difficulties into which this purchase threw him. Marshal Davoust was in the same case. The Emperor prescribed to each of his marshals the purchase of a house, which involved a great establishment and large expenditure in furniture. Rich stuffs and precious objects of all kinds adorned these dwellings; splendid services of plate glittered on the Marshals' tables. Their wives wore valuable jewels; their equipages and dress cost great sums. This display pleased Bonaparte, satisfied the shopkeepers, dazzled everybody, and, by removing individuals from their proper sphere, augmented their dependence on the Emperor—in fact, perfectly carried out his intentions.

During this time the old nobility of France lived simply, collecting its ruins together, finding itself under no particular obligations, boasting of its poverty rather than complaining, but in reality recovering its estates by degrees, and reamassing those fortunes which at the present day it enjoys. The confiscations of the National Convention were not always a misfortune for the French nobility, especially in cases where the lands were not sold. Before the Revolution that class was heavily in debt, for extravagance was one of the luxuries of our former *grands seigneurs*. The emigration and the laws of 1793, by depriving them of their estates, set them free from their creditors, and from a certain portion of the charges that weighed upon great houses; and, when they recovered their property, they profited by that liberation, which, in truth, they had bought at a high price. I remember that M. Gaudin, Minister of Finance, related once before me how the Emperor had asked him which was the most heavily taxed class in France, and he had answered that it was still that of the old nobility. Bonaparte seemed uneasy at this, and remarked, " But we must take order with that."

Under the Empire a certain number of tolerably large fortunes were made; several persons, military men especially, who had nothing formerly, found themselves in possession of ten, fifteen, or twenty thousand livres per annum, because, in proportion as they were remote from the observation of the Emperor, they could live according to their own fancy, and expend their income with order and economy. Of those immense fortunes with which the grandees of Bonaparte's Court were so gratuitously accredited, but little remains; and on this point, as on many others, the party who, on the return of the King, thought that the state might be enriched by seizing upon the treasures supposed to be amassed under the Empire, advised an arbitrary and vexatious measure which led to no result.

At this period my family had a share in the gifts of the Emperor. My brother-in-law, General Nansouty, was given the Grand Cross of the Legion of Honor. He had been First Chamberlain to the Empress, and was made First Equerry, replacing M. de Caulaincourt in his absence. He received a grant of thirty thousand francs in Hanover, and one hundred thousand francs for the purchase of a house, which might, if he chose, be of greater value, but which became inalienable by the fact of this grant. The amount went toward its price.

CHAPTER XXVII

(1807-1808.)

I THINK it well to devote a separate chapter to the events which were taking place at Fontaine-bleau in connection with the Emperor's divorce at this time. Although Bonaparte had not spoken to his wife on the subject for some years, except on occasions when he had some quarrel with her, and those occasions had become exceedingly rare in consequence of the amiability and self-control of the Empress, it is nevertheless probable that he never entirely lost sight of the idea. The death of the eldest son of Louis had deeply impressed him. His victories, while increasing his power, had also expanded his ideas of greatness; and his policy, as well as his vanity, was concerned in an alliance with a European sovereign. The rumor was at first spread that Napoleon had cast his eyes on the daughter of the King of Saxony; but an alliance with that Princess would not have procured him any valuable support for his continental authority. The King of Saxony reigned only because France authorized him to reign. Besides this, his daughter was now at least thirty years of age, and by no means handsome. Bonaparte, on his return from Tilsit, spoke of her to his wife in a manner which set Josephine's mind completely at ease.

The conferences at Tilsit very reasonably inflated Napoleon's pride. The admiration which the young Czar felt for him, the assent which he yielded to certain of his projects, especially to the dismemberment

674

of Spain, the complaisance of his new ally with regard to his wishes, all combined to lead Napoleon to
form designs of a closer alliance. No doubt he spoke
openly of these to M. de Talleyrand, but I do not
think that anything was said about them to the Czar;
the whole matter was referred to a future, more or
less near, according to circumstances.

The Emperor returned to France. On rejoining
his wife, he once more yielded to that sort of affection
with which she always inspired him, and which was
sometimes a trouble to him, because it rendered him
uncomfortable when he had deeply grieved her.

On one occasion, when he was talking with her
about the quarrels of the King of Holland and his
wife, the death of the young Napoleon, and the delicate health of the only child remaining to the
ill-assorted pair, he spoke of the obligation which
might one day be imposed upon himself of taking a
wife who should give him children. He approached
the subject with some emotion, and added: " If such
a thing should happen, Josephine, it will be for you
to help me to make the sacrifice. I shall count upon
your love to save me from all the odium of a forced
rupture. You would take the initiative, would you
not? You would enter into my position, and you
would have the courage to withdraw?" The Empress
knew her husband's character too well to facilitate
beforehand, by one imprudent word, the step which
she repelled as much as she could; so that during this
conversation, far from leading him to hope that she
would contribute to soften the effect of such a pro- '
ceeding by her conduct, she assured him that she
would obey his orders, but that she would never anti-
cipate them. She made this reply in that calm and
dignified tone which she always did well to assume
toward Bonaparte, and it was not without effect.

"Sire," said she (it should be remarked that from the beginning of his reign she always addressed him, even when they were alone, with the forms of ceremonious respect), "you are the master, and you shall decide my fate. If you should order me to quit the Tuileries, I will obey on the instant; but the least you can do is to give me that order in a positive manner. I am your wife; I have been crowned by you in the presence of the Pope. Such honors, at least, demand that they should not be voluntarily renounced. If you divorce me, all France shall know that it is you who send me away, and shall be ignorant neither of my obedience nor of my profound grief." This manner of replying, which was always the same, did not annoy the Emperor, and even seemed occasionally to touch him; for, when on several occasions he recurred to the subject, he frequently wept, and was genuinely agitated by contending feelings.

Mme. Bonaparte, who retained her self-control so admirably while in his presence, gave way to excessive emotion on relating to me all that had passed. Sometimes she wept bitterly; at other moments she would dwell on the ingratitude of such conduct. She recalled to mind that when she married Bonaparte he had considered himself highly honored by her alliance, and she asserted that it was an odious deed to repudiate her in his greatness, after she had consented to share his low fortunes. Sometimes she became so excited that she even yielded to apprehensions concerning her personal safety. "I will never give in to him; I will demean myself entirely as his victim; but, if I stand too resolutely in his way, who can tell of what he would be capable, or whether he would resist the necessity of getting rid of me!" When she spoke thus, I made every effort to calm her imagination, which no doubt led her too far. Whatever I might think of the facility with which Bonaparte yielded to political necessity, I did not believe for a moment that he would be capable of conceiving and executing the black designs of which she then suspected him. But he had acted in such a way on several occasions, and he had used such language, that it was not wonderful that misery such as hers should inspire her with suspicions of the sort. And, although I solemnly declare that in my conscience I did not believe he had ever contemplated such a means of getting out of his difficulty, I was unable to make any other reply to the Empress than, " Madame, be quite sure that he is not capable of going so far."

For my own part, I was astonished that a woman so completely disenchanted concerning her husband, tortured by a dreadful suspicion, detached from every affection, and indifferent to fame, should hold so strongly to the enjoyment of such a precarious royalty; but, seeing that nothing availed to disgust her with it, I contented myself with entreating her, as I had always done, to keep silence, and to maintain her calm, sorrowful, but determined attitude in the presence of the Emperor, for I knew well that by these means only could she turn aside or delay the storm. He knew that his wife was generally beloved. Day by day public opinion was becoming alienated from him, and he was afraid of incensing it.

When the Empress confided her sorrows to her daughter, she did not, as I have already said, find her very capable of understanding her. Since the death of her child, the sorrows of vanity had appeared more than ever inexplicable to Queen Hortense, and her sole answer to her mother always was, " How can any one regret a throne? "

Mme. de la Rochefoucauld, to whom Mme. Bonaparte also spoke, was, as I have said, somewhat frivolous, and passed over everything as lightly as she could. The burden of the Empress's confidence fell, therefore, upon me. The Emperor was aware of the fact, but did not at that time resent it to me. I know he even said to M. de Talleyrand, "It must be acknowledged that the Empress is well advised." When his passions gave his intellect a chance, he could estimate fairly and wisely enough conduct which embarrassed him, provided it only embarrassed him a little, because he always knew that when he chose he could surmount the light obstacles that were opposed to him; and he allowed one to play one's own cards, because he knew that in the end he should none the less surely win the game.

Meanwhile we went to Fontainebleau, and the fêtes, the presence of foreign princes, and above all the drama which Bonaparte was preparing for Spain, diverted his mind from the question of the divorce, and at first everything went smoothly enough.

My friendship with Talleyrand became confirmed, and the Empress was rejoiced at this, because she hoped that when occasion arose it would be useful, or at least convenient, to herself. I have said that just then the sovereigns of the duchy of Berg and Fouché the Minister of Police were scheming in concert. Mme. Murat always contrived to quarrel with anybody who was about the Empress, and spared no pains for that end. Talleyrand and Fouché were jealous and distrustful of each other, and at this period the great importance of the former gave umbrage to all.

About two or three weeks before the end of our sojourn at Fontainebleau the Minister of Police arrived one morning. He remained a long time in the Emperor's cabinet, and was afterward invited to dine with him, an honor rarely accorded to any one.

During dinner Bonaparte was in high spirits. Some sort of amusement, I forget what, filled up the evening. Toward midnight, when every one had retired, one of the Empress's attendants knocked at my door. My maid told him I had gone to bed. The man replied that I need not get up, but that the Empress begged my husband would come to her at once.

M. de Rémusat, who had not yet left my room, immediately repaired to the Empress's apartment. He found her half undressed, pale, and in great agitation. She sent away her women, and, exclaiming that she was lost, placed in my husband's hands a long letter, written upon large paper, and signed by Fouché himself. In this letter Fouché began by protesting that his former devotion to her was quite unaltered, and assuring her that it was in consequence of that sentiment he ventured to ask her to consider her position and the Emperor's. He represented the Emperor as all-powerful, depicted him at the height of his glory, sovereign master of France, but accountable to that same France for the present and for the future which were confided to him. "We must not disguise from ourselves, Madame," said he, "that the political future of France is compromised by the want of an heir to the Emperor. As Minister of Police, I am placed in a position to judge of public opinion, and I know that the succession to such an empire gives rise to public uneasiness. Picture to yourself what would be the strength of his Majesty's throne to-day, if it were supported by the existence of a son." This advantage was dwelt upon skillfully and at length, as indeed it might well be. Fouché then spoke of the opposition between the conjugal affection of the Emperor and his policy. He foresaw that he would never bring himself to prescribe so grievous a sacrifice, and he therefore ventured to advise Mme.

Bonaparte to make a courageous effort on her own part, to resign herself, to immolate herself for France; and he drew a very pathetic picture of the *éclat* which such an action would cast upon her now and in the future. Lastly, the letter ended with a declaration that the Emperor was quite ignorant of its having been written, that the writer knew it would be displeasing to him, and earnestly entreated the Empress to keep it a profound secret.

We may easily imagine all the oratorical phrases that adorned this letter, which had every appearance of having been written with care and reflection. The first thought of M. de Rémusat was that Fouché had not attempted such a proceeding without an understanding with the Emperor; he, however, took good care not to indicate this conviction to the Empress, who was making visible efforts to repel the same suspicions on her own part, while her tears and agitation proved that she dared not count upon the Emperor on this occasion. " What shall I do? " asked she. " How shall I avert this storm? " " Madame," said M. de Rémusat, " I strongly advise you to go this instant to the Emperor's room, if he has not yet retired, or, at all events, to go to him very early to-morrow. Remember that you must seem to have consulted nobody. Make him read that letter; watch him if you can, but at any rate show him that you are angry at this side-winded advice, and declare to him anew that you will only obey positive orders pronounced by himself."

The Empress adopted this advice. She begged my husband to tell M. de Talleyrand all that had occurred, and to report to her what he said; then, as it was late, she put off her conversation with the Emperor until next morning. When she showed Bonaparte the letter, he affected to be extremely angry, and declared that he was totally ignorant of this proceeding; that Fouché had exhibited quite uncalled-for zeal, and that, if he had not set out for Paris, he should have been severely reprimanded. The Emperor added that he would punish the Minister of Police if the Empress wished it, and would even go so far as to remove him from the Ministry, should she exact such a reparation. He accompanied this declaration with many caresses; but his manner did not convince the Empress, who told me the same day that she was aware he was greatly embarrassed during this explanation.

In the mean time the matter was discussed between my husband and myself. We saw very clearly that Fouché had been induced to take this step by a superior order, and we said to each other that, if the Emperor was seriously thinking of divorce, it was exceedingly unlikely Talleyrand would be opposed to the step. What was our surprise to find that at this moment he was so! Talleyrand listened to us very attentively, and like a man who was totally unaware of what had happened. He considered Fouché's letter improper and ridiculous, and added that the idea of the divorce appeared to him utterly mistaken. He took my view, and that vehemently; advised that the Empress should take a very high tone with the Minister of Police, and should tell him that he had no business to interfere in such a matter. He added that, if the affair were ever arranged, it ought to be settled without any go-between. The Empress was delighted with this advice, and she and I together composed a cold and dignified reply to Fouché's letter. Talleyrand read and approved of this, and desired us to show it to the Emperor, who, he said, would not venture to find fault with it. He was right; and Bonaparte, who had not yet made up his mind, con-

tinued to play the same part, to exhibit increasing
anger, to indulge in violent threats, and to declare
with so much iteration that he would dismiss the Minister of Police if she wished it, that the Empress,
tranquillized by degrees and deceived anew, ceased to
feel any resentment toward Fouché, whom she no
longer feared, and refused the offered reparation,
telling her husband that she would not on any account
have him deprive himself of the services of a man
who was useful to him, and that it would be enough
if he " scolded him well."

Fouché came back to Fontainebleau a few days
afterward. In Mme. Bonaparte's presence her husband treated him with scrupulous coldness; but the
Minister did not seem to mind that in the least, which
confirmed me in my belief that the whole thing had
been arranged. He repeated to the Empress all that
he had written. The Emperor told his wife that he
went over precisely the same ground with him. " It
is an excess of zeal," said he. " We must not be
angry with him for it; it is quite enough that we are
determined to reject his advice, and you know well
that I could not live without you." Bonaparte repeated these same words to his wife day and night.
He was much more with her than he had recently
been, was really agitated, would take her in his arms
and protest the most passionate love; and in these
scenes, which were at first, as I believe, acted for a
purpose, he involuntarily became quite carried away,
and ended by experiencing sincere emotion.

All that he said was confided to me, and I repeated
it to Talleyrand, who dictated the line of conduct to
be observed. His advice steadily tended to avert the
divorce, and he guided Mme. Bonaparte very well. I
could not refrain from letting him see that I was
somewhat astonished he should oppose a project which

had certainly a reasonable political aspect, and that he should take so much interest in the purely domestic side of the affair. He replied that it was not altogether so domestic as I imagined. "There is nobody," he said, "in the palace who ought not to desire that this woman should remain with Bonaparte. She is gentle and good, she has the art of keeping him quiet, and she enters quite sufficiently into everybody's position. She is a refuge for us on a thousand occasions. If a Princess were to come here, we should find the Emperor break with all the Court, and we should all be crushed."

Giving me these reasons, Talleyrand convinced me that he was speaking sincerely; but yet he was not telling me all his secret, for, while he repeated to me that we must all unite to avert the divorce, he frequently asked me what would become of me if by any chance the Emperor carried the plan into effect. I replied that without hesitation I should share the fate of my Empress. "But," said he, "do you love her well enough to do that?" "Certainly," I replied, "I am attached to her; nevertheless, as I know her well, as I know her to be frivolous and hardly capable of a steady affection, it would not be the dictates of my heart that I should follow on this occasion, so much as those of propriety. I came to this Court through Mme. Bonaparte's influence; I have always passed in the eyes of the world as her intimate friend; I have had the burden and the confidence of that friendship; and, although she has been too much taken up with her own position to care much about me, although she has thrown me aside and taken me up again, as it suited her convenience, the public, who can not enter into the secrets of our mutual relations, and to whom I shall not confide them, would, I am sure, be astonished if I did not share her exile."

"But," said Talleyrand, "this would gratuitously put you into a position which might be very unpleasant for yourself and your husband, and would perhaps separate you. You would have to encounter many small difficulties, for which assuredly she would not pay you." "I know that as well as you," said I. "She is changeable and even whimsical. I can foresee that in such a case she would be at first very grateful for my devotion, then she would get used to it, and finally she would think no more about it. But her character shall not prevent me from acting in accordance with my own, and I will do what seems to be my duty without expecting the smallest reward."

In fact, when speaking, about this time, of the chances of the divorce, I promised the Empress that I would leave the Court if she ever left it. She seemed deeply touched by this declaration, which I made with tears and sincere emotion. Assuredly she ought to have resisted the suspicions which she afterward conceived against me, and of which I shall give an account in due time. I placed only one restriction upon the promise which I made: "I will not be Lady-in-Waiting to another Empress. If you retire into some country place, I will follow you, being always happy to share your solitude; and I will never leave you, except you should quit France."

No one could tell what was really passing in the Emperor's mind, and he had once said to his wife: "If you quit me, I would not have you lose state or rank by it; you shall reign somewhere, perhaps even at Rome." It is to be remarked that when he was thus speaking the Pope was in that same Rome, and that there was no reason to suppose he would have to leave the city. But the most serious events seemed perfectly simple to Napoleon; and from time to time, if one listened attentively, a word dropped here and there sufficed to indicate the succession of projects which he was forming.

M. de Rémusat thought with me respecting my proper line of conduct. He was perfectly alive to the inconvenience which might possibly result from it; but that consideration did not deter him, and he repeated to the Empress that she might count upon my fidelity in her misfortunes, should they ever fall upon her. We shall see that she was afterward induced to place no reliance upon a promise which was given with perfect sincerity.

It was at this period, and upon the subject of the divorce, that we had certain conversations with Mme. de la Rochefoucauld, which brought about the explanations to which I have previously referred, and that M. de Rémusat became acquainted with what had passed respecting him on his return from the Prussian campaign. These new lights added considerably to the painful impression of our successive discoveries relating to the Emperor's character.

I will now tell what I learned of the motives which induced Talleyrand and the Minister of Police to act in the manner which I have just recorded. I have said that Fouché, who was fascinated by Mme. Murat, was forced in consequence to break with what was called " the party of the Beauharnais." I do not know whether he really wished to do so; but, when a man mixes himself up in certain intrigues in which women play a part, he can not tell at what point he may be able to stop, because there are so many little sayings, little denunciations, and little treacheries, that in the end he gets lost among them. Mme. Murat, who detested her sister-in-law, and did all in her power to drive her off the throne, longed for an alliance with a European Princess for her own pride's sake, and plied the Emperor with flattery on this point. Fouché thought that it would be useful to the new dynasty to be supported by a direct heir. He knew Bonaparte too well not to foresee that, sooner or later, policy would take precedence of every other consideration with him. He was afraid that he himself might not be employed in this affair, which seemed to be entirely in Talleyrand's line, and he was anxious to deprive him of the honor and the advantages of such a negotiation. With this intention he broke the ice with the Emperor, and spoke to him on the important point. Finding him disposed to entertain it, he dwelt upon all the motives which were so easy to urge, and ultimately succeeded in extracting from Bonaparte an order, or at least a proposal, that he should play the part of mediator between the Emperor and the Empress in all negotiations on the point. He went further; he made public opinion declare itself! With the assistance of the police, he got speeches made on the subject of the divorce at several places of general assembly in Paris. The people began to discuss in the cafés the necessity of the Emperor's having an heir. These utterances, which were prompted by Fouché, were reported by him and the rest of the police, who gave an exact account of all that took place; and the Emperor believed that the public were far more occupied with this subject than they really were.

On his return from Fontainebleau, Fouché told the Emperor that there was great excitement in Paris, and that the populace might possibly assemble under his windows and ask him to contract another marriage. The Emperor was at first taken with this idea, from which M. de Talleyrand adroitly contrived to turn him aside. Not that the latter had really any repugnance to the divorce, but he wanted it to be effected in his own way, at his own time, and with great utility and dignity. He was quick to perceive that the zeal of Fouché tended to deprive him of the palm, and he could not endure that any other scheme should take the place of his on his own ground.

France had formed a close alliance with Russia, but M. de Talleyrand, who was very able in the use he made of his knowledge of the actual state of Europe, thought it necessary to keep a close watch on Austria, and had already come to the conclusion that another tie between us and that Power would be the most useful move for us. Besides, he knew that the Empress-Mother of Russia did not share the Czar's admiration for Napoleon, and that she would refuse to give us one of her daughters for an Empress. Again, it was possible that a hurried divorce might not be quickly followed by a marriage, and the Emperor would in that case be placed in a disagreeable position. The contest which might break out at any moment in Spain would rouse the attention of Europe, and it was not a moment to engage ourselves in two enterprises, both of which would demand grave deliberation.

These were, no doubt, the considerations which led M. de Talleyrand to thwart Fouché, and to espouse the interests of Mme. Bonaparte for the time being. Neither she nor I was clever enough to see through his motives at the time, and it was not until afterward that I became aware of them. M. de Rémusat had not so much confidence in M. de Talleyrand's apparent acquiescence in what we desired, but he was of opinion that we might turn it to account; so that, with various intentions, we were all pursuing the same course.

While the Emperor was in Paris, in the short interval between his journey to Italy and his journey to Bayonne, while Fouché was constantly plying him with what he stated to be popular opinions, M. de Talleyrand seized an opportunity of showing him that in this instance the Minister of Police was misleading him. "Fouché," he said to the Emperor, "is, and always will be, a revolutionist. Look well to it, and you will see that he would lead you, by factious means, to an act that should only be accomplished with the parade and pomp befitting a monarch. He wishes that a mob, collected by his orders, should come and vociferously demand of you an heir, just as they forced concessions from Louis XVI., who was never able to refuse them. When you have accustomed the people to meddle with your affairs after this fashion, how do you know that it will not occur to them to do so again, and how can you tell what they may subsequently demand of you? And, after all, no one will be duped by these gatherings, while you will be accused of having got them up." The Emperor was impressed by these observations, and imposed silence upon Fouché.

From that moment the question of the divorce was no longer discussed in the cafés, and the "national wish" remained unexpressed. The effect on the Emperor of this silence was favorable to his wife, and she felt somewhat reassured. He continued, however, to show great agitation at times, and their intercourse was constrained and often interrupted by long fits of silence; after which he would return to the subject, dwelling upon the disadvantage of not having a direct posterity on which to found his dynasty, and saying that he did not know what to do. He suffered much from conflicting feelings at this time.

He was particularly confidential with M. de Talleyrand, who repeated to me a portion of their conversations. "In separating myself from my wife," Bonaparte said, "I renounce all the charm which her presence gives to my home-life. I should have to study the tastes and habits of a young wife. This one accommodates herself to everything; she understands me perfectly, and I should be making her an ungrateful return for all she has done for me. The people care little for me as it is, and then it would be much worse. She is a link between me and them, and especially between me and a certain party in Paris, which I should have to give up." After regrets of this kind, he would dwell upon the reasons which made it a state question; and M. de Talleyrand told my husband it was his conviction that this creditable hesitation would one day give way before political considerations—that the divorce might be delayed, but that it was vain to hope that it could be ultimately avoided. He concluded by saying that we might rely upon it he had no influence in the matter, and that the Empress would do well to adhere to the course which she had adopted.

M. de Rémusat and I agreed that we would say nothing to the Empress about the first part of this statement, which would have so much increased her apprehensions as perhaps to betray her into some false step; and we saw no use in inspiring her with distrust of M. de Talleyrand, who had at that time no interest in injuring her, but who might have had such an interest had she allowed an imprudent word to escape her. For my part, I resolved to await the future without trying to foresee it, and to be guided by the prudence and dignity which should always distinguish those who hold a prominent position, and who are surrounded by a hundred eyes that watch, and a hundred mouths ready to repeat all they say. It was at this period that the Emperor said to M. de Talleyrand, " The Empress is well advised."

Shortly before his departure for Bayonne, another

explanation on the subject of the divorce took place. This was the last at this time, and it showed that the Emperor, willful as he was, was yet capricious in his moods, and that he was sometimes carried away by genuine feeling.

M. de Talleyrand, coming out of the Emperor's cabinet one morning, met M. de Rémusat, and said to him, as they walked toward his carriage: "I think your wife will have to meet the trial that she fears sooner than she anticipates. The Emperor is again most eager on the subject of a divorce; he has spoken to me of it as of a thing almost decided upon, and we shall all do well to take it as such, and not vainly oppose it." My husband repeated these words to me; they caused me great pain. There was to be a reception at Court that evening. I had just lost my mother, and did not go into society. M. de Rémusat returned to the palace to superintend the play that was to be performed. The apartments were crowded. Princes, ambassadors, and courtiers were all assembled, and at length the order was given to begin the play, without waiting for their Majesties, who would not appear. The fête went off badly, and the guests dispersed as soon as they could.

M. de Talleyrand and M. de Rémusat, before leaving the palace, went to the private apartments of the Emperor, where they were told that he had retired with his wife at eight o'clock, that he had ordered the door to be closed, and that he should not be disturbed until the next day. M. de Talleyrand went away in dudgeon. "What a devil of a man!" said he. "How he yields to sudden impulses, as if he did not really know what he wanted! Why can he not come to some decision, and cease making us the puppets of his moods, not knowing what attitude we are to assume toward him?"

The Empress received my husband the next day, and told him that at six o'clock she had joined the Emperor at dinner; that he was then sad and silent; that afterward she had left him to dress for the evening, and while she was preparing for the reception an attendant came to fetch her, saying that the Emperor was ill. She found him suffering from severe spasms, and in a highly nervous state. On seeing her, he burst into tears, and, drawing her toward the bed on which he had thrown himself, without taking heed of her elegant attire, he folded her in his arms, repeating again and again, " My poor Josephine, I can not leave you." She added that his state inspired her with more compassion than tenderness, and that she kept saying to him time after time: " Sire, be calm; make up your mind what you really want to do, and let us have an end of these scenes." Her words seemed only to add to his excitement, which became so excessive that she advised him to give up the idea of appearing in public, and to go to bed. He consented to this, but only on condition that she would remain with him; and she was obliged at once to undress and to share that bed, which, she said, he literally bathed with his tears, repeating constantly, " They harass me, they torment me, they make me miserable!" and the night was thus passed in alternate fits of tenderness and intervals of agitated sleep. After this evening he gained command over himself, and never again gave way to such vehement emotion.

The Empress alternated between hope and fear. She placed no reliance on these pathetic scenes, and declared that Bonaparte passed too quickly from tender protestations to quarreling with her about flirtations of which he accused her, or to other subjects of complaint; that he wanted to break down her resistance, to make her ill, or perhaps even worse—for, as

I have already said, her imagination pictured every extreme. Sometimes she would say that he was trying to disgust her with him by incessantly tormenting her. It is true that, either intentionally or because of his own agitation, he kept her in a constant state of unrest, which affected her health.

Fouché talked openly of the divorce, to the Empress, to me, and to every one, saying that he might be dismissed, but that he should not be prevented from offering good advice. M. de Talleyrand listened to him in disdainful silence, and consented to being considered by the public to be opposed to the divorce. Bonaparte saw through all this, without blaming the conduct of the one or the other, or, indeed, that of any one.

The Court observed even stricter silence than usual, for there was no positive indication as to which of these great personages it would be prudent to side with.

In the midst of these troubles the tragic event in Spain took place, and the divorce question was for a time laid aside.

CHAPTER XXVIII
(1807-1808.)

AT or about this time M. Molé was nominated Prefect of the Côte-d'Or. The Emperor, who had remarked his abilities on many occasions, had to a certain extent adopted him, and in his own mind decided on his promotion. He was more and more pleased by his conversations with him, in which he brought out all that was most remarkable in Molé's mind, and Bonaparte knew how to attract the sympathies of youth. M. Molé showed some dislike to the idea of leaving Paris, where he was pleasantly settled with his family. " We must not hurt people's feelings," the Emperor said to him, " by sudden promotions. Besides, some experience in the affairs of administration will be very useful to you. I will only keep you one year at Dijon, and then you shall return, and you will have reason to be pleased with me." He kept his word to M. Molé.

The sojourn of the Court at Fontainebleau came to an end toward the middle of November, at which there was general satisfaction; for every one was tired of the fêtes, and the restraint which they occasioned. Most of the foreign princes returned to their homes, dazzled by our magnificence, which had been " administered," if I may be permitted the expression, with the most perfect order; for the Emperor would not have allowed any other system in the management of his private affairs. He was very much pleased when M. de Rémusat asked of him only 150,-

ooo francs for the expenses incurred for the fêtes and plays; and certainly, if this sum be considered relatively to the results produced, it is evident that minute attention must have been paid to every detail of the expenditure. The Emperor, who wished to be informed of all these details, referred on this occasion to the sum that it formerly cost the Court of France to make such journeys, and he drew the comparison with a complacency justified by the facts. The household was strictly administered by the Grand Marshal, and the accounts were kept and paid with the utmost regularity.

Duroc acquitted himself remarkably well of this charge, but with a harshness of manner which was doubtless inspired by his master's severity. When the Emperor scolded, the consequences were felt by every servant in the palace, in the rude treatment to which they were subjected. Discipline was strict, and punishments were severe; vigilance was never relaxed, so that each one was always to be found at his post, and everything was done with silent regularity. Every abuse was guarded against, and all wages were paid punctually and in advance. In the offices, and in the kitchens, a plate of soup or a glass of *eau sucrée* was not given out without the authorization of the Marshal, who was invariably informed of all that happened in the palace. His discretion never failed, and he repeated whatever occurred to the Emperor only.

The Emperor left Fontainebleau to make a short tour in Italy. He wished to visit Milan again, to show himself in Venice, and to communicate with his brother Joseph; and I believe he wished to arrive, above all, at a decision with regard to the kingdom of Italy—a decision by which he hoped to reassure Europe. He also intended to signify to the Queen of Etruria, daughter of the King of Spain, that she must quit her kingdom. As he was secretly preparing to invade Spain, he admitted that the idea of the union of the crowns of France and Italy had alarmed Europe. In naming Eugène as successor to the throne of Italy, he wished it to be understood that this union was not to last for ever, and believed that the concession which did not dispossess him would be received, and the power of his successor be thus limited.

Murat, who had every interest in keeping up daily communication with his brother-in-law, obtained permission to accompany him in this little tour, to the great annoyance of M. de Talleyrand, who foresaw that advantage would be taken of his absence to frustrate his plans.

The Emperor left Fontainebleau on the 10th of November, and the Empress returned to Paris. The Prince Primate remained there some time longer, as well as the Princes of Mecklenburg. They came to the Tuileries every evening, where they played or conversed, and listened to the music.

The Empress talked more with the Prince of Mecklenburg-Schwerin than with the others: this was remarked upon, as I have mentioned before. Most people laughed, and attached so little importance to it as even to joke with the Empress herself about it. Others viewed the subject more seriously, and wrote to the Emperor; and on his return he rebuked her severely. Although accustomed to gratify all his own fancies, he was very severe on those of others.

During this journey, a vaudeville was represented at one of the small theatres with such success that every one wished to see it, Mme. Bonaparte as well as others. She requested M. de Rémusat to get her a box, and in a simple dress, and in a carriage without arms, she went privately to the theatre, accompanied by some ladies and the two Princes of Mecklenburg. This was immediately reported at Milan, and the Emperor wrote a furious letter to his wife, and on his return reproached her for a want of dignity. I even remember that, in his annoyance, he reminded her that the last Queen of France had done herself the greatest harm by forgetting what was due to her rank, and indulging in frivolities of a similar kind.

During his absence the Imperial Guard made a triumphal entry into Paris. The Prefect received them with a speech, and many fêtes were given in their honor.

As I have said elsewhere, the Sisters of Charity were reëstablished. They assembled, by order of the Minister of the Interior, in the apartments of Mme. Mère, where he distributed medals to them. The Emperor wished his mother to be at the head of every charitable institution, but there was nothing in her manner to make her popular, and she acquitted herself of the task imposed on her without ability or taste.

The Emperor appeared to be satisfied with the administration of affairs in Italy, and traveled from one end of the country to the other. He went to Venice, where he was joined by his brother Joseph, and by the King and Queen of Bavaria. Mme. Bacciochi went to solicit an extension of her estates.

During this time Russia broke completely with England. A part of our army, still in the north of Germany, held the King of Sweden in check. Bernadotte was at Hamburg in communication with the malcontent Swedes, and he acquired a personal reputation which he carefully maintained. He expended large sums in bribes. It is not likely that he could have had an idea at that time of what was afterward to happen; but his ambition, as yet vague, led him to turn every happy chance that befell him to account, and at that period one might, in certain situations, undertake everything and hope for anything.

The Prince of Brazil left Lisbon on the 29th of November, and General Junot entered that city a few days afterward with our army, declaring, according to custom, that we came to free the Portuguese from the yoke of the English.

Toward the end of the month the Emperor, having assembled the Corps Législatif at Milan, declared that he solemnly adopted Eugène, who became heir to the crown of Italy should the Emperor have no male issue. At the same time he endowed him with the title of Prince of Venice, and he created the little princess, who was just born, Princess of Bologna. He then returned to Paris, where he arrived on the 1st of January, 1808.

I was engrossed just then by melancholy duties. On my return from Fontainebleau, I had found my mother ill. She continued for some time in a languid state without actually causing me anxiety. Notwithstanding her illness, she evinced great satisfaction at the improvement that had taken place in our position, and I began during the first days of her illness to put our establishment on the footing which the Emperor desired. Toward the end of December my mother's state became so alarming, that we thought of nothing but the care she needed, and our house was closed to visitors. Three weeks afterward we had the misfortune to lose her, and one of the most tender ties of my life, one of its dearest enjoyments, was lost to me for ever. My mother was in every way a remarkable person. She was possessed of great talent and judgment, which were much appreciated in society. She was useful and agreeable to us at every moment of the day. She was universally regretted, and her loss overwhelmed us with grief. My husband wept for her like a son; we were pitied even at Court, because even there her worth was appreciated. The Emperor expressed himself kindly on hearing of our calamity, and spoke of it in suitable terms to M. de Rémusat when he saw him; but, as I have already said, the life of retirement, into which good taste, as well as my sorrow, caused us to withdraw, was opposed to his views, and two or three months afterward he deprived us of that increase to our income which he had granted us that we might entertain in good style, on the pretext that it was now useless to us. Thus we were left encumbered with debts which he had obliged us to contract.

I passed that winter very sorrowfully. I wept bitterly for my mother; I was separated from my eldest son, whom we had placed at college, so that he might cultivate those talents for which he has since been remarkable, and which were even then noticeable; my health was bad, and my spirits were depressed. My society could not have been very amusing to M. de Talleyrand, yet he did not forsake me in my sadness. He was, on the contrary, one of the most assiduous and attentive of our visitors. He had known my mother formerly, and he liked to speak of her, and to listen to all my recollections of her. In the depth of my sorrow I lost all my little ambition to appear clever, and I did not endeavor to check my tears in his presence.

When alone with my husband and me, he showed no impatience with my grief nor with the tenderness of M. de Rémusat's efforts to console me. It seems to me now, on thinking of it, that he observed us with curiosity. His own life had been devoid of natural affections, and ours was a novel spectacle to him, which touched him not a little. He then learned for the first time what mutual love, united with moral principle, can do to give comfort and courage amid the trials of life. That which he witnessed in my house appeared to rest him after what passed elsewhere, and colored even his recollections, for more than once at this time he spoke to me of himself with regret, and, I might almost say, with disgust. We responded to his affection with gratitude which sprang from our hearts. He came to see us more and more frequently, and he remained a long time at each visit. We no longer jested at or ridiculed others. Restored to my better self, I let him see to the depths of a sensitive nature, which domestic happiness had rendered sympathetic. In my sorrow and deep melancholy, and in my ignorance of all that was taking place outside, I led him into regions until then unknown to him; their discovery seemed to give him pleasure, and by degrees I might say what I chose to him. He even allowed me to censure and judge him severely, which I occasionally did. He never grew angry at my sincerity; and from this time there existed between us a friendship very precious to both. When I succeeded in awakening any emotion in him, I was as much elated as if I had gained a victory; and he was grateful to me for having stirred his soul, which had fallen asleep from habit or through indifference.

On one occasion, when, impatient at his inconsistency, I went so far as to say, " Good heavens! what a pity it is that you have taken such pains to spoil yourself, for I can not help believing that the real *you* is better than you are," he smiled and said: " Our entire life is influenced by the manner in which we pass the early years of it; and, were I to tell you how my youth was spent, you would cease to wonder at many things that now astonish you."

Then he told me that, being lame and the eldest of his family, and having by this accident disappointed the hopes and prevented the fulfillment of that custom which before the Revolution destined the eldest son of every noble family to a military career, he had been discarded from his home, and sent to live with an old aunt in one of the provinces. Without returning to his parents' roof, he had then been placed in a seminary, and it was intimated to him that he was to become an ecclesiastic—a profession for which he had not the slightest taste. During the years which he passed at Saint Sulpice, he was almost always obliged to stay in his room and alone, his infirmity rarely permitting him to remain long standing, or to take part in the active amusements of the young. He then fell into a deep melancholy, formed a low opinion of social life, and revolted against the priestly state, to which he had been condemned in spite of himself. He held that he was not bound scrupulously to observe the duties that had been imposed upon him without his consent. He added that he felt a profound disgust to the world, and anger at its prejudices, and that he only avoided falling into despair by encouraging in himself complete indifference toward all men and all things. When at length he returned to his parents, he was received by them with the greatest coldness, and as if he were displeasing in their sight, and he never had a word of consolation or kindness addressed to him.

" You see," he would say to me, " that I must either have died of grief, or become callous to all that must ever be wanting in my life. I chose the latter alternative, and I am now willing to admit to you that I was wrong. It would have been better to have resigned myself to suffer, and to have kept alive the faculty of feeling with acuteness; for this cold-heartedness, with which you reproach me, has often disgusted me with myself. I have not loved others enough, but I have loved myself no better. I have never taken sufficient interest in myself.

" On one occasion I was drawn out of this indifference by my love for the Princess Charlotte de Montmorency. She was much attached to me, and I rebelled more than ever against the obstacle which prevented my marrying her.

" I made several efforts to get a dispensation from vows that were odious to me. I think I should have succeeded if the Revolution, which then broke out, had not prevented the Pope from granting me what I wished. You will easily understand that, in the disposition of my mind, I hailed that Revolution with eagerness. It attacked the principles and the customs of which I had been a victim; it seemed to me just what I wanted to break my chains, and so in every way it was pleasing to me. I espoused it readily, and, since then, events have disposed of me."

When M. de Talleyrand spoke to me in this manner, I pitied him with my whole heart, because I fully understood the sad influence which his unhappy youth had exercised over all the rest of his life; but I felt persuaded, too, that a more vigorous character might have avoided falling into such errors, and I frankly deplored to him that he should have so stained his life.

A most fatal indifference to good and evil, right and wrong, formed the basis of M. de Talleyrand's nature; but we must do him the justice to admit that he never sought to make a principle of what was immoral. He is aware of the worth of high principles in others; he praises it, holds it in esteem, and never seeks to corrupt it. It appears to me that he even dwells on it with pleasure. He has not, like

Bonaparte, the fatal idea that virtue has no existence, and that the appearance of it is only a trick or an affectation the more. I have often heard him praise actions which were a severe criticism of his own. His conversation is never immoral or irreligious; he respects good priests, and applauds them; there is in his heart both goodness and justice; but he does not apply to himself the rule by which he judges others. He regards himself as a being apart; all things are different for him. He has long been *blasé* on every point, and he seeks for excitement as a fastidious palate seeks pungent food. All serious reflections applied to moral or natural sentiments are distasteful to him, because they lead him into a train of thought which he fears, and from which he tries to escape by a jest or a sarcasm. A combination of circumstances has surrounded him with persons of light or depraved character, who have encouraged him in a thousand follies. These people are congenial to him, because they draw him away from his own thoughts; but they can not save him from profound weariness, and from that he seeks refuge in great affairs. These affairs do not fatigue him, because he rarely enters into them completely; indeed, he seldom enters heart and soul into anything. His intellect is lofty, and often just; he perceives correctly; but he has a certain carelessness and desultoriness about him, which make him disappoint one's hopes. He pleases much, but satisfies never, and at last inspires one with a sort of pity, which leads, if one sees much of him, to real affection.

I believe that our intimacy did him good while it lasted. I succeeded in rousing in him feelings that had long slumbered, and in awakening him to more elevated thoughts; I interested him in many subjects that were new to him, or which he had forgotten. To me he owed many fresh sympathies; he owned this, and was grateful for it. He often sought my society, and I appreciated his doing so, because I never flattered his weaknesses, but spoke to him in a style that he had not been accustomed to.

He was at that time strongly opposed to the plots that were being concocted against Spain. The truly diabolical artifices employed by the Emperor, if they did not offend his moral sense, were at least very displeasing to that good taste which M. de Talleyrand displayed in political as well as in social life. He foresaw the consequences, and prophesied to me what they would be. "This ill-advised man," he said, "will call his whole position in question again." He was always anxious that war should be frankly declared against the King of Spain, if he would not accede to what was required of him; that advantageous conditions should be dictated to him; that the Prince of the Peace (Godoy) should be sent away, and an alliance by marriage effected with the Infante Ferdinand.

But the Emperor conceived that additional security would be guaranteed to him by the expulsion of the house of Bourbon, and was obstinate in his views, being once more the dupe of the schemers by whom he was surrounded. Murat and the Prince of the Peace flattered themselves with the hope of gaining two thrones, but the Emperor had no notion of giving them any such satisfaction. He deceived them, and believed too easily in their readiness to facilitate his plans in the hope of securing their own. Thus every one in this affair overreached every one else, and was at the same time deceived.

The winter passed brilliantly. The theatre in the Tuileries was finished; on reception days theatrical representations were given, most frequently in Italian, and sometimes in French. The Court attended in full dress, and tickets for the upper galleries were distributed to the citizens. We, too, formed a spectacle to them. Everybody was eager to be present at these representations, where there was a great display of splendor.

Full-dress and masked balls were given. These were novelties to the Emperor, and he liked them. Some of his Ministers, his sister, Murat, and the Prince de Neufchâtel, received orders to invite a certain number of persons belonging to the Court or to the city. The men wore dominoes, the women elegant costumes, and the pleasure of being disguised was almost the only one they enjoyed in these assemblies, where it was known that the Emperor was present, and where the fear of meeting him made the guests silent and circumspect.

He was closely masked, and yet easy to recognize by that peculiar air and gait which he could not disguise, as he walked through the rooms, generally leaning on the arm of Duroc. He accosted the ladies freely, and was often very unscrupulous in his remarks to them; and, if he was answered, and unable at once to recognize who it was that spoke to him, he would pull off the speaker's mask, revealing himself by this rude act of power. He also took great pleasure, under cover of his disguise, in seeking out certain husbands and tormenting them with anecdotes, true or false, of their wives. If he learned afterward that these revelations had been followed by unpleasant consequences, he became very angry; for he would not permit the displeasure which he had himself excited to be independent of him. It must be said, because it is the truth, that there is in Bonaparte a natural badness, which makes him like to do evil in small as well as in great things.

In the midst of all these amusements he worked

hard, and was much occupied by his personal strife with the English Government. He devised various methods for sustaining his continental policy. He flattered himself that, by articles in the newspapers, he could subdue the discontent caused by the increase in the price of sugar and coffee, and the scarcity of English merchandise. He encouraged every new invention, and believed that the sugar extracted from beet-root and other things would enable us to dispense with the help of foreigners in certain productions, such as the making of colors. He caused the Minister of the Interior to address a public report to him, stating that he had obtained, through the Prefects, letters from the Chambers of Commerce in approbation of the system, which, although it might involve some temporary privations, must ultimately secure the freedom of the seas.

The English were molested everywhere. They were made prisoners at Verdun; their property was confiscated in Portugal; Prussia was forced into a league against them; and the King of Sweden was menaced because he obstinately persisted in maintaining his alliance with them.

The cord was thus tightened at both ends and stretched to its utmost. It became impossible not to see that only the ruin of one or the other of the contending parties could terminate the quarrel, and wise people became profoundly anxious. As, however, we were always being deceived, we regarded the journals with constant distrust. We read them, indeed, but without believing what they stated.

The Emperor exhausted himself in writing, but he did not convince us. He became deeply incensed at this want of confidence, and each day his aversion to the Parisians increased. It hurt his vanity to find that he was not believed, and the exercise of his power was incomplete when its influence could not be extended to the very thoughts of the people. In order to please him, one had to be credulous. "You like Berthier," said M. de Talleyrand to Bonaparte, "because he believes in you."

Occasionally, as a change from political articles, the newspapers would relate the daily words and actions of the Emperor. For example, we were told how he had gone to see the picture of his coronation painted by David, and had much admired it, and how he had surprised the painter by his acute observations; also, that when he was leaving the studio he had taken off his hat and saluted David, in proof of *" the sentiments of benevolence which he bestowed on all artists."*

This reminds me that he once found fault with M. de Luçay, one of the Prefects of the Palace, who had the superintendence of the Opéra, with being too distant in his manner to the actors who went to him on business. "Are you aware," he said, "that talent of any kind is positive power, and that even I take off my hat when I receive Talma?" There was, no doubt, some exaggeration in this statement; but it is nevertheless true that he was very gracious to artists of any distinction, that he encouraged them by his liberality and his praise; provided, however, that they were always willing to dedicate their art to his praises, or to the furtherance of his projects; for any great reputation acquired without his concurrence seemed to offend him, and he had no sympathy with glory that he had not bestowed. He persecuted Mme. de Staël because she overstepped the line he had laid down for her, and he neglected the Abbé Delille, who lived in retirement far from him.

At this period two distinguished artists, Esménard and Spontini, produced the opera entitled "La Ves-

tale," which had an immense success. The Emperor
—I know not for what reason—was determined to
prefer the French music of Lesueur, the author of
" Les Bardes," and was greatly displeased with the
Parisians for not thinking as he did in the matter.
He thenceforth cherished a prejudice against all Ital-
ian music, and the influence of this was felt when the
distribution of the decennial prizes took place.

On the 21st of January, 1808, the assembled Senate granted a levy of eighty thousand men on the conscription of 1809. Regnault, the Councilor of State,
who was, as usual, the speaker on the occasion, argued
that even as the preceding levies had served to secure
the continental peace, so this one would at length obtain for us the freedom of the seas; and no one opposed this reasoning. We knew that Senator Langue-
nais and some others occasionally tried, during the
Emperor's reign, to make certain representations to
the Senate on the subject of these severe and numerous
levies; but their observations dispersed themselves in
the air of the senatorial palace, and effected no change
in decisions which had been arrived at beforehand.
The Senate was timid and submissive; it inspired no
confidence in the national mind, and had even come
by degrees to be regarded with a sort of contempt.
Men are severe toward their fellows; they do not pardon each other's weaknesses, and they applaud virtues of which they themselves are seldom capable. In
short, whatever tyranny may be exercised, public opinion is more or less avenged, because it is invariably
heard. No despot is ignorant of the feelings which he
inspires and the condemnation which he excites. Bonaparte knew perfectly well how he stood in the estimation of the French nation, for good or evil, but he
imagined that he could override everything.

In the report made to him by his Minister of War,

General Clarke, on the occasion of the fresh levies, we find these words: "A vulgar policy would be a calamity for France; it would hinder those great results which you have prepared." No one was duped by this formula. The question in the comedy, *"Qui est ce donc qu'on trompe ici?"* was appropriate to the occasion; but everybody kept silence, and that was enough for Napoleon. Shortly after, the towns of Kehl, Cassel, Wesel, and Flushing were united to the Empire, being regarded as keys which it was necessary we should hold in our hands. At Antwerp great works were carried on, and all was stir and activity.

When the English Parliament opened, the Emperor evidently hoped for a disagreement between the English Government and the nation. There was a great deal of sharp dissension, and the Opposition declaimed in its usual style. The Emperor helped it with all his might. The tone or the notes in the "Moniteur" was very violent; certain English journalists were subsidized, and there is no doubt Bonaparte flattered himself that he would be able to bring about a revolt. But the English Ministry was pursuing a course which, though difficult, was honorable to the country, and it had a majority at every vote. The Emperor was incensed, and declared that he "could not understand that form of liberal government in which the voice of the popular party never had any weight." Sometimes he would say, with a sort of paradoxical audacity: "In reality, there is more liberty in France than in England, because nothing can be worse for a nation than the power of expressing its will without being listened to. When all is said, that is the merest farce, a vain semblance of liberty. As for me, it is not the case that the true state of France is kept from me. I know everything, for I have exact reports, and

I would not be so mad as to venture on doing anything in direct opposition to French interests or to the French character. Intelligence of all kinds comes to me as to a common center, and I act in accordance with it; whereas our neighbors never depart from their national system, maintaining the oligarchy at any price; and in this age men are more ready to accept the authority of one able and absolute man than the humiliating power of an effete nobility."

When Bonaparte talked thus, it was hard to know whether he was trying to deceive others or to deceive himself. Was it that his imagination, which was naturally lively, exerted its influence over his intellect, which was generally mathematical? Did the lassitude and inaction of the nation deceive him? Was he trying to persuade himself that what he desired was the case? We have often thought that he forced himself to do this, and that he sometimes succeeded.

Besides, as I have already said, Bonaparte always believed that he was acting in conformity with the spirit of the Revolution, by attacking what he called oligarchs. At every turn he would insist upon equality, which in his mouth meant leveling. Leveling is to equality exactly what despotism is to liberty; for it crushes those faculties and neutralizes those situations to which equality opens a career. The aristocracy of classes levels, in fact, all that exists outside those privileged classes, by reducing strength to the condition of weakness, and merit to the condition of mediocrity. True equality, on the contrary, by permitting each to be that which he is, and to rise as high as he can, utilizes every faculty and all legitimate influence. It also forms an aristocracy, not of class, but of individuals—an aristocracy which draws into it all who deserve to form a portion of it.

The Emperor felt this distinction, and, notwithstanding his nobles, his decorations, his senatorships, and all his fine talk, his system tended solely to base his absolute power upon a vast democracy, also of the leveling order, with political rights which, although they had the appearance of being accorded to all, were in reality within the reach of none.

Toward the beginning of February the marriage of Mlle. de Tascher, Mme. Bonaparte's cousin, was solemnized. She was raised to the rank of Princess, and her husband's relatives were in the greatest delight, and remarkably obsequious on the occasion. They flattered themselves that they would be exalted to a great position; but the divorce undeceived the D'Arenberg family, and they quarreled with the young Princess, who had not brought them quite so much as they expected.

At this time Count Romanzoff, the Russian Minister of Foreign Affairs, arrived in Paris. He was a man of knowledge and of sense, and he came there full of admiration for the Emperor, and affected by the genuine enthusiasm that his own young sovereign felt for Napoleon. He was, however, sufficiently master of himself to observe the Emperor with close attention. He perceived the constraint of the Parisians, who looked on at all the glory of the army without appropriating it to themselves. He was struck with certain remarkable disparities, and he formed a modified judgment which, no doubt, had afterward some influence on the Czar. The Emperor said to him on one occasion, "How do you consider that I govern the French?" "Sire," he replied, "a little too seriously."

Bonaparte, with the aid of a *senatus consultum,* created a new "grand dignity of the Empire," under the title of "Governor-General beyond the Alps"; and he conferred this dignity on Prince Borghese, who was sent to Turin with his wife. The Prince was obliged to sell the finest statues in the Villa Borghese to the Emperor, and they were placed in our Museum. This collection of all the masterpieces that Europe had possessed was superb. They were grouped in the Louvre with the greatest care and elegance, and that was a conquest of a kind which appealed eloquently to French vanity and French taste.

Bonaparte had a report made to him, in a sitting of the Council of State, upon the progress of science, letters, and art since 1789, by a deputation, at the head of which was M. de Bougainville. After the report had been read, he replied in these terms: "I have heard you upon the progress of the human mind in these latter days, in order that what you say to me may be heard by all nations, and may silence the detractors of our age, who are endeavoring to force the human mind to retrograde, and who seem to aim at its extinction. I desired to know what remains for me to do for the encouragement of your labors, in order to console myself for being unable to contribute otherwise to their success. The welfare of my people and the glory of my throne are equally interested in the prosperity of the sciences. My Minister of the Interior shall make me a report upon all your demands; you may confidently count upon my protection." Thus did the Emperor occupy himself with everything at the same time, and thus ably did he associate all that was illustrious with the *éclat* and the grandeur of his reign.

I have already said that he was desirous of founding families which should perpetuate the remembrance of the dignities that he had accorded to those whom he favored. He was greatly annoyed at the resistance he had met with from M. de Caulaincourt, who had gone away to Russia, declaring very positively that, as he could not marry Mme. de——, he would never marry.

The Emperor did his best to overcome the opposition which he also encountered from the man for whom he cared most—Marshal Berthier, Prince de Neufchâtel. Berthier had been for many years deeply attached to an Italian lady, who, although she was nearer fifty than forty, was still remarkably beautiful. She exercised supreme influence over him, even to the extent of making him pardon several acts of levity which she did not hesitate to indulge in before his eyes. These she represented in any colors which she chose, and he forgave them.

Marshal Berthier, who was importuned on this point by the Emperor, would often entreat his master to spare him with respect to this cherished weakness, for the sake of his fidelity; and Bonaparte would laugh at him, get angry, return to the charge, but could never conquer his resistance. This went on for years; but at length, by dint of talking and urgency, he carried his point, and Berthier, although he shed bitter tears on the occasion, consented to marry a princess of the house of Bavaria. The Princess Marie was brought to Paris, and the marriage was solemnized in the presence of the Emperor and Empress. Berthier's bride was by no means handsome, or calculated to make her husband forget the sentiments which he had cherished for so long; and, indeed, his passion for the Italian lady ended only with his life. The Princess was an excellent person, but in no way remarkable. She was liked at the French Court, and she was always of the opinion that she had made a good marriage. The Prince de Neufchâtel, who was largely endowed with gifts by the Emperor, possessed an immense revenue, and the household of three lived on the best possible terms. After the Restoration they lived in Paris. The Marshal, who was ill with fever when Bonaparte returned from Elba on the 20th of March, 1815, was so terrified by that event that he lost his senses, and either threw himself or fell out of a window, and was killed. He left two sons. The Princess remained in Paris, and the fair Italian keeps up her former relations with her.

At this time the Emperor showed more plainly than ever what a monarchical turn his ideas were taking, by founding the institution of the " Majorats." That institution was approved by many, blamed by others, envied by a certain class, and readily adopted by many families, who welcomed this opportunity of conferring importance on their eldest sons and perpetuating their name. The Arch-Chancellor carried the decree to the Senate, and represented in his speech that hereditary distinctions were of the essence of monarchy, that they kept alive what is in France called honor, and that our national character should lead us to approve them. He then proceeded to pacify the men of the Revolution by adding that all citizens would be none the less equal before the law, and that distinctions impartially accorded to all who merited them ought to stimulate the zeal of all without exciting the jealousy of any. The Senate received all this with its ordinary approbation, and voted an address of thanks and admiration to the Emperor.

M. de Talleyrand warmly praised this new institution. He could not understand a monarchy without a nobility. A council was created to superintend the administration of the laws by which the foundation of a Majorat was to be obtained. M. de Pasquier, chief Master of Requests, was named Procurator-General; titles were granted to those who held great offices in the state. This was at first ridiculed, because certain names allied themselves oddly enough to the title of Count or Baron; but the public soon got accustomed to it, and, as all hoped to arrive at some distinction, they tolerated and even approved the new system.

The Emperor was ingenious in his method of demonstrating to all parties how entirely they ought to approve of these creations. " I am securing the Revolution," said he to one party; " this intermediate class which I am founding is eminently democratic, for everybody is called to it." " It will support the throne," said he to the *grands seigneurs*. Then he added, turning toward those who wanted a modified monarchy: " It will oppose itself to the encroachments of absolute authority, because it will itself be a power in the state." To genuine Jacobins he said, " You ought to rejoice, for here is the old *noblesse* finally annihilated;" and to that old *noblesse* he said, " By arraying yourselves in new dignities, you resuscitate yourselves and perpetuate your ancient rights." We listened to him; we wished to believe him; and, besides, he did not give us much time to reflect—he carried us away in the whirlwinds of contradictions of every kind. He even imposed his benefits by force when it was necessary; and this was an adroitness the more, for there were people who wanted to be forced to accept.

Another institution which seemed really grand and imposing succeeded this one. I allude to the University. Public instruction was concentrated in a clear and comprehensive system, and it was admitted that the decree was very nobly conceived.

Ultimately, however, that which happened to everything else happened to the University; Bonaparte's own despotic disposition took fright at the powers which he had accorded, because they might possibly become obstacles to certain of his desires. The Min-

ister of the Interior, the Prefect, the general administration—that is to say, the absolute system—mixed
itself up with the operations which the University
corps were attempting, contradicted them, and over-
ruled them when they indicated the very least traces
of independence. In this respect also we present the
spectacle rather of a fine façade than of a solid building.

M. de Fontanes was nominated Grand Master of
the University. This choice, which was also generally
approved, suited the purpose of the master, who was
so jealous of preserving his daily and hourly authority over men and things. M. de Fontanes, whose
noble intellect and reputation for perfect taste had
procured him a very distinguished position, injured
these qualities by carelessness and inertness, which
rendered him incapable of making a stand when it was
necessary. I must place him also, I fear, among the
fine façades.

Nevertheless, something was gained by this creation; order was restored to education, the scope of
study was extended, and young people were occupied.
It has been said that under the Empire education at
the Lycées was entirely military, but that was not the
case. Letters were carefully cultivated, sound morals
were inculcated, and strict surveillance was practiced.
The system of education was, however, neither sufficiently religious nor sufficiently national, and the time
had come when it was necessary that it should be both
one and the other. No effort was made to impart to
young people that moral and political knowledge
which trains citizens, and prepares them to take their
part in the labors of their Government. They were
obliged to attend the schools, but nobody spoke to
them of their religion; they heard much more about
the Emperor than they heard about the state, and they

were incited to a desire for military fame. Yet, notwithstanding these drawbacks, and although the youth of the French nation is not all that it ought to be, it has been developed to a remarkable extent, and a great difference may be discerned between those who have availed themselves of the public education offered to all and those who have held aloof from it. Mistrust, party spirit, and a sort of general misgiving induced the old French nobility and a portion of the wealthy class to keep their children with themselves, and to rear them in a number of prejudices, for which they are now suffering. The pupils of the Lycées acquired a superiority by their public education, which it would now be vain to dispute.

The decree which created the University, after having regulated the functions of those who were to compose it, fixed their salaries at high rates. The officials were given a handsome costume and an imposing organization. After the Grand Master (the Bishop of Bazas) came M. de Villaret as Chancellor. M. Delambre, permanent secretary of the first class of the Institute, who was held in high consideration, both for his learning and character, was Treasurer. The Council of the University was composed of distinguished men; the names of M. de Beausset, formerly Bishop of Alais, and now Cardinal, of M. Cuvier, M. de Bonald, M. de Frayssinous, Royer-Collard, etc., were included in the number. The professors were chosen with great care. In short, this creation met with universal approbation; but ensuing events hindered its action in the first place, and afterward disorganized it like all the rest.

On the 23d of March, 1808, the Court went to Saint Cloud. The Emperor always left Paris as soon as he could: he disliked living at the Tuileries, because of the impossibility of walking about there freely;

and then, the greater his power and splendor became, the more ill at ease he found himself in the presence of the Parisians. He could not endure any restraint, and he knew that in the city people were aware of the language which he was in the habit of using, and the violence to which he gave way. He excited curiosity, which annoyed him; he was coldly received in public; a number of stories about him got into circulation; in short, he was obliged to put some constraint upon himself. Thus his sojourns in Paris became more and more brief, and he began to talk of inhabiting Versailles. The restoration of the palace was decided upon, and Bonaparte observed more than once that in reality he had no occasion to be in Paris, except during the session of the Corps Législatif. When he rode or drove to any distance from the town, he used to say, as he approached it on his return, " Here we are again, in the great Babylon." He even formed plans for the transplantation of the capital to Lyons. It was only in imagination that he contemplated such a displacement, but he took pleasure in the idea, and it was one of his favorite dreams.

The Parisians were perfectly well aware that Bonaparte did not like them, and they avenged themselves by sarcastic jests and anecdotes, which were for the most part pure inventions. They were submissive to him, but cold and satirical. His courtiers adopted the antipathy of their master, and never spoke of Paris without some disparaging epithet. More than once I have heard the Emperor say, moodily, " They have not yet pardoned me for pointing my guns upon them on the 13th Vendémiaire."

An authentic collection of the observations that Bonaparte made upon his own conduct would be a very useful book to many sovereigns, and to their advisers. When at the present time (I write in 1819)

I hear people, who seem to me to be mere novices in the art of governing men, affirm that nothing is so easy as to impose one's will by force, and that by trusting to the bayonet one may constrain a nation to endure any *régime* which may be inflicted upon it, I recall what the Emperor used to say about the difficulties which had arisen from his first steps in his political career, the complications produced by the employment of force against the citizens, which beset him from the very day after that on which he had been obliged to avail himself of so terrible a resource.

I have heard his Ministers say that, when any violent measure was proposed in the Council, he would put the question, " Can you answer for it that the people will not rise? " and that the smallest popular movement always appeared to him grave and ominous. I have seen him take pleasure in describing, or in listening to a description of, the various emotions that are experienced upon the field of battle, and turn pale at a narrative of the excesses of a people in revolt; and, if, when riding through the streets of Paris on horseback, a workman threw himself in his way to implore some favor, Bonaparte's first movement was always to shudder and recoil.

The generals of the Guard had strict orders to prevent contact between the people and the soldiery. " I could not," said Bonaparte, " take the part of the latter." If any quarrel took place between soldiers and citizens, the soldiers were invariably punished and sent away. It is true they afterward received compensation money, which quieted them.

All this time the north of Europe was in a state of agitation. The King of Sweden was too faithful to the policy imposed upon him by the English Government for the interests of his subjects. He excited increasing discontent among the Swedes, and his conduct bore witness to the condition of his brain. The Emperor of Russia having declared war against him, and having at the same time commenced an expedition to Finland, M. d'Alopeus, the Russian ambassador at Stockholm, was placed under arrest in his own house, contrary to all the rights of nations.

On this occasion the notes in the " Moniteur " were eloquent indeed. One of them was as follows: " Poor Swedish nation, into what hands have you fallen? Your Charles XII. was, no doubt, a little mad, but he was brave; and your King, who went to play braggart in Pomerania while the armistice existed, was the first to run away when the same armistice, which he broke, had expired." Such language as this could only announce an impending storm.

At the beginning of the month of March the King of Denmark, Christian VII., died; and his son, who had long been Regent, ascended the throne under the title of Frederick V., in the fortieth year of his age.

It is remarkable that, at a period when the troubled nations seemed to have need of sovereigns of more than ordinary intelligence and wisdom, several of the thrones of Europe were filled by princes who had but little use of reason, and in some instances had none at all. Among those unfortunate sovereigns were the Kings of England, Sweden, and Denmark, and the Queen of Portugal.

Popular discontent manifested itself on the occasion of the arrest of the Russian ambassador at Stockholm. The King left that city and retired to the Castle of Gripsholm, from which he issued orders for war, either against the Russians or against the Danes.

All eyes were, however, soon turned away from what was passing in the north, to fix themselves upon the drama which was beginning in Spain. The Grand Duke of Berg had been sent to take the command of

our army on the banks of the Ebro. The King of
Spain, who was feeble, timid, and ruled by his Minister, made no opposition to the passage of the foreign
troops through his country, toward Portugal as it was
represented. The national party of the Spaniards, at
whose head was the Prince of the Asturias, were incensed at this invasion, for they discerned its consequences. They saw that they were sacrificed to the
ambition of the Prince of the Peace. A revolt against
that Minister broke out; the King and Queen were
attacked, and prepared to quit Spain. This was what
the Emperor wanted, for he was bent upon dethroning the Prince of the Asturias afterward, and believed
that he should easily succeed in doing so. I have already said that the Prince of the Peace, won by the
promises that had been made to him, had devoted
himself to the policy of the Emperor, who began by
making the tremendous mistake of introducing French
influence into Spain under the auspices of a detested
Minister.

Meanwhile the people of Madrid flocked to Aranjuez, and sacked the palace of the Minister, who was
obliged to hide himself to escape the fury of the mob.
The King and Queen, greatly alarmed at the danger
of their favorite, and almost equally grieved, were
forced to demand that he should resign; and on the
16th of March, 1808, the King, yielding to pressure
from all sides, abdicated in favor of his son, announcing that his health compelled him to seek a better
climate. This act of weakness checked the revolt.
The Prince of the Asturias took the name of Ferdinand VII., and his first act of authority was to confis-
cate the property of the Prince of the Peace. But he
had not sufficient strength of character to profit fully
by the new situation. He was frightened by his rupture with his father, and hesitated at the moment

when he ought to have acted. On the other hand, the King and Queen played the game of the Emperor by calling the French army to their aid. The Grand Duke of Berg joined them at Aranjuez, and promised them his dangerous assistance. The vacillation of the authorities, the fear inspired by our arms, the intrigues of the Prince of the Peace, the severe and imperious measures of Murat, all combined to produce trouble and disorder in Spain; and the unfortunate reigning family speedily perceived that this disorganization was about to turn to the advantage of the armed mediator, who assumed the position of a judge. The " Moniteur " gave an account of these events, deploring the misfortune of King Charles IV.; and a few days later the Emperor, accompanied by a brilliant Court, left Saint Cloud, under the pretext of making a journey into the south of France.

I shall give the details of all these events when I reach the fourth epoch of these Memoirs. We were in the dark about them at the time of their occurrence. We asked ourselves, what was the Emperor going to do? Was this new journey an invasion? All these secret intrigues, to which we had no clew, excited our attention and curiosity, and the public disquiet increased daily.

M. de Talleyrand, whom I saw frequently, was exceedingly dissatisfied, and openly blamed all that was done and was about to be done. He denounced Murat, declaring that there was perfidy somewhere, but that he was not mixed up with it, and repeating that had he been Minister of Foreign Affairs he would never have lent his name to such devices. The Emperor was exceedingly angry at this freely expressed condemnation. He saw that approbation of a new kind was felt for M. de Talleyrand; he listened to denunciations of his Minister, and their friendship was interrupted. He has frequently asserted that M. de Talleyrand advised this Spanish affair, and only attempted to get out of it when he perceived that it was a failure. I can bear witness to the fact that M. de Talleyrand severely condemned it at the period of which I am writing, and expressed himself with so much vehemence against such a violation of all the rights of nations that I had to advise him to moderate his language. What he would have advised I can not say, because he never explained himself on that point, and I have now stated all that I know. It is, however, certain that the public were with him at this time, and declared for him because he did not dissemble his dissatisfaction. "This," he said, "is a base intrigue. It is an enterprise against a national aspiration; we declare ourselves thereby the enemy of the people; it is a blunder which will never be repaired." Events have proved that M. de Talleyrand was right, and that from that fatal event the moral decline of him who at that time made all Europe tremble may be dated.

About this time the mild and gentle Queen of Naples set out to rejoin her husband in Spain, and to take her place upon a throne from which she was destined to descend before very long.

CHAPTER XXIX
(1808.)

ON the 2d of July, 1808, the Emperor set out on the pretext of visiting the southern provinces, but in reality to watch what was going on in Spain. I will give an idea of what that was as succinctly as possible.

The transactions of Charles IV. with the different Governments of France were well known. After having vainly attempted in 1793 to save the life of Louis XVI., at the close of a war nobly undertaken but unskillfully conducted, the Spaniards had to submit to the dictation of the conqueror, and the French Government had always meddled more or less in their affairs since that time.

At the head of the administration was Emanuel Godoy—a man of ordinary capacity, who had risen to the position which he now held, and was governing the Spains, as the result of the feelings with which he had inspired the Queen. On him had been heaped all the dignities, honors, and treasures which any favorite could possibly obtain. He was born in 1768, of a noble family, and placed in the royal Bodyguard in 1787. The Queen took him into favor, and he rose rapidly from rank to rank, becoming lieutenant-general, Duke of Alcudia, and in 1792 Minister of Foreign Affairs. In 1795 he was made Prince of the Peace. After the treaty which he concluded with France in 1798, with so little honor to himself, he ceased to be Minister; but he still directed affairs, and all his life he exercised complete empire over King Charles IV., who strangely shared the infatuation of the Queen his wife. The Prince of the Peace married a niece of the King.

The good understanding which existed between France and Spain appeared to be intact until the opening of the Prussian campaign, when the Prince of the Peace, believing that the war would injure the fortunes of the Emperor, proposed to arm Spain, so that the country should be ready to profit by events which might enable it to shake off the French yoke. He issued a proclamation, inviting all Spaniards to enroll themselves. This proclamation reached the Emperor on the battle-field of Jena, and many persons have said that from that moment he was resolved on the destruction of the house of Bourbon in Spain. After his great victories he distributed the Spanish troops over all points of Europe, and the Prince of the Peace obtained his protection only at the price of submitting to his policy.

Bonaparte often asserted in 1808 that at Tilsit the Czar had approved his designs upon Spain; and, in fact, the interview of the two Emperors took place so amicably at Erfurt, immediately after the overthrow of Charles IV., that it is very likely they had mutually authorized each other to pursue their projects, the one toward the north and the other toward the south. But I can not tell to what extent Bonaparte deceived the Emperor of Russia, nor whether he did not begin by hinting to him the division of the states of King Charles IV., which he was pretending to prepare, and the equivalent in Italy which he feigned to intend to give him. Perhaps he had not yet arranged his plan for entirely dispossessing him, and it is quite certain that M. de Talleyrand was not in the plot.

Murat, in his correspondence with the Prince of the

Peace, bribed him with the government of a portion of Portugal, which, he said, should become the kingdom of the Algarves. Another portion of Portugal was to belong to the King of Etruria, and Etruria was thenceforth to become the empire of King Charles IV., who was to keep the American colonies, and at the general peace to take the title of Emperor of the Two Americas.

In 1807 a treaty on these bases was concluded at Fontainebleau, without the knowledge of M. de Talleyrand, and the passage of our troops through Spain for the conquest of Portugal was granted by the Prince of the Peace. At Milan the Emperor signified to the Queen of Etruria that she was to return to her father. Meanwhile the Prince of the Peace was becoming more and more odious to the Spanish nation, and was especially hated by the Prince of the Asturias. The latter, impelled by his own feelings and by the advice of those who surrounded him, distressed by the increasing alienation of his mother and the weakness of his father, alarmed at the entry of our troops, which made him suspect some fresh plot, and especially indignant that the Prince of the Peace should endeavor to make him contract a marriage with the sister of the Princess, wrote to Bonaparte to apprise him of the grievances of the Spaniards against the favorite, and to request his support and the hand of a lady of the Bonaparte family. To this request, which was probably inspired by the ambassador of France, the Emperor made no immediate reply. Shortly afterward the Prince of the Asturias was denounced as a conspirator and arrested, and his friends were exiled. Several notes denunciatory of the exactions of the Prince of the Peace were found among his papers, and on this a charge of conspiracy was founded. The Queen pursued her son with determined enmity, and

the Prince of the Asturias was about to be brought
to trial when letters from the Emperor, signifying
that he would not permit a question of the project of
marriage to be raised, reached Madrid. As it was
upon this point that the accusation of conspiracy was
to bear, the charge had to be abandoned. The Prince
of the Peace wanted to take credit for indulgence, and
pretended that he had solicited and obtained pardon
for the Prince of the Asturias. King Charles IV.
wrote to the Emperor, giving him an account of the
affair and of his own conduct; and Bonaparte became
adviser and arbitrator in all these difficulties, which
so far were favorable to his own designs. These
events took place in October, 1807.

Meanwhile our troops were establishing themselves
in Spain. The Spaniards, surprised by this invasion,
complained bitterly of the weakness of their sovereign
and the treason of the favorite. It was asked why the
Spanish armies were sent to the frontiers of Portugal,
far from the center of the kingdom, which was thus
delivered over without defense. Murat was marching
toward Madrid. The Prince of the Peace sent a
creature of his own, one Izquierdo, to Fontainebleau
for final instructions. This man had an interview with
M. de Talleyrand, in which the latter informed him
of the error into which the Prince of the Peace had
fallen, and showed him that the treaty just signed at
Fontainebleau involved the complete destruction of the
power of Spain. Izquierdo, thunderstruck at all he
heard, returned immediately to Madrid, and the Prince
of the Peace began to perceive how he had been
tricked. But it was too late. The troops were recalled, and a project of imitating the conduct of the
Prince of Brazil by abandoning the Continent was
discussed. The Court was at Aranjuez; its preparations, however, could not be so secretly conducted but

that they transpired in Madrid. The excitement in the city was increased by intelligence of the approach of Murat and of the intended departure of the King, and soon broke out into a revolt; the people went in crowds to Aranjuez, the King was detained as a prisoner in the palace, and the house of the Prince of the Peace was sacked, while he himself was thrown into prison, barely escaping from the fury of the populace. Charles IV. was forced to disgrace his favorite and banish him from Spain. On the following day the King, either feeling himself too weak to rule over a country about to become the scene of discord, or successfully coerced by the opposite party, abdicated in favor of his son.

All this took place at a few leagues' distance from Madrid, where Murat had established his headquarters. On the 19th of March, 1808, Charles IV. wrote to the Emperor that, on account of his health, he was unable to remain in Spain, and that he had just abdicated in favor of his son. This occurrence upset all Bonaparte's plans. The fruit of the device which he had been planning for six months was snatched from him; Spain was about to pass under the sway of a young Prince who, judging by recent events, appeared capable of taking strong measures. The Spanish nation would, no doubt, eagerly embrace the cause of a sovereign whose aim would be the deliverance of his country. Our army was coldly received at Madrid. Murat had already been obliged to have recourse to severe measures for the maintenance of order. A new plan was necessary, and it was needful, above all, to be nearer the theatre of events, so as to estimate them aright.

For these reasons the Emperor resolved on going to Bayonne. He left Saint Cloud on the 2d of April, parting with coolness from M. de Talleyrand, and abstaining from any disclosure of his plans. The " Moniteur " announced that the Emperor was about to visit the southern departments, and not until the 8th of April, after meager accounts of what was taking place in Spain, did we learn that his presence at Madrid was not only desired, but expected.

The Empress, who was both fond of traveling and averse to being separated from her husband, obtained permission to make the journey after his departure, and she soon joined him at Bordeaux.

M. de Talleyrand was uneasy and displeased at the Emperor's movements. I am inclined to think that for a long time past, as much from his dislike to Murat as on account of other projects of which I am ignorant, he had favored the party by whom the Prince of the Asturias was guided. On this occasion he found himself put aside, and realized for the first time that Bonaparte was learning to do without him. In Paris we were all mystified at what was going on. The official articles in the " Moniteur " were extremely obscure; nothing that emanated from the Emperor could surprise us; but even curiosity was at last wearing out, and, moreover, no great interest was felt in the royal house of Spain. There was, therefore, very little excitement, and we waited for time to enlighten us. France was growing used to expect that Bonaparte would use her simply for his own personal ends.

Meanwhile Murat, who was acquainted with some of the Emperor's projects, and who saw that some of them must fail through the abdication of Charles IV., acted with skillful duplicity at Madrid. He contrived to avoid recognizing the Prince of the Asturias, and all the evidence leads to the conclusion that he contributed to excite the old King's desire to resume his crown. A dispatch from General Monthion, who had been sent as envoy to Charles IV. at Aranjuez, was published in the " Moniteur," and Europe was informed that the King had made bitter complaints of his son, had declared that his abdication was forced, and had placed himself in the Emperor's hands, with a special request that the life of the Prince of the Peace should be spared. The Queen, in still more passionate terms, accused her son, and seemed entirely engrossed by anxiety for the fate of her favorite.

The Spaniards had accepted the abdication of their King, and were rejoiced to be rid of the yoke of the Prince of the Peace. They were impatient, especially at Madrid, of the presence of the French, and of their reserved behavior toward the young sovereign; and Murat could repress the growing excitement only by measures of severity, necessary under the circumstances, but which completed the detestation in which we were held.

On the Emperor's arrival at Bayonne, he took up his abode at the Château de Marrac, about a mile from the town. He was uncertain as to what might come of his present undertaking, and as a last resource was prepared to go to Madrid; but he was fully determined not to let the fruit of his endeavors escape him. No one about him was in the secret: he controlled the actions of all without confiding in any one. In the Abbé de Pradt's " History of the Revolution in Spain," there are some interesting notes and comments on the force of character which enabled the Emperor to bear quite alone the secret of his vast conceptions. The Abbé de Pradt was at that time Bishop of Poitiers, and Bonaparte, on passing through the city, attached him to his suite, believing he should be able to make use of his well-known talent and inclination for intrigue.

Several persons who accompanied the Emperor on

this journey told me that their sojourn at Marrac was dull, and that they all wished for a climax to the events then taking place, in order that they might return to Paris.

Savary was dispatched to Madrid, and in all probability received orders to bring back the Prince of the Asturias at any cost. He accomplished his mission with the exactitude for which he was remarkable, and which forbade him from criticising either the orders he received or the means necessary to their fulfillment. On the 7th of April Savary presented himself to the Prince of the Asturias at Madrid. He announced the Emperor's journey into Spain as certain, assumed the character of an ambassador coming to congratulate a new King, and bound himself, in the name of his master, not to meddle with any Spanish affairs if the sovereign's dispositions were friendly toward the Emperor. He next insinuated that negotiations would be greatly expedited by the Prince's moving forward to meet the Emperor, who intended very shortly to repair to Madrid; and to the surprise of every one, to the surprise of posterity also, he contrived to persuade the Prince of the Asturias and his Court to undertake the journey. We can hardly doubt that advice on this occasion was backed by threats, and that the unfortunate young Prince was caught in a multitude of snares, all spread for him at once. He was, no doubt, given to understand that this was the price at which his crown must be purchased, and that, as the Emperor wished him to take this step, no help would be afforded him unless he consented to it; the bait that the Emperor would meet him on the way was also held out, and nothing was at first said about his crossing the frontier.

The Prince of the Asturias found himself involved by circumstances in an enterprise beyond his strength;

he was more the puppet than the chief of the party who had placed him on the throne, and he could not quite reconcile himself to the position of a son in open rebellion against his father. Moreover, he was intimidated by the presence of our troops, and dared not answer to his people for the safety of their country if he resisted us. His advisers were alarmed. Savary's counsels were mingled with threats, and the unhappy Prince, who was influenced by the most generous sentiments, consented to a step which was the proximate cause of his ruin. I have heard Savary say that the orders he had received were so positive that, when once he had him on the road to Bayonne, he would not have suffered him to turn back for any consideration in the world; and, some faithful adherents having conveyed a warning to the Prince, he watched him so closely that he felt assured no human power could snatch him from his grasp.

To further this wicked and ably laid plot, the Emperor wrote the following letter, which was subsequently published. It was handed to the Prince of the Asturias at Vittoria, and I transcribe it here, as it throws a light on the events which followed:

"BAYONNE, *April, 1808.*

" MY BROTHER: I have received your Royal Highness's letter. In the papers of the King, your father, you must have seen proofs of the interest I have always felt in your Royal Highness. You will permit me, under present circumstances, to address you loyally and frankly.

" I hoped, on reaching Madrid, to have persuaded my illustrious friend to undertake some necessary reforms in his states, and to satisfy in some measure the public opinion of the country. The dismissal of the Prince of the Peace seemed to me to be necessary both for his own happiness and that of his subjects. Affairs in the north have delayed my journey. Certain events have taken place at Aranjuez. I pronounce no judgment on these, nor on the conduct of the Prince of the Peace; but I know this well, that it is dangerous for kings to accustom their people to shed blood and to administer justice to themselves. I pray God that your Royal Highness may not learn this one day by your own experience. It is not in the interest of Spain to injure a Prince who is husband to a Princess of the blood royal, and who has so long reigned over the kingdom. He has now no friends, nor will your Highness have any if misfortune overtake you. Men are always ready to make us suffer for the honors they have paid us. Besides, how could proceedings be taken against the Prince of the Peace without implicating the Queen and the King, your father? Such a lawsuit will encourage dissensions and faction, and the consequences will be fatal to your crown. Your Royal Highness has no other claim to it than that conferred on you by your mother; if the lawsuit reflects dishonor on her, your Royal Highness's rights will be thereby destroyed. Close your ears, therefore, to weak and perfidious counsel; you have no right to sit in judgment on the Prince of the Peace. His crimes, if he is accused of any, are absorbed in the rights of the throne. I have often expressed a desire that the Prince of the Peace should be removed from the conduct of affairs. The friendship of King Charles has often induced me to keep silence, and to turn away my eyes from his weak attachment. Wretched creatures that we all are! our motto should be, 'Weakness and Error.' But all may be arranged. Let the Prince of the Peace be banished from Spain; I will offer him a refuge in France.

"As to the abdication of King Charles IV., he made it at a time when my army was occupying Spain, and in the eyes of Europe and of posterity I should appear to have sent large numbers of troops thither merely in order to turn my ally and my friend off his throne. As a neighboring sovereign, I may be allowed to wait for full and entire information before recognizing this abdication. I say to your Royal Highness, to all Spaniards, and to the whole world, if the abdication of King Charles IV. is spontaneous, if it has not been forced on him by the insurrection and the tumult at Aranjuez I will make no difficulty about recognizing it, and will acknowledge your Royal Highness to be King of Spain. I desire, therefore, to converse with you to this end. The caution with which I have watched these things for the last month should be a guarantee of the support I would afford you if, in your turn, a factious spirit, of whatever kind, should disturb you on your throne. When King Charles informed me of the events of last October, I was painfully impressed by them, and I may have contributed, by the suggestions I then made, to the happy ending of the Escurial affair. Your Royal Highness was greatly to blame: no other proof of this is needed than the letter you addressed to me, which I have persistently ignored. When, in your turn, you are a King, you will know how sacred are the rights of a throne. Any advances made to a foreign sovereign are criminal. Your Royal Highness must be on your guard against outbursts of popular feeling. A few of my soldiers might be murdered in isolated situations, but the destruction of Spain would be the result. I already perceive with regret that letters from the Captain-General of Catalonia have been distributed about Madrid, and that everything has been done to promote disturbance there.

"I have now fully explained myself to your Royal Highness; you perceive that I am hesitating between various ideas, which require confirmation. You may be assured that, in any case, I shall treat you as I would treat the King, your father. I beg you to believe in my desire for conciliation, and to grant me an opportunity of proving my good will and high esteem."

We see by this letter that the Emperor still reserved to himself the right of judging of the validity of the abdication of Charles IV. It appears, however, that Savary flattered the young King into the belief of more positive approbation than was actually contained in the letter, while Murat was secretly urging King Charles to retract. By thus writing to the Prince of the Asturias, the Emperor contrived a means of saving the Prince of the Peace, if necessary, from taking part with Charles IV., and finally of blaming the first symptom of rebellion against his father on the part of the Prince of the Asturias. It was known, however, at this period that the ambassador of France had suggested to the Prince the demand which he had made for the hand of a Princess of the Imperial family in marriage. It was this demand which had most deeply offended the favorite.

The Prince of the Asturias left Madrid on the 10th of April. He received tokens of affection from his people on his way, and great anxiety was everywhere displayed at his approach to the frontier. Savary reiterated his assurances that by pushing on farther they must meet the Emperor, and kept the Prince under strict guard. On reaching Burgos, the Prince's council began to take alarm; but they continued their route to Vittoria, where the people unharnessed the horses from the carriage, the guard had to force a passage, and this was done almost against the will of the Prince, whose hopes were fading.

"At Vittoria," Savary told me afterward, "I thought for an instant that my prisoner was about to escape, but I took care he should not. I frightened him." "But," I answered, "do you mean that, if he had resisted, you would have killed him?" "Oh no," he said; "but I protest that I would never have let him go back."

The Prince's councilors, however, were reassured by the reflection that a marriage would conciliate all parties, and, being unable to understand the immensity of the Imperial projects, they looked upon such an alliance, together with the sacrifice of a few men and of the liberty of trade, as the conclusion of a definitive treaty. They yielded, therefore, to the soldierly arguments of Savary, and finally crossed the frontier.

The royal party entered Bayonne on the 21st of April. Those persons of the household who were then in attendance on the Emperor discovered, by the change in his temper, how important for the success of his projects was the arrival of the Infantes. Until then he had seemed full of care, confiding in no one, but dispatching courier after courier. He dared not reckon on the success of his plan. He had invited the old King to come to him, who, as well as the Queen and the favorite, had just then nothing better to do; but it seemed so likely that the new King would take advantage of the revolt about to break out in Spain and would rouse the new-born enthusiasm of all classes for the deliverance of their country, that, until the actual moment when he was informed that the Prince had crossed the Pyrenees, the Emperor must have looked on the event as wellnigh impossible. He has since said that, dating from this blunder, he had no longer a doubt of the incapacity of King Ferdinand.

On the 20th of April the Queen of Holland gave birth to a son who was named Louis.

At this time the painter Robert died. He was famous for his artistic talent, his taste in architecture, and was, besides, an excellent and very clever man.

The Abbé de Pradt has narrated all the circumstances of the arrival of the Princes; and, as he witnessed it, I again refer to his work, without feeling bound to quote from it here. He says that the Emperor came from Marrac to Bayonne; that he treated the Prince of the Asturias as an equal; that he invited him the same day to dinner, treating him with royal honors; and that it was not until the evening of that day, when the Prince had returned to his dwelling, that Savary again came to him, with orders to inform him of Bonaparte's intentions. These intentions were to overthrow the reigning dynasty, in order to put his own in its place, and consequently the abdication of the whole family was demanded. The Abbé de Pradt is naturally astounded at the part which the Emperor played during the day, and one can hardly conceive why he gave himself the trouble to act a character in the morning so contrary to that of the evening.

Whatever were his motives, one can understand the amazement of the Spanish Princes, and what must have been their regret, having thus delivered themselves into the hands of their inflexible enemy. From that time they made efforts, not to fly—for they quickly perceived that flight was impossible—but to inform the Junta, sitting at Madrid, of their captivity and of the intentions which would cause the ruin of the last Bourbons. The greater number of their messengers were stopped, but some few got away safely; the news they carried excited indignation in

Madrid, and thence throughout Spain. Some provinces protested; in several towns the people rose in revolt; in Madrid the safety of the French army was endangered. Murat redoubled his severity, and became an object of hatred, as well as terror, to all the inhabitants.

Every one knows now how greatly the Emperor deceived himself as to the condition of Spain and the character of the Spaniards. He was influenced in this odious undertaking by those same defects of character and judgment which had on other occasions led him into such grave errors: first, his determination to prevail by sheer force, and his thirst for instant submission, which made him neglect intermediaries, who are not always to be despised with impunity; and, secondly, an obstinate conviction that men are but very slightly influenced by their mode of government, and that national differences are so unimportant that the same policy will answer equally well in the north or in the south, with Germans, Frenchmen, or Spaniards. He has since admitted that he was greatly mistaken in this. When he learned that there existed in Spain a higher class, aware of the bad government under which it lived, and anxious for some changes in the constitution, he did not doubt but that the people too would swallow the bait if a revolution like that of France were offered to them. He believed that in Spain, as elsewhere, men would be easily roused against the temporal power of the priesthood. His keen perception appreciated the movement which had caused the revolt of Aranjuez, and had placed the reins of power in the hands of a weak Prince, too evidently lacking ability to make or control a revolution; and he imagined, overleaping time and the obstacles or circumstances which cause delay, that, the first impulse of movement having been given to Spanish institutions, a complete change would ensue. He believed himself to be even rendering a service to the nation in thus fore-stalling events, in seizing on the Spanish revolution beforehand, and in guiding it at once to the goal which he thought it destined to reach.

But even were it possible to persuade a whole nation, and to induce it to accept, as the outcome of a wise foresight, those things which it can never understand except through the teaching of facts and often of misfortune, the hatefulness of the means employed by the Emperor blasted him in the eyes of those he wished to win, and whom he believed he was serving; *" for the heart of Jehu was not upright, nor his hands clean,"* that Spain should receive him as the reformer whom she needed. Moreover, a foreign yoke was offensive to Spanish pride; while secret machinations, the imprisonment of the sovereigns, unconcealed contempt for religious beliefs, the threats that were used, the executions that followed on them, and, later, the exactions and cruelties of war, all concurred to prevent any concord. The two contending parties, each inflamed against the other, were soon filled with a furious longing for mutual destruction. The Emperor himself sacrificed everything rather than yield; he was lavish of men and money only that he might prove himself the strongest, for he could not endure the shame of defeat before the eyes of Europe, and a bloody war, terrible disasters, were the result of his wounded pride and his tyrannical will. All he did, therefore, was to throw Spain into a state of anarchy. The people, finding themselves without an army, believed that the defense of the soil devolved upon them; and Bonaparte, who took pride in being the elect of the people, and who also felt that therein lay his security—Bonaparte, who, to be consistent in his theories, should never have waged war except on kings —found himself, after a few years, cut adrift from that policy on which he had founded his power while he revealed to the whole world that he used that power for his personal advantage only.

Although he was conscious of some of these future difficulties, he continued to tread the devious path on which he had entered. The Prince of the Asturias refused to sign an act of abdication, and this caused him great perplexity. Fearing that the Prince might escape him, he caused him to be strictly watched; he tried him by every kind of persuasion and threat, and all who surrounded the Emperor soon became aware of the state of perturbation into which he had again fallen. Duroc, Savary, and the Abbé de Pradt were enjoined to bribe, to persuade, or to terrify the Prince's councilors. But how is it possible to persuade people to consent to their own fall from power? If we abide by the Emperor's opinion, that every member of the reigning family was equally stupid and incapable, the wiser course would still have been to have left them in possession of the throne; for the necessity of taking action in times that were becoming so difficult must have led them into many faults, of which their enemy might have taken advantage. But, by the outrageous insults put upon them, by the violation of every human right in their regard, by the inaction to which they were forced, by imposing on them the simple and pathetic character of victims, their part was made so easy to play that they became objects of interest without having to take the smallest pains to excite that sentiment. With respect to the Spanish Princes and the Pope, the Emperor committed the same blunder and incurred the same penalty.

Meanwhile, he was determined to end this state of mental anxiety, and he decided on sending for King

Charles IV. to Bayonne, and on openly espousing the cause of the dethroned old monarch. He foresaw that this course of action must be followed by war, but he flattered himself—his vivid imagination was always ready to flatter him when he had fully decided on any step—that this war would resemble all the others. "Yes," he said, "I feel that I am not doing right; but why do not they declare war on me?" And when it was pointed out to him that he could scarcely expect a declaration of war from persons removed from their own territory and deprived of their liberty, he exclaimed: "But why did they come, then? They are inexperienced young men, and have come here without passports. I consider this enterprise as very important, for my navy is defective, and it will cost me the six vessels I have now at Cadiz." On another occasion he said: "If this were to cost me eighty thousand men, I would not undertake it; but I shall not need twelve thousand. It is a mere trifle. The people here don't know what a French brigade means. The Prussians were just the same, and we know how they fared in consequence. Depend upon it, this will soon be over. I do not wish to harm any one, but, when my big political car is started, it must go on its way. Woe to those who get under the wheels!"

Toward the end of April the Prince of the Peace arrived at Bayonne. Murat had released him from the captivity in which he was held at Madrid. The Junta, under the presidency of Don Antonio, brother to Charles IV., gave him up unwillingly, but the time for resistance was over. The favorite had lost any hope of future sovereignty, his life was in danger in Spain, and the Emperor's protection was his only resource; therefore there was little doubt but that he would agree to anything required of him. He was instructed to guide King Charles in the path the

Emperor wished him to follow, and he acquiesced without a word.

I can not refrain from transcribing some reflections of the Abbé de Pradt, which seem to me to be very sensible and appropriate here.

" At this period," he says, " that part of the scheme which concerned the translation of Joseph to Madrid was not as yet made public. It may have been discerned, but Napoleon had not disclosed it. In the interviews with Napoleon which the negotiation with M. Escoiquiz procured for me he never made any allusion to it. He left to time the task of unfolding each feature of a plan which he revealed cautiously and by slow degrees, and after he had cherished it for a long succession of days in his own mind, without relieving himself of the burden by one indiscreet word. This was sad misuse of moral strength, but it proves how great is the self-mastery of a man who can thus control his words, especially when naturally inclined to indiscretion, as Napoleon was, particularly when he was angry."

King Charles IV. reached Bayonne on the 1st of May, accompanied by his wife, their youngest son, the daughter of the Prince of the Peace, and the Queen of Etruria and her son. Shortly afterward Don Antonio arrived also; he had been obliged to leave the Junta and to join his relatives.

CONCLUSION

THE Memoirs of my grandmother came to an end here, and general regret will, no doubt, be felt that she was prevented by death from continuing them, at any rate so far as the divorce from the Emperor, which, from the very beginning, hangs threateningly over the head of the fascinating, lovable, and yet somewhat uninteresting Josephine. No one can supply what is wanting here; even the correspondence of the author affords little political information respecting the succeeding period, and during the latter part of her life she seldom spoke of what she had witnessed or endured. My father entertained at times the idea of continuing her narrative, by putting together what he had heard from his parents, anecdotes of expressions of their opinions in the last days of the Empire, and what he himself knew concerning their lives. He did not carry out his plan in its entirety, nor did he leave anything on the subject complete. His notes, however, seem to me to be valuable, and give the ending of the great drama which has been described in the foregoing pages. It will be interesting to read them as a continuation of the Memoirs, which they complete, although he has recorded his opinions concerning the latter days of the Empire, and the period when he himself entered political life, in a more extensive work. His political views and clear definition of the conduct of officials and of citizens in times of difficulty deserves to be made known. I have added this chapter to the Memoirs, and published the notes of which I speak in their original unstudied form, confining myself to the slight modifications necessary to make the narrative succinct and clear.

The Spanish sovereigns arrived at Bayonne in May, 1808. The Emperor dispatched them to Fontainebleau, and sent Ferdinand VII. to Valençay, an estate belonging to M. de Talleyrand. Then he himself returned, after having traveled through the southern and western departments, and made a political journey into La Vendée, where his presence produced a great effect. He reached Paris about the middle of August. Count de Rémusat writes:

" My father, who was then First Chamberlain, was appointed to receive the Spanish Bourbons at Fontainebleau. He accomplished his task with the attention and courtesy habitual to him. Although on his return he gave us an account which conveyed no exalted idea of the King, the Queen, or the Prince of the Peace, who accompanied them, he had treated these dethroned Princes with the respect due to rank and misfortune. It would seem that some of the other Court officials had behaved in a different fashion, rather from ignorance than from ill feeling. Charles IV. noticed this, and said, ' Rémusat, at any rate, knows that I am a Bourbon.'

" M. de Talleyrand happened to be actually staying at Valençay when the Emperor sent him orders to proceed thither, with an evident intention of committing him to the Spanish affair, to receive the three Infantes. He was not altogether pleased with the task, nor on his return did he refrain from sarcastic remarks concerning these strange descendants of Louis XIV. He used to tell us that they bought children's toys at all the booths at the neighboring fairs, and when a poor person begged an alms of them they would give him a doll. He afterward accused them of dilapidations at Valençay, and cleverly mentioned the fact to Louis XVIII., who, being desirous to dismiss him from Court, while he had not the courage to order him to go, took occasion to praise the beauty and splendor of his seat at Valençay. 'Yes, it is pretty fair,' he said, 'but the Spanish Princes entirely spoiled it with the fireworks on St. Napoleon's Day.'

"Although M. de Talleyrand was aware that his position with the Emperor was altered, yet he found Bonaparte when he joined him well disposed and inclined to trust him. There was no perceptible cloud between them. The Emperor had need of him for the conference at Erfurt, to which they went together at the end of September. My father was in attendance on the Emperor. The letters which he doubtless wrote thence to my mother have not been found; but their correspondence was so strictly watched, and must therefore have been so reserved, that its loss is, I fancy, of little importance. My father's general letters referred to the good understanding between the two Emperors, their mutual finessing, and the fine manners of the Emperor Alexander.

"M. de Talleyrand composed a narrative of this Erfurt conference, which he was in the habit of reading aloud. He used to boast, on his return, that as the two Emperors entered their respective carriages, each about to journey in a different direction, he had said to Alexander, while attending him, 'If you could only get into the wrong carriage!' He had discerned some fine qualities in the Czar, and had endeavored to win favor, by which he profited in 1814; but, at the time of which I am writing, he looked on a Russian alliance as a merely accidental necessity during a war with England, and he persistently held that friendship with Austria, which would eventually become a basis for an alliance with England, was the true system for France in Europe. His conduct of political affairs, whether at the time of Napoleon's marriage, or in 1814, in 1815, or, again, in the reign of Louis Philippe, was always consistent with this theory. He often spoke of it to my mother.

" My mother, in order to complete the history of the year 1808, would have had to narrate, first, the Erfurt conference, according to the narratives of M. de Talleyrand and of my father; and, secondly, the reaction of the Spanish affair on the Court of the Tuileries and on Parisian society. The Royalist section of the Court and society was deeply moved by the presence of the ancient Bourbons at Fontainebleau. Here, I think, she would have placed the disgrace and exile of Mme. de Chevreuse.

" The Emperor came back from Erfurt in October, but he merely passed through Paris, and started immediately for Spain, whence he returned at the beginning of 1809, after an indecisive campaign.

" Public opinion was far from favorable to his policy. For the first time the possibility of his loss had occurred to the minds of men, especially of his sudden death in the course of a war in which a motive of patriotism might nerve an assassin's hand. Various reports, partly loyal and partly malicious, had made the progress of disapprobation and discontent known to him. Talleyrand and Fouché had not hesitated to confirm those reports. The former, especially, was always bold, and even imprudent, as are all men who are proud of their powers of conversation and believe in them as in a force. Fouché, who was more reserved, or less often quoted in society, probably went further in fact. After his positive fashion, he had been practically considering the hypothesis of the opening up of the Imperial succession, and this con-

sideration had brought him nearer to M. de Talleyrand's opinions.

"The Emperor returned in an angry mood, and
vented his irritation on the Court, and especially at the
Ministerial Council, in the celebrated scene in which he
dismissed M. de Talleyrand from his post of Grand
Chamberlain, and put M. de Montesquiou in his place.

"That important functionaries of the Empire, such
as Talleyrand and Fouché, as well as other less prominent persons, should have behaved as they did on this
occasion, has been severely commented on. I am
ready to admit that vanity and talkativeness may have
led Talleyrand and Fouché to say more than was prudent; but I maintain that, under an absolute government, it is necessary that men holding important
offices should, in the case of public danger, or on perceiving that affairs are being badly directed, not be
afraid to encourage, by a prudent opposition, the moral
resistance which alone can slacken or even divert the
mistaken course of authority. Still more, if they foresee the possibility of disaster, against which no
preparations have been made, they should take thought
concerning what may yet be done. That the pride of
absolute power should be mortified, that endeavors
should be made to overcome and to suppress that
resistance when it is too isolated to avail, I understand. But it would be none the less a boon to the
state and for the ruler, if this opposition were sufficiently powerful to oblige him to modify his plans and
to reform his life.

"With regard to the case in point, let us suppose
that, instead of imputing the disapprobation of Talleyrand or of Fouché to intrigue or treason, Napoleon
had received reports from Dubois, or others who had
presented it as a proof of the universal discontent;
that his Prefect of Police, himself sharing them, had

pointed out to him that these sentiments were felt and expressed by Cambacérès, by Maret, by Caulaincourt, by Murat, lastly by the Duc de Gaëta, whom Thiers quotes on this occasion—in short, by every important personage in the Court and the Government—would the service rendered to the Emperor have been an evil one? And would not this unanimous opposition have been the only means likely to enlighten him, to arrest his steps, to turn him from the way of perdition at a period when it was not yet too late?

"As to the reproach addressed to Talleyrand or others, that they censured the Government after having approved and served it, that is a natural one in the mouth of Napoleon, who, moreover, did not hesitate to exaggerate it by falsehood. But in itself it is foolish; otherwise all honest men must hold themselves forbidden, because they have once belonged to a certain government, because they have formerly supported, cloaked, or even justified its faults, either in error or from weakness, to grow wiser as dangers thicken and circumstances become developed. Unless we are resolved on unceasing opposition or on unlimited submission, a time must come when we no longer approve what we approved yesterday, when we feel bound to speak although hitherto we have been silent, and when, drawbacks striking us more forcibly than advantages, we recognize defects which we had hitherto endeavored or pretended to ignore, and faults which for a long time we have palliated! After all, this is what happened in France with regard to Napoleon, and the change took place in the mind of officials and citizens alike, except when the former were blinded by servility or corrupted by a base ambition.

"In our own modest sphere we never had to decide under the Empire, except upon the direction of our wishes and feelings, for we never took any part in politics; yet we had to solve for ourselves that question which continually recurs to me when I reperuse the Memoirs or the letters in which my mother has preserved her impressions and her thoughts.

" My mother would have had to allude, at any rate indirectly, to this grave subject in narrating the disgrace of M. de Talleyrand. She saw him, at that time, at least as often as formerly; she heard his own statements. Nothing was better known just then to the public than the cold silence (equally far removed from weakness and from insolence) with which, leaning against a console on account of his lameness, he listened to the Emperor's philippic. As is the custom under absolute monarchy, he swallowed the affront, and continued to present himself at Court with a coolness which was not to be mistaken for humility; and I have no recollection that his attitude under the Empire was ever accused of weakness from that day forth. It must, of course, be understood that the rules of the point of honor are not in this case as they are understood in a free country, nor the philosophic laws of moral dignity as they are understood outside the world of courts and politics.

" My mother would, after this, have had to relate our own little episode in the drama. I am not sure whether the Emperor, on his arrival, felt or showed any displeasure toward my father. I do not know whether it was not subsequent reports which caused our disgrace. In any case, my father did not become immediately aware of the truth, either because it was so far from his thoughts that he suspected nothing, or because the Emperor did not think of him at first. He was a friend of M. de Talleyrand's, and in his confidence up to a certain point: this in itself was a motive for suspicion and a cause of disfavor. We had written no letter and taken no step that could tell against us, and I remember that even our speech was very guarded, and that, could the police spies have witnessed the interviews with M. de Talleyrand in my mother's little drawing-room, where my parents habitually received him alone, they could have discovered nothing whereon to found a police report. Such reports were made, however; my father felt no doubt about that, although the Emperor never displayed his resentment by any outbreak, nor did he even enter into any serious explanation. But he acted toward him with a cold malevolence and harshness which made his service intolerable. Thenceforth my parents felt themselves in a painful position with the sovereign, which might, perhaps, lead to their quitting the Court.

"There was no amelioration in this state of things when Napoleon, who had gone to Germany in April, 1809, came back to Fontainebleau on the 6th of October, the conqueror of Wagram, and proud of the peace just signed at Vienna. Victories, however dearly bought, did not make him more generous or kindly. He was still performing work important enough to be vain of his power, and, if it had been put to severe tests, that was a stronger reason why he desired it to be respected. However, he found, in reverting to the recent souvenir of the descent of the English upon Walcheren, a state of things in Spain quite unsatisfactory, a quarrel with the Holy See pushed to its last extremities, and public opinion more restless about his inclination for war than reassured by his victories— defiant, sad, even critical, and besetting with its suspicions the man whom it had so long environed with its fallacies.

"This time Fouché was the object of his thoughts. Fouché had acted in his own way at the moment of the descent of the English. He had assumed authority,

he had made an appeal to public sentiment, he had
reorganized the national guard, and employed Bernadotte on our side. Everything in these proceedings,
both the conception and the details, had greatly displeased the Emperor. All his ill-temper was concentrated upon Fouché; and, besides, as he had come
back resolved upon the divorce, it was difficult to hold
M. de Talleyrand aloof from a deliberation in which
the knowledge of the condition of Europe should have
a decisive weight. In this must be still seen one of
those proofs, at that time less frequent each day, of
the almost impartial justice of his mind. He was
sometimes heard to say: 'It is Talleyrand alone who
understands me; it is only Talleyrand with whom I
can talk.' He consulted him, and at other moments
spoke of placing him at Vincennes. Thus he did not
fail to call him when he deliberated upon his marriage.
M. de Talleyrand strongly insisted that he should unite
himself to an Archduchess. He even thought that the
Emperor had sought an interview with him because
his intervention in this matter would contribute to
decide Austria. What is certain is the fact that he has
always alluded to his conduct in this instance as one
of the guarantees he had given of his fundamental
opinion in regard to the alliances of France and the
conditions of the independence of Europe.

"It is seen how, in all these matters—the state of
opinion during the campaign of the Danube, the
deliberations relative to the divorce, those which preceded the marriage with Marie Louise—the Memoirs
of my mother would have been instructive and interesting. It is unhappily impossible to supply this last
link. I am only able to recall that she said that the
Empress was wrong in doubting her fidelity on one
occasion, probably relative to the divorce. She has
announced that this matter was explained. I can not

explain it in its place, and I have no recollection that she ever spoke to me of it. At the moment of the divorce her devotion was appreciated, and Queen Hortense went so far as to consult with her in regard to it twice before enlisting her irrevocably in favor of her mother. I have no wish to over-estimate the value of what she did in that matter; the most refined delicacy dictated her conduct; and, besides, with her deplorable health, her forced inactivity, her former relations to Josephine, and our new situation near the Emperor, she would have had in a renovated Court, near a new Empress, a most awkward and painful position. It may be conceived, indeed, that nothing in all that I am going to recall restored our credit at the Court, and my family remained there irreparably lessened in its influence. The Emperor, however, approved of my mother's remaining with the Empress Josephine. He even praised her for it; this suited her. He regarded her as a person on the retreat, with whom he no longer needed to concern himself. Having less to expect from him, less to demand from him, he reproached us less in his thought for omitting to do anything on our part to please him. He left my father in the circle of his official duties, to which his character and a certain mingling of discontent and fear kept him closely enough confined. It was almost established in the mind of Napoleon that he had nothing more to do for us, and he no longer thought of us.

"This new situation makes it evident that the Memoirs of my mother would have lost their interest. She no longer visited the Court, going once only to be presented to the Empress Marie Louise; then she had later an audience of the Emperor, who wrote to her asking it. She would, therefore, have had nothing to relate of which she had been a witness in the imperial palace. She was no longer placed under obligations by any relations with the great personages of the state—at least she considered herself relieved of them; and yielding, perhaps too readily, to her tastes, and her sufferings, she gradually isolated herself from everything that would remind her of the Court and of the Government.

"However, as my father did not cease to frequent the palace to the end, as the confidence in M. de Talleyrand seemed not to diminish, and, finally, as the rapid and declining steps in the affairs of the Emperor more and more affected public opinion, and soon stirred up the restless attention of the nation, my mother had still much with which to become acquainted, and much to observe, and she would have been able to give to the painting of the last five years of the Empire a positive historic value.

"Some reflections on many events of those five years will be taken, if it is desired, as a remembrance of what I have heard, during this same time, from the lips of my parents.

"Among the events of that year, 1809, one of the most important, and which made the least noise, was the action of the Emperor in regard to the Pope. The facts were not well understood when they took place, and, it is necessary to say, that among the nation that Louis XIII. put under the protection of the Holy Virgin no one thought of them. The Emperor had begun by causing the Roman States to be occupied, then went on by dismembering them, then by demanding from the Pope that he should make war upon England, then by driving him from the city of Rome, then by depriving him of all temporal power, then, finally, by causing him to be arrested and guarded as a prisoner. How strange all this, assuredly! And yet it seemed that no government of Catholic Europe seriously offered assistance to the common father of the faithful. The Pope certainly, deliberating in 1804 whether he should crown Napoleon, had not objected on the ground that it was he who, in that year, had caused the Duc d'Enghien to be shot. The Emperor of Austria, deliberating in 1809 whether he should give his daughter to Napoleon, did not object on the ground that it was he who, in that same year, had placed the Pope in prison. It is true that at that time all the sovereigns of Europe had, in that which relates to pontifical authority, entirely different ideas from those ascribed to them, and from those attributed to them to-day. The house of Austria, in particular, had for a traditional rule that political testament in which the Duke of Lorraine, Charles V., recommends that the Pope should be reduced to the single domain of the court of Rome, and makes sport 'of the delusion of excommunications, when the real point is that Jesus Christ never established the temporal power of the Church, and that the latter can possess nothing without contradicting his example and without compromising his Gospel.'

"In a letter of my mother she advised my father, in the autumn of 1809, not to allow 'Athalie' to be represented at Court, at a moment when it might be said that there were some allusions to papal affairs in that struggle of a queen and a priest, and in presence of a prince so pious as the King of Saxony, who was preparing to visit the Emperor. In this incident was the *maximum* of evidence of the direction of her thoughts excited by a tyrannic act of which so much would now be heard, and in regard to which public opinion would certainly be no more divided. I have not heard it said that a single officer in this immense empire would have separated himself from a government of which the head was excommunicated, if not by name, at least impliedly, by the bull launched against all the authors or abettors of the attempts against pontifical authority. I can not refrain from alluding to the Duc de Cadore. He was a man not without intelligence nor without honesty; but, accepting as indisputable laws the intentions of the Emperor, after having employed his ministry in the spoliation of the Spanish dynasty, he concurred with the same docility in that of the sovereign Pontiff, and, himself excommunicated as a *mandatory, abettor, and counselor*, he maintained with great composure that Napoleon could resume that which Charlemagne had given, and that now France was in the presence of Rome by the rights of the Gallic Church.

" The situation of the Empire at the end of 1809 is summarized in these words by the great historian of the Empire: ' The Emperor had made himself, at Vincennes, the rival of the regicides; at Bayonne, the peer of those who would declare war on Europe to establish a universal republic; at the Quirinal, the peer certainly of those who had dethroned Pius VI. to create the Roman Republic.'

" I am not one of those who assist by declamation in intensifying the odium of these acts. I do not regard them as unheard-of monstrosities reserved to our century; I know that history is full of examples with which it is not difficult to compare them, and that analogous outrages can be found in the life of sovereigns for whom posterity has preserved some respect. It would not be difficult to find in the history of the severities of the reign of Louis XIV. executions which are not incomparable with the death of the Duc d'Enghien. The affair of the Man in the Iron Mask, especially if, as it is difficult not to believe, this man was a brother of the King, is nothing that the murder of Vincennes need be envious of; and power and deception are not less worthily arrayed in the act by which Louis XIV. seized Lorraine in 1661 than in the fraudulent dismemberment of Spain in 1808. I see in the abduction of the Pope hardly more than its equivalent if we revert to the middle ages. I will add that, even after these acts, for ever to be condemned, it was still possible, by the use of a little wisdom, to have assured the repose, the prosperity, and the grandeur of France to the extent that no name in history would have been more honored than that of Napoleon. But if any one imagines that this is what he has not done; that all the wars thereafter undertaken were no more than the mad preparatory steps to the ruin of the country; and that thenceforward the character of the man already loaded with such misdeeds was afflicted with a superciliousness and a harshness which were discouraging to his best servants, it is essential to clearly understand that, even at Court, all those whom the servile complaisance of false judgment had not led astray, sadly disabused, could rightly serve without confidence, admire without affection, fear more than hope, desire lessons of opposition to a terrible power, in his successes to dread his intoxication, and in his misfortunes to weep for France rather than him.

" Such, in fact, is the spirit in which these Memoirs would have been continued, and it will even be found that, by a kind of retroactive effect, this spirit is shown in the recitals anterior to 1809. At the epoch in which history was enacting, this spirit was slow in manifesting itself, as I have now described it. Years glided away in sadness timid and defiant, but without hate, and each time that a happy circumstance or a wise measure gave their light to them, the star of hope resumed the ascendant, and one tried to believe that the progress in the direction of evil would have an end.

" The years 1810 and 1811 are the two tranquil years of the Empire. The marriage in the one and the birth of the King of Rome in the other seemed pledges of peace and stability. The hope would have been without shadows, the security entire, if the torn veil through which the Emperor could be seen had not revealed passions and errors, seeds always productive of gratuitous mistakes and senseless attempts. It was seen that the love of excess had taken possession of him, and was carrying all before it. Besides the interminable duration of a war with England, with no possibility of gloriously conquering her, or of doing her any injury that was not damaging to us, and the continuation of a struggle in Spain difficult and unfortunate, were two trials that the pride of the Emperor could not long endure in peace. It was necessary that he should preserve his reputation at all cost, and that by some astounding successes he should cause to be forgotten those obstinate checks to his fortune. Sound judgment pointed out that the Spanish question was the one to end, I do not say by a return to justice and by a generous concession—the Bonapartes are not among those to whom such measures suggest themselves—but by force. It can readily be believed that, had the Emperor concentrated all the resources of his genius and of his Empire upon the resistance of the Peninsula, he would have conquered it. Unjust causes are not always destined to fail in this world, and the Emperor ought to have seen that, in humiliating Spain, he was preparing the occasion, so vainly sought, for striking England, since that nation rendered itself vulnerable by landing her armies on the Continent. Such an occasion made it worth while that something should be risked. Napoleon should have gone there in person, and himself entered the lists with Arthur Wellesley. What glory, on the other hand, and what fortune did he not reserve to himself and to his nation, in persistently adjourning the struggle, and in confronting them both finally on the mournful plains of Waterloo!

"But the Emperor had no relish for the Spanish question; he was tired of it. It had never yielded a pleasant or glorious moment. He half understood that he had begun it unjustly and conducted it feebly; that he had singularly misconceived its difficulty and importance. He tried to have a contempt for it, in order not to be humiliated by it; he neglected it, in order to avoid its anxieties. He had a childish repugnance, if it was nothing worse, to risking himself in a war which did not appeal to his imagination. Shall we dare say that he was not absolutely sure of doing the work well, and that the dangers of reverses turned him from an enterprise which, even well carried to its conclusions, would have gone too slowly and with too many difficulties to have increased his grandeur? A ready extemporizer, his plan seemed to be to allow everything to die of old age that displeased him, and to build up his fortune and fame in some new enterprise. These causes, joined to the logical developments of an absurd system, and to the developments natural to an uncontrollable temper, annulled all the guarantees of prudence and safety that the events of the years 1810 and 1811 seemed to have given, turned him from Spain to Russia, and brought about that campaign of 1812 which logically drew him on to his destruction.

"Two years in which hope had the ascendency of fear, and three years in which fear left very little place for hope—here we have the division of the five last years of the reign of Napoleon.

"In speaking of 1810 and 1811, my mother would have had to show how the two events, which ought to have inspired in the Emperor the spirit of conservation and of wisdom, his marriage and the birth of his son, served in the sequel only to exalt his pride. In the interval all the obstacles between him and the execution of his will are seen to be removed. For instance, since, long ago, he does not pardon Fouché for having a will of his own. Fouché showed that he desired peace. A violent scene occurs to recall that of which Talleyrand had been the object, and the Duc de Rovigo becomes Minister of Police, a choice which beguiles, without doubt, the hopes of the Emperor and the fears of the public, but which seems, however, to expand still more the area in which arbitrary power has sway. The existence of Holland and the indocible character of its King are still an obstacle, at least a limit. The King is compelled to abdicate, and Holland is declared French. Rome itself becomes the capital of a department, and the domain of St. Peter is united, as formerly Dauphiné was, to furnish a title for the heir to the Empire. The clerical order, driven with a high hand, is violated in its customs and in its traditions. An appearance of a council is attempted and broken up, and prison and exile impose silence on the Church. A councilor, submissive but modest, executes the wishes of his master, but does not glorify him; he lacks enthusiasm in his servitude: Champagny is set aside for Maret and the lion is let loose in Europe, and no voice is heard which rouses it to madness. And as, during this time, the fortune of the conqueror and the liberty of the people have found the one its limit, the other its bulwark in those immortally celebrated lines of Torres-Vedras, it becomes essential that this restless and maddened force should dash itself in pieces upon Moscow.

" This last period, so rich for the political historian in its terrible pictures, has but little value to the simple

observer of the interior scenes of the government.
The cloud became dense around power, and France
knew as little what was done as if she had been lost
by a throw of dice. Nevertheless, there was still the
work of drawing the instructive picture of hearts and
of minds ignorant and restless, indignant and submissive, desolated, reassured, imposed upon, unconcerned,
depressed—all that at intervals, and sometimes concentrated into an hour; for despotism, which always
feigns to be happy, ill prepares the masses of the
people for misfortune, and believes in courage only
when it has deceived it.

" It is, I think, to this description of public sentiments that my mother would have been able to con-
secrate the end of her Memoirs, for she knew something of what everybody saw. M. Pasquier, whom
she saw every day, observed, by taste as well as by a
sense of duty, the discretion prescribed to his functions.
Accustomed to conversations with the class of persons
whom he ruled without restraint, he was during a
great length of time careful to take political notes,
when all the world was free to talk politics. The Duc
de Rovigo, less discreet, divulged his opinions rather
than the facts; and the conversations of M. de Talleyrand, more frank and more confident, were hardly
more than the disclosure of his judgments and of his
predictions."

POSTSCRIPT

I N the first volume of these Memoirs I attempted to retrace the chief events of my grandmother's life, and I also narrated the circumstances which induced her to rewrite the manuscript unhappily destroyed in 1815. I considered it necessary to a right comprehension and appreciation of her views that the reader should learn how she had been brought up, what were the position and circumstances of her parents, for what reasons she accepted a place at Bonaparte's Court, through what phases of enthusiasm, hope, and disenchantment she passed, how by degrees liberal opinions gained a hold upon her, and what influence her son, when he began to make a figure both in society and in political life, exercised over her.

However strong may be his confidence in the success of a publication, it is the duty of an editor to avail himself of every aid, and to make sure, or nearly so, that the author shall in everything be understood. This was all the more necessary in the present instance, because the editor, brought up to entertain the same sentiments, and accustomed to hear the same opinions and the same anecdotes repeated around him, might well be afraid of deceiving himself respecting the worth or the success of these reminiscences. Relatives are seldom good judges either of the intellectual or physical attributes of their kin. Family beauties or prodigies, admired by the fireside or in select coteries, are frequently found to be insignificant personages on a larger stage, and when seen in broader daylight. I therefore thought it well to relate all that might be needed for the instruction of the reader, and, by introducing him into the private life of the author, to account for a mixture of admiration and severity in these Memoirs which sometimes appears contradictory. I should have been excused for adding my own comments upon the ability of the writer and the character of her hero; indeed, such comments would have furnished the subject of a preface, of the kind that we are told ought to precede every work of serious importance. But I carefully avoided writing any such preface, because I had one to offer which would enhance the value of the book to the public, as it enhances it to myself—a preface written by my father more than twenty years ago. I may print that preface now, for success has justified his previsions and our hopes.

When my father wrote the pages that I am about to lay before the reader, the Second Empire was still in existence, and to all appearance secure. Nothing short of a persistent trust in the undeviating principles of justice and liberty could have led any one to believe that its fall was possible or probable. Since then the fullness of time has come, and events have marched with a rapidity which could not have been foreseen. Similar errors have brought about similar reverses; the moody and wavering mind of Napoleon III. has led him to adopt the same course which ruined the brilliant and resolute genius of the great Emperor. My father for the third time beheld the foreigner in France, and vanquished France seeking in liberty a consolation for defeat. He suffered by our misfortunes, as he had suffered by them fifty years earlier, and he had the melancholy honor of repairing a portion of those misfortunes, of hastening the day of the final deliverance of our soil. He contributed to the foundation of a liberal and popular Government on a heap of ruins. The last years of the Empire, the War, the Commune, the difficult accession of the Republic through so many perils, had no power to change his convictions; and he would think to-day just what he wrote twenty-two years ago of the vices of absolute power, of the necessity for teaching nations what conquerors cost them, of the right of his mother to set down her impressions, and of the duty of his son to publish them.

PAUL DE RÉMUSAT.

II

LAFFITTE, *November,* 1857.

" I have once more taken up, after a long lapse of time, the manuscript of these Memoirs, which my mother composed nearly forty years ago; and, having attentively reperused it, I now leave it to my sons and to their children, with an injunction to publish it. I believe that it will prove a useful historical testimony, and, combined with her correspondence, will be a most interesting monument to the intellect and the heart of a gifted and good woman. This work will perpetuate the memory of my mother.

" At whatever epoch these Memoirs may appear, I foresee that they will not find the public ready to receive them entirely without protest, and with satisfaction complete at all points. Even should the Imperial restoration which we now witness not be destined to a prolonged future—should it not be, as I hope it may not be, the final government of the France of the Revolution—I suspect that, whether through pride, weakness, or imagination, France, as a whole, will continue to entertain a tolerably exalted opinion of Napoleon, which it will be reluctant to submit to the free examination of politics and philosophy. He was one of those great men who are placed from the beginning in the sphere of fancy rather than in that of reason, and in his case poetry has taken the lead of history. A somewhat puerile sympathy, a somewhat weak generosity, has almost always made the nation refuse to impute to Bonaparte those awful ills which he brought down upon France. The nation has pitied him the most for its own misfortunes, and thought of him as the noblest victim of the calamities of which he was the author. I know that the sentiments which have led France to make this strange mistake are excusable and even praiseworthy; but I also know that national vanity, the lack of seriousness of mind, levity which takes little heed of reason and justice, are the sources of this patriotic error. Let us lay aside the question of principle—since the nation chooses to resolve that question differently at different times, and glories in despising liberty at intervals —and let us speak only the language of national independence. How can he be in the eyes of the people the hero of that independence who twice brought the foreign conqueror into the capital of France, and whose government is the only one which, for five hundred years, since the time of the mad King Charles VI., left French territory smaller than it found it? Even Louis XV. and Charles X. did better than that. Nevertheless, I am convinced the multitude will abide in its error, and *non auferetur ab ea.*

" It is, then, very unlikely that the spirit in which my mother has written will ever be popular, or that all her readers will be convinced. I am prepared for this, but I also think that among thoughtful people the truth will make its way. Infatuation will not have an endless duration, and, notwithstanding certain obstinate prejudices, public opinion—especially if liberty be at length restored to us and remain with us —will be enlightened, and will never again sacrifice the rights of reason and those of the public conscience to glory. Will my mother appear sufficiently impartial to these more impartial judges? I believe she will, if they take account of the time at which she wrote, and also of the sentiments and ideas which inspired her; and so I have no hesitation in delivering up her Memoirs to the judgment of the world.

" 'The further I go,' wrote my mother to me, ' the more I am resolved that, until my death, you shall be my only reader, and that is enough for me.' And again: ' Your father says he knows no one to whom I could show what I am writing. He says nobody carries so far as I do " the talent of being true." That is his expression. Well, then, I do write for no one, but one day you will find this among my effects, and you may do with it what you will.' She was not without some apprehensions. ' There is a thought which sometimes troubles me. I say to myself, " If one day my son should publish all this, what will be thought of me! " The idea that I may be supposed to be evil-minded, or, at least, ill-natured, makes me uneasy. I exhaust myself with the effort to find something to praise, but this man was such an exterminator (*assommateur*) of worth, and we were brought so low, that I grow utterly disheartened, and the cry of truth utters itself irresistibly. I know no one but you to whom I would intrust such confidences.'

" I hold myself formally authorized by these passages to bequeath the work which my mother confided to me to the public. As for the opinions which it expresses, taking them upon myself, I will explain myself freely respecting the Emperor and the Empire, but not from the purely political point of view. All that I might say on the subject of despotism (which I hate) would be without importance in this case, since the question is, What would be a just judgment of the Emperor and the Empire formed by one who had witnessed the 18th Brumaire, and shared the confident readiness of the nation to divest itself of the charge of its own destinies, by placing them in the hands of one man? I deal with the moral, and not the political, aspect of the matter.

" Let us first consider the Emperor, and discuss him with those only who, while finding much to admire in him, are willing to exercise their judgment upon what they admire. It was commonly said, under his reign, that he despised men. The motives by which he defended his policy in his conversations were not taken from among the noble qualities of the human heart, but from that which he thoroughly understood, the imagination of the people. Now, imagination is naturally captivated by grand and beautiful things, and the imagination of the Emperor, which was vivid and daring, was accessible to this kind of charm. His extraordinary faculties rendered him capable of great things, and he employed them, with others, to captivate France, the world, and posterity. Thence came what was thoroughly admirable in his power and his life; and, if we were to consider that only, we could not place him too high. Nevertheless, a close observer will discern that it was by that intelligence and imagination, rather than the purely moral sentiments of justice and of right, that all was done. Take, for example, religion. It was not the truth of religion, it was its influence and its prestige, which dictated what he did for its cause; and so with all the rest. In his contemptuous estimate of humanity, he recognized only two springs of action—vanity and self-interest; and to the masterly handling of these he applied himself with remarkable ability. While by the *éclat* of his acts, by the glory of his arms, by a permanent embellishment of conservative social principles, he gave to his government what was essential to prevent self-love from blushing at the fact of its connection with it, he carefully manipulated, he caressed, he even exalted other sentiments more humble, which may oftentimes be harmless, but which are not noble and virtuous principles. Love of repose, fear of responsibility, preoccupation with the pleasures of private life, the desire of personal comfort, the taste of riches, as well in the individual as in the family; finally, all the weaknesses which usually accompany these sentiments when they are exclusive, found in him a protector. It is from this point of view that he was everywhere recognized as essential to the preservation of order. But, when men are governed by the springs I am about to call to mind, and when the governor is not upheld or restrained by the sentiment of pure and true glory, by the instinct of a soul naturally frank and generous, it is an easy step to the thought that imagination, vanity, interest are paid with counterfeit as well as good money; that abuses of power, appearances of grandeur, success attained at all cost, tranquillity maintained by oppression, riches distributed by favor, prosperity realized by force or made to seem to exist by falsehood—that, finally, all the triumphs of artifice or of violence, all that despotism can wrest from credulity and fear, are things which also prosper among men; and that the world is often, without serious objection, the plaything of the strongest and most shrewd. But nothing in the nature of the Emperor preserved him from the temptation of employing such means for the advancement of his power. Not satisfied with meriting power, he consented, when he could not merit it, to take it by force

is the controlling thought of the Memoirs.   This is
the basis of those of my mother.

" She had suffered intensely during the years in
which her opinions were in opposition to her interests,
and during which the former could have triumphed
over the latter only *per abrupta,* as Tacitus says,
speaking of this same thing, *sed in nullum reipublicæ
usum.*   Attempts of this kind, besides, never fall to
the lot of a woman; and, in a remarkable letter that
my mother wrote to one of her friends, she said to her
that women at least had always the expedient of saying in the palace of Cæsar:

> 'Mais le cœur d'Emilie est hors de ton pouvoir.'

And she declared to her that this line had been her
secret consolation.

" Her correspondence will reveal in its lightest
shades, in its deepest recesses, the sentiments of a pure
and active soul.   It will there be seen how she united
a generous kindness to a penetrating observation of
all those weaknesses, of all those unhappy circumstances of our nature, which give opportunity to the
painters of morals to display their talents.   It will
there also be seen how, after having caused her much
suffering, Napoleon had kept a place in her thoughts;
how this memory still moved her; and how, when the
unhappiness of his exile at St. Helena was described,
she was deeply affected.   When, in the summer of
1821, the news of the death of Napoleon was brought
to Paris, I saw her melt with tears, and she always
became sad when uttering his name.   As to the men
of her time, I will say only one thing: she had learned
to know them at Court.   The recollection she had preserved of it left her no pleasure.   I have somewhere
seen related a little circumstance that greatly interested
those who witnessed it.   It was the time when the

French imitation of Schiller's 'Marie Stuart' was in fashion. There was a scene in which Leicester repels, by pretending not to know him, a devoted young man who, relying on his secret thoughts, comes to him with a proposal to save the Queen of Scotland. Talma represented admirably the haughty cowardice of the courtier, who disavows his own affection for fear of being compromised, and insolently repels the man who makes him afraid: 'What do you want of me? I do not know you.' The act terminated, and in the box in which we were seated the entire company was struck with this scene, and my mother in her agitation suffered some words to escape whose import was: 'That was it precisely! I have seen the same thing!' When suddenly appeared at the entrance of the box M. de B——, to whom no special application could assuredly have been made, but who had been chamberlain of the Emperor, my mother could no longer restrain herself. She said to Mme. de Catellan, 'If you knew, madame!' . . . and she wept!

"It may be said that this condition of her mind has influenced her in coloring her pictures. I do not think it so. Saint-Simon has also painted a Court, and the despotism in it was more becoming, more natural, and the characters, perhaps, a little more strong in our days. What does he do, however, if not justify, in his truthful painting, what the teachers of his time and the moralists of all times have said of Courts in general? The exaggeration of Saint-Simon is in the language. Of a fault he makes a vice; of a weakness, a cowardice; of a negligence, a treason; and of a hesitation, a crime. The expression is never strong enough for his thought, and it is his style which is unjust rather than his judgment.

"Let us mention a person of a less impulsive mind, more reserved in her language, and who certainly had her reasons for seeing with more indulgence than Saint-Simon the people over whom Louis XIV. reigned. How did Mme. de Maintenon speak of the Court? 'As to your friends of the Court,' she wrote to Mlle. de Glapion, 'they are always with you, and, if you could see what we see, you would find yourself seeing (at Saint-Cyr) only irregularities, wayward conduct, want of light; while we see murders, jealousies, hatreds, treacheries, insatiable desires, degradations, which are covered up by the name of grandeur, of courage, etc., for I fly into a passion in merely permitting myself to think of them.' The judgments of my mother are not characterized by such vivid expressions. But, like Saint-Simon, like Mme. de Maintenon, she had good reason to think that a constant personality, which betrays itself by fear, jealousy, complaisance, flattery, forgetfulness of others, contempt of justice, and desire to injure others, reigns at the Court of absolute kings, and that self-love and interest are the two keys of every Court secret. My mother has said no more; and her diction, without being cold and tame, never exaggerates the facts with which she deals, and allows, in almost everything she has been compelled to relate, that excuse demanded by human weakness in its struggle with bad example, with the temptation of fortune, and with the seductions of a power that does not find itself compelled to respect its promises. It is not without reason that, when we speak of the Empire, our eulogies are almost exclusively addressed to its armies, because, at least, in the business of war, intrepid contempt of death and of suffering is such a triumphant victory over the selfishness of ordinary life, that it covers up whatever this selfishness can suggest, even to the soldiers themselves, of bitter sacrifices to pride, to envy, to cupidity, to ambition.

"Look through the centuries in which historians and moralists endeavor to paint in its true colors every evil that incessantly increases within the sphere of government, especially in the shadow, or, if Louis XIV. demands it, in *the sun* of absolute power. It is strange, in fact, how that which ought to bring into play only devotion, and to place the benefit of all above personal interest—I mean the service of the state—furnishes to human selfishness occasions to make mistakes and means of being satisfied by the art of concealing itself. But it is apparent that this has not been said often enough, for I have not discovered that the evil is soon to end, or even become less conspicuous. Truth alone, incessantly presented to public opinion, can arm it against falsehoods, of which party spirit and state government raise a cloud concealing the misfortunes of the body politic. The masses of the people can never know too well at what price human insolence sells them the necessary service of a government. In times of revolution especially, misfortune sometimes renders it indulgent to the forms of government which have fallen, and the system which triumphs covers with a deceptive veil everything which makes its victory odious. Truthful books must, some time or other, cause all masks to fall, and leave to all our weaknesses the salutary fear of being some day revealed."